52 WEEKS OF

PRACTICAL APPLICATIONS
TO BIBLICAL PRINCIPLES

A Guide To Practice What You Preach Or Teach.

How To Live The Word Of God From Day To Day

Dr. Catherine Braswell

Library of Congress Control Number:	2022943092
Paperback:	978-1-958169-14-8
eBook:	978-1-958169-15-5

Contents

Introduction

In walking daily as a Christian, I know that reading, studying, and learning the Word of God (Bible) is very important. But over the course of years I have noticed that, as Christians, it is very hard for many of us to take what we have learned and walk it out from day to day. We can read the Bible and tell others what we have read but very few of us can actually take the words of Scripture and apply them to daily crisis.

For this reason I would like to introduce you to a guide that will teach you how to walk daily in the Word of God! This is a book of 52 weeks of Biblical Principles with weekly applications to help the reader or Christian practice as you go through life challenges.

As you apply these principles you should be able to see growth and maturity in life and learn how to trust God in every area and situation that you may encounter in this life.

When we learn how to trust God in every situation we will find ourselves stronger, more faithful to God, and more willing to commit and surrender to His divine will for our life.

Now let us get ready to walk the walk that we have been talking about for so long!

Week 1

I MUST LOVE THE LORD TOTALLY

BIBLICAL PRINCIPLE: DEUTERONOMY 6:5 - *⁵And thou shall love the Lord thy God with all your heart, and with all your soul, and with all your might.*

M oses was reminding the children of Israel not to forget God! God had done so many things for them and worked so many miracles in their life after bringing them out of bondage in Egypt. God had promised to bring them into a land of plenty, not because they earned it but because he loved them. God did not want the people to get in their new land and forget all about Him. So, Moses began to tell and remind Israel to remember to love God with all their heart (not equate him with other gods of the nations), but to remember that God is the Great I AM! They needed to love God with all of their being (everything within them), not only when they were in trouble or needed something, but always. Also with all of their might (strength), they were to love God with every fiber of their being!

God knew if his people would love Him at this magnitude with all their heart, there would not be a chance of them falling in love with other gods. The only way for them to do this was by surrendering totally to God! They needed to always remember what God did for them when they cried unto Him for HELP!!

So many times we forget all that the Lord did has done for us and sometimes (not meaning to) we start placing our love and loyalty in other things instead of in God!

How do I give God the love and loyalty that is due to Him?

PRACTICAL APPLICATIONS:

1. Start first by recommitting yourself to God! As you look deep within your heart (being honest) and see where you started drifting into other things. Recognize what things became more important and valuable to you than loving God as you once did. Study Scriptures such as these and apply (practice) them daily:

   A. Psalm 37:5

   [5]Commit your way into the Lord; Trust also in Him; and he shall bring it to pass (stop living as you please, allow God to lead you).

   B. 1 Peter 5:6

   [6]Humble yourselves therefore under the mighty hand of God, that he may exalt you in due time (do not walk in pride).

   C. Psalm 51:10-12 [10]Create in me a clean heart, O God; And renew a right spirit within me. [11]Cast me not away from your presence; And take not your Holy Spirit from me. [12]Restore unto me the joy of your salvation; And uphold me with your free Spirit (ask God to keep your heart clean daily).

2. Accept your fresh start in Christ and your new attitude toward loving Him. Start by reading and studying his Word DAILY! Also while studying his Word allow Him the time to speak to you through His Word. Do not rush through you study. Read Scriptures such as:

A. Psalm 42:1-2

[1]As the hart (deer) pants after the water brooks, So pants my soul after thee, O God. (The deer life depends on water for survival, our soul depends on Jesus, the Living Water for survival). [2]My soul thirsts for God, for the living God: When shall I come and appear before God? (Wait for the presence of the Lord and allow him to speak to you).

B. Psalm 119:9-12

[9]Wherewithal shall a young man cleanse his way? By taking heed thereto according to your word. [10]With my whole heart have I sought you: O let me not wander from your commandments. [11]Thy word have I hid in my heart, that I might not sin against you. [12]Blessed are you, O Lord: Teach me your statures (realize that the word of God cleanse and keep you when hidden in your heart daily).

3. Start developing a personal relationship all over again with the Lord by keeping your focus on what God wants from you. Do not waste your time on what others are doing because it has nothing to do with you. Read Scriptures such as:

A. Psalm 9:1-2

[1]I will praise you, O Lord, with my whole heart; I will show forth all your marvelous works. [2]I will be glad and rejoice in you: I will sing praises to your name, O most High (get involved in praising and giving thanks unto the Lord daily).

B. Psalm 18:1-3a

   [1]I will love you, O Lord, my strength. [2]The Lord is my rock, and my fortress, and my deliverer; My God, my strength, in whom I will trust; My buckler, and the horn of my salvation, and my high tower. [3a]I will call upon the Lord, who is worthy to be praised: (realize how powerful and faithful our God truly is).

C. Proverbs 3:5-8

   [5]Trust in the Lord with all your heart; And lean not unto thine own understanding. [6]In all thy ways acknowledge him, And he shall direct your paths. [7]Be not wise in your own eyes: Fear the Lord, and depart from evil. [8]It shall be health to your navel, and marrow to thy bones (always know that you do not know everything and always acknowledge Him in all you do).

4. Now, keeping God as Priority Number ONE in your life, Do not allow yourself to slip back into the habit of doing God when you have time. It is so important that you (not someone else for you) stay in constant contact with the Lord by reading, studying His word, and communicating with Him daily! Do not let days and things separate you from the relationship you desire with God. Read Scriptures such as:

A. Romans 12:1-2

   [1]I beseech (calling a person, meaning to produce a particular effect) you therefore, brethren, by the mercies of God, that you present your bodies a living sacrifice, holy, acceptable unto God, which is your reasonable service (not doing God's service as a duty or ritual but make sure you are servicing him with the involvement of your whole heart, mind, and will). [2]And be not conformed to this world (have different morals and priorities

than the world system): but be ye transformed by the renewing of your mind (change your mind to fit God's plan for you), that you may prove what is that good, and acceptable, and perfect will of God (what God wants from you here and now).

5. Always remember that God does not expect you to accomplish any of this on your own, but with the abiding aid of His Holy Spirit this can be achieved! You must realize that you must give God the permission to move in your life to produce the needed changes for this relationship. This is called submission to God! Read Scriptures such as:

A. James 4:7-8a

[7]Submit yourselves therefore to God. Resist the devil, and he will flee from you. [8a]Draw nigh to God, and he will draw nigh to you.

Remember: It is entirely up to you to have the type of relationship you desire with God. Only you can make this happen! Take the time out to fall in love with Jesus all over again!!!

Notes:

_____

_____

_____

_____

_____

_____

_____

_____

_____

_____

_____

_____

_____

_____

_____

_____

_____

_____

_____

_____

_____

_____

_____

_____

_____

_____

Week 2

START BY FORGIVING ALL DEBTS

BIBLICAL PRINCIPLE - MATTHEW 6:12 - ¹²And forgive us our debts, as we forgive our debtors.

In this particular passage of scripture Jesus was asked by His disciples to teach them how to pray. During this teaching session they were told to ask God to forgive (pardon, let go of the debt, wipe the slate clean) us (you and I) our debts (whatever we owe to others) as we forgive our debtors (all the people that owe us a debt) whether great or small. We are instructed by God to stop holding onto things such as: anger toward others that have angered us, hurt from both old and new relationships, being misused by people you thought would never misuse you, and anything that is in your heart that you cannot seem to get rid of.

It is very important that I understand the true meaning of this scripture because I am praying to God to forgive me only as I forgive others. So everything that I hold in my heart or charge others with, I am telling

The Lord to do the exact same thing to me!! I am required by God to realize that all people are human just as I am and that they also make mistakes too. So to hold a debt on someone else is like saying that I am this perfect person and I don't need forgiveness from anyone. I am sure you have hurt and mistreated someone else in your lifetime, did you not want forgiveness?

So how do I learn how to forgive others?

PRACTICAL APPLICATIONS:

1. I must first humble myself and admit that I have something in my heart against someone else. It does not matter who was wrong.

   A. Matthew 18:21-22

   [21]Then came Peter unto him, and said, Lord, how often shall my brother sin against me, and I forgive him? till seven times? [22]Jesus said unto him, I say not unto you, seven times, but, until seventy times seven (the point is there is no number or count as to how many times we are expected to forgive).

   B. Luke 17:3-4

   [3]Take heed to yourselves: If your brother trespass against you, rebuke him; and if he repent, forgive him. [4]And if he trespass against you seven times in a day, and seven times in a day turn again to you, saying I repent; you shall forgive him (forgiveness is to be unlimited, practice forgiving).

2. I must speak out with my mouth (confess) that I really feel this way and that I need God to forgive and help me. I must repent of my heart condition so that I can move forward.

   A.   Proverbs 28:13

[13]He who covers his sins shall not proper: But whoso confesses and forsakes them shall have mercy (I must confess and stop sinning).

3. I must realize that the Word of God is my basic source of information on why I must do this. So I will take unto me the word of God and began to read and study Scriptures like these and start applying them daily:

    A. Matthew 6:14-15

        [14]For if you forgive men their trespasses, your heavenly Father will also forgive you. [15]But if you forgive not men their trespasses, neither will your Father forgive your trespasses.

    B. Matthew 18:27

        [27]Then the lord of that servant was moved with compassion, and loosed him, and forgave him the debt.

    C. Luke 6:37

        [37]Judge not, and you shall not be judged: condemn not and you shall not be condemned: forgive and you shall be forgiven.

Please take the time to find other scriptures on forgiveness and study them until you are able to forgive!

4. There are some debts that you may need to go to the individual(s) to discuss and settle just to clear your heart.

    A. Matthew 18:15-17

        [15]Moreover if your brother shall trespass against you, go and tell him his fault between you and him alone: if he shall hear you, you have gained your brother. [16]But if he will not hear you, then take with you one or two more, that in the mouth

of two or three witnesses every word may be established. [17]And if he neglect to hear them, tell it unto the church: but if he neglect to hear the church, let him be unto you as a heathen man and a publican.

5. Make a point of not looking at everyone else and their problems. This is one area that is sure to keep you in bondage! Right now I am working on my heart and I must focus on my issues. I must examine (look into your own heart) my dealings and not measure myself by anyone but the WORD of GOD. I am taking this principle very personal.

   A. 2Corinthians 13:5

   [5]Examine yourselves, as to whether you are in the faith; prove your own selves. Know ye not your own selves, how that Jesus Christ is in you, except ye be reprobates (you are responsible for your own heart).

   B. 1Corinthians 11:28

   [28]But let a man examine himself, and so let him eat of that bread, and drink of that cup (know the true condition of your heart).

6. Just let it all go! Now every day I will practice, do, and live out forgiveness. Every encounter with others, I will be careful not to hold on to JUNK in my heart. I will purposefully let it go and start handling things that need to be handled and forgetting things that need to be forgotten. Remember you cannot control how others feel or think about you but you can control how you are toward others. You must give an account of your own dealings to the Almighty God Himself!!! Do not just practice this application for one week but make this something you will do for the rest of your life!

7. If I do not forgive others, I am not forgiven! When I choose not to forgive others for what they have done to or against me, I am saying to God "do not forgive me for what I have done to others." Read Scriptures such as:

A. Matthew 6:14-15

    [14]For if you forgive men their trespasses, your heavenly Father will also forgive you: [15]But if you forgive not men their trespasses, neither will your Father forgive your trespasses. (If you want to be forgiven you must be forgiving).

B. Luke 6:37

    [37]Judge not, and ye shall not be judged: condemn not, and ye shall not be condemned: forgive, and ye shall be forgiven.

C. Ephesians 4:32

    [32]And be ye kind one to another, tenderhearted, forgiving one another, even as God for Christ's sake hath forgiven you.

Remember: Because God loves me so much, he sent his only begotten Son into this world to die for and forgive me of all my sins, I should always remember to forgive others because of how much I have been forgiven!

Notes: _____

_____

_____

_____

_____

_____

_____

_____

_____

_____

_____

_____

_____

_____

_____

_____

_____

_____

_____

_____

_____

_____

_____

_____

_____

_____

_____

_____

Week 3

LOVE IS WHAT I DO

BIBLICAL PRINCIPLE - 1 JOHN 3:18 - [18]**My little children, let us not love in word, neither in tongue; but in deed and in truth.**

In this Scripture the Apostle John was speaking to the Christians to DO the kind of Love that God expects from the Church! He was telling them that love is not to be done out of an obligation, it must come directly from the heart! When love comes from the heart it flows freely to others and it compels others to love. When love is what I do, deeds follow my words. The person that the love is directed to will know as well as you that your love is real. Why? **People will know that you love them by the action it produces. This is called Love in Action!!**

If the love I give is not real, it will be hard to continue in it. Real love has a way of being there even when the person does not deserve it. You see this is exactly what Jesus gave and did for you and me. We were very undeserving of a second chance because we all have sinned. Jesus looked beyond all of my faults and realized that I could not stop doing sin without His help. So he took all of my sins to the cross and relieved me of the debt. Now it is my turn to relieve the debts of others by loving them in ACTION! How do I make this happen? Is this really possible? Can I really possess this kind of love in my heart? The answer is yes!!!

Let us look in the Word of God and see what is said regarding such love and start applying it to my everyday life:

PRACTICAL APPLICATIONS:

1. I must realize that in God's Word Jesus commanded such love from you and I. Since it is commanded by Jesus himself it is not optional. I need to stay in the Word of God daily to produce such love. I must pray to God for his help in producing this great fruit of the Spirit. Instead of trying to change people to fit me I need to change my love to fit the individual. Scriptures to read and practice daily:

   A. Matthew 5:44

   [44]But I say unto you, Love your enemies, bless them that curse you, do good to them that hate you , and pray for them which despitefully use you, and persecute you. (In this particular teaching Jesus began to instruct us on how to handle and conquer these difficult situations. First of all, instead of arguing and mouthing off with the person start practicing a quiet tongue. Yes start learning how to take what is said or done negatively to you and let it go, yes let it go. When you know that you are right about something you do not have to always explain it or justify what you know. Just let it go)!

   B. Matthew 22:37-39

   [37]Jesus said unto him, thou shall love the Lord your God with all your heart, and with all your soul, and with all your mind.

^{38}This is the first and great commandment. ^{39}And the second is like unto it, You shall love your neighbor as yourself (love, love, love).

2. I know by now you are probably saying "whatever", right. But when I say that I am a child of God and that I love the Lord with all my heart, I must recognize that to love God is to obey Him. To obey Him is to practice LOVE to everyone! Because I want others to love me, should not I try and try hard to love others. If for no other reason, just because God said so. Let the Holy Spirit inside of you teach you how to love. Practice loving and watch Him show you how it is done.

   A. 1 John 4:21

   ^{21}And this commandment have we from Him, that he who loves God love his brother also (always remember how much you want to be loved).

3. Sometimes we have been mistreated by so many people in this life until we think that we cannot take it anymore. I know that I am a Christian and I know that I love the Lord, but this need to stop. Yes, people do hurt us , shame us, and even disappoint us but let us remember how at some point in life we did the same to someone else. But God in his great mercy and grace erased all of our debts and gave us a new chance at life now we are determined to give the same to others even if we have to humble ourselves to make it happen. Why? Because love is what we are determined to do!!

   A. 1 John 4:7-8

   ^{7}Beloved, let us love one another: for love is of God; and everyone that loves is born of God, and knows God. ^{8}He that loves not , does not know God; for God is love (if I say I know God, I must love others).

B. This Scripture alone should prompt me practice loving others daily. Since God is love and His Holy Spirit lives inside of me, I know that He is able to produce the type of love in me for my brethren. I just need to stay in the word of God until I find this word actively flowing from my heart. For me nothing else will do.

Study Scriptures on love and pray that God will teach you how to love and how to receive love from others.

Remember: Jesus said in John 15:9 - As the Father hath loved me, so have I loved you: continue ye in my love. This is so very powerful and possible because Jesus would not have told us to continue in His love if we could not perform it. He made it possible through the abiding presence of His Holy Spirit, now all I need to do is JUST DO IT !!!

Notes: _____

_____

_____

_____

_____

_____

_____

_____

_____

_____

_____

_____

_____

_____

_____

_____

_____

_____

_____

_____

_____

_____

_____

_____

_____

_____

_____

_____

_____

Week 4

FAITH TO PLEASE GOD

BIBLICAL PRINCIPLE - HEBREWS 11:6 - ⁶But without faith it is impossible to please Him: for he that cometh to God must believe that he is, and that he is a rewarder of them that diligently seek him.

What is faith? Faith is the substance of things hoped for, the evidence of things not seen (Hebrews 11:1). So what is faith? Faith is having confidence that someone or something is reliable or trustworthy. Faith is knowing that I can depend on someone or something without a doubt. The only one I know who is of such reputation and good report is God the Father, God the Son, and God the Holy Spirit.

We as humans will and can do all we know to be reliable but somehow we still seem to come up short and fail people from time to time. But God is always faithful and reliable. He can always be trusted to come through no matter the circumstances. His testimonies and His reputation speak volume as to why He can be trusted!!!

First of all we must realize that all humans have some type of faith in objects. So for the Christians our faith must have an object or something to place that faith into! Our object is God and all that He says in his word regarding his son Jesus Christ!! The first test of my faith is to believe that God is or shall I say that God Exist, and not only does he exist but that he is a perfect promise keeper to them that seek or trust him.

To receive God one must trust that God is real. After establishing that God is real then I must trust that He will do everything He said He would do in his word regarding me (make the word of God personal). He will fill me with his Spirit and give me the power of Grace and Mercy to live the life of a true Christian! I must trust that God will keep me in his care and create in me a desire to please Him no matter what I may face or go through in this life.

To have Faith in God is to believe that God will never fail me because He is true to His word. There are things that I as a Christian must do to experience the rewards of God in my life and to please my God!!

What must I do to please God and have the rewards of God active in my life? Let us go to the word of God and see what God has to say about such things:

PRACTICAL APPLICATIONS:

1. When I first received Christ as my Personal Savior I had to believe that He is GOD! Now that I am in this relationship with Him I must continue to believe that He is still God!

   A. Hebrews 11:6

      ⁶But without faith it is impossible to please him: for he who comes to God must believe that he is, and that he is a rewarder

of those that diligently seek him. (God rewarded me by accepting me as his child).

2. Now that I am in this relationship it is so important that I began to build upon a closer walk with God. This is the time I start to read, eat, breath, and meditate upon the word of God. This is how the relationship began to grow stronger.

A. 2Timothy 2:15

[15]Study to show yourself approved unto God, a workman that needs not to be ashamed, rightly dividing the word of truth. (Start learning the truth of God's word for yourself).

B. Psalm 119:9-11

[9]Wherewithal shall a young man cleanse his way? By taking heed thereto according to thy word. [10]With my whole heart have I sought thee: O let me not wander from thy commandments. [11]Your word have I hid in mine heart, that I might not sin against you. (I must realize that my way will stay clean as long as I hide the word of God in my heart and stay before him through his word).

3. As I stay in the word of God and began to learn of his promises, I must teach my mind to start trusting that God loves me and he is true to his word! (Starting to build upon my faith by reading the results of his testimonies).

A. Romans 12:2

[2]And be not conformed to this world: but you be transformed by the renewing of your mind, that you may prove what is that good, and acceptable, and perfect will of God. (My mind must

be changed to accept the fact that God is trustworthy and that I now belong to him and he must take care of me).

B. Mark 9:23

[23]Jesus said unto him, If you can believe, all things are possible to him that believes. (As I read the word of God and see for myself that God has never failed, I will begin to develop a new desire to start trusting that he can and will do just what he said he would do, even for me).

C. Colossians 1:10

[10]That you might walk worthy of the Lord unto all pleasing, being fruitful in every good work, and increasing in the knowledge of God. (The closer I walk with the Lord the more I learn of and about him, this teaches me what God really like and want from me as his child).

D. 1Peter 5:6-7

[6]Humble yourselves therefore under the mighty hand of God, that he may exalt you in due time: [7]Casting all your care upon him; for God cares for you. (The word of God have a way of making me humble because it shows me how great my GOD really is! Therefore I gain confidence enough to lean on him through all of life challenges one day at a time).

4. I encourage you to read and study Hebrews Chapter 11 in its entirety to see how the great men and women of God in the bible believed God through thick and thin! They were normal human beings just as you and I and they suffered through the cares of this life but they found God to be faithful in all of His doings. Allow God to be the one you lean on and trust to bring you to your expected end!!

5. Faith is ACTIVE and therefore it has to be exercised daily. When life get hard and you do not know what to do, lean on Jesus. He is strong enough to carry you. When life is going fine, lean on Jesus because He delights in caring for you. The more you lean on him the more you began to trust him. This is how your faith is developed and finally matured.

   A. Romans 10:17

   [17]So then faith comes by hearing, and hearing by the Word of God (you must Read the Word to Hear the Word).

Once you learn that God can be trusted you will have a faith that is STEADFAST and UNMOVABLE!! Try trusting The Almighty God Daily, just because you can!

Remember: MY GOD IS ABLE and IS THERE ANYTHING TOO HARD FOR GOD???

Notes: _____

_____

_____

_____

_____

_____

_____

_____

_____

_____

_____

_____

_____

_____

_____

_____

_____

_____

_____

_____

_____

_____

_____

_____

_____

_____

_____

_____

_____

_____

Week 5

PRAISE IS WHAT I DO

BIBLICAL PRINCIPLE - PSALM 9:1-2 - ¹I will praise thee, O Lord, with my whole heart; I will show forth all thy marvelous works. ²I will be glad and rejoice in thee: I will sing praise to thy name, O thou most High.

What is praise? According to the American Heritage College Dictionary, praise is defined as: 1) Expression of approval, commendation, or admiration; 2) The extolling or exaltation of a deity, ruler, or hero.

In this particular Psalm David is expressing his approval of his GREAT GOD! He is giving as an award or sacrifice of honor and admiration for all that the Lord has done for him. He is lifting God up high above the earth as the one and only true and living God, the ruler of the universe, and as his great hero! He is conscious of the marvelous works that God is doing in the earth and in his life. Because of this he experience this overflow of gratitude, thanksgiving, and joy in his soul and spirit and began to give God the honor, the glory, and the reverence that is due to his name and to who he is!!! He realized that God is so worthy of all praise, every honor, all exaltation, and all that is within him, because of who GOD is!!!

Because God has been and is so good to me, praise is what I do. Because he makes ways for me even when I do not deserve it, praise is what I do. Because God is who he is, praise is what I do. I will bless Thee O Lord at all times and your praise shall constantly be in my mouth because praise is what I do!

Instead of mumbling, grumbling, and complaining about the things I do not have or the things I think I should have, I should praise God for all the things that he has done for me. When I mumble, grumble, and complain I am telling The Lord that he does not know what is best for me. I am saying that I am not thankful for what he do for me. I may not say it in words but by my actions and my complaining attitude, this is exactly what I am saying. Let us change our attitudes and behaviors to praising and thanking God for his greatness!!!

Let us go to the word of God and find out what the word says about praising our Great God!

PRACTICAL APPLICATIONS:

1. I will praise the Lord because I am designed or fashioned in such a way that I cannot comprehend or understand how great you have made me!!! For this I will look upon you with great AWE and forever praise you.

   A. Psalm 139:14

   ¹⁴I will praise thee; for I am fearfully and wonderfully made: Marvelous (causing wonder or astonishment) are thy works; and that my soul knows right well.

2. I will praise the Lord because His Name alone prompt praise!

   A. 1Chronicles 29:13

      ^{13}Now therefore, our God, we thank thee, and praise thy glorious name.

3. Knowing the names of God will teach me to have a holy respect and honor to the Great God of this universe. Let us look at a few of the names of our God with their meanings! His name is:

   A. Jehovah - He is the eternal "I AM", He is the self-existent One", He reveals Himself! (Exodus 3:13-14).

   B. Jehovah-Ropheka - "The God that Heals" (Exodus 15:26). He heals me!

   C. Jehovah-Meqaddeshkem - "The God who Sanctifies" (Exodus 31:13). I cannot sanctify myself, it is God who cleanses me!

   D. Jehovah-Jireh - "The Lord will Provide" (Genesis 22:14). Only God is able to meet all of my needs, He provides for me!

   E. Jehovah-Nissi - "The Lord is my Banner" (Exodus 17:15). As a child of God I do not have to fight for myself! My God will fight for me!

   F. Jehovah-Shalom - "The Lord is my Peace" (Judges 6:24). As this world change with all of its uncertainties and the changes in my life, I can find great confidence that my God will keep me in perfect peace! He is my peace!!!

   G. Jehovah-Tsabaoth - "The Lord of Host" (1Samuel 1:3). Whatever comes up against me, rest with assurance that my God will take care of me always!!

H. Jehovah-Shammah - "The Lord is there" (Ezekiel 48:35). Sometimes I become fretful when God sends me to places that I am not familiar with, but because His Spirit lives within me, God is always there!

I. Jehovah-El Elyon - "The Lord Most High" (Psalm 7:17). I will praise Him for the rest of my life because God is The Lord Most High and there is no other God like unto Him!!!

J. Jehovah-Tsidkenu - "The Lord is our Righteousness" (Jeremiah 23:6). Now, more praise is sufficient because I am the righteousness of God through Jesus Christ His Son. I cannot achieve such righteousness on my own, for this I give God all the praise!!

4. I will praise God because of His eternal plan of salvation! He has made it possible for me to have eternal life, something I would never have received if Jesus did not give His life for all of us!! God sent His son Jesus to implement His eternal plan of SALVATION for all mankind!!! Now I do not have to perish because of what Jesus did just for me. I will praise His Holy Name!!!

A. Matthew 1:21

   ^{21}And she shall bring forth a son, and thou shall call His name JESUS: for He shall save His people from their sins.

B. John 3:16

   ^{16}For God so loved the world that He gave his only begotten Son, that whosoever believeth in Him should not perish, but have everlasting life.

5. This is personal for me: I will praise Him because he first loved me!! Even when I was so unlovable, so awful, so full of hate, so mean,

and just downright disgusting, God still loved me. Me a nobody! When others counted me out, Jesus never gave up on me. He saw something in me that no one else could see. Lord I truly do thank you!!! For this I praise your Holy and Righteous name!!!

A. Psalm 103:1-3

[1]Bless the Lord, O my soul: And all that is within me, bless His holy name. [2]Bless the Lord, O my soul, and forget not all His benefits: [3]Who forgives all my iniquities; Who heals all my diseases.

B. Psalm 104:1

[1]Bless the Lord, O my soul. O Lord my God, thou art very great; Thou art clothed with honor and majesty.

C. Psalm 107:1

[1]O give thanks unto the Lord, for He is good: For his mercy endures forever.

D. Psalm 113:1-2

[1]Praise ye the Lord. Praise, O ye servants of the Lord. [2]Blessed be the name of the Lord from this time forth and for evermore.

E. Psalm 34:1-3

[1]I will bless the Lord at all times: His praise shall continually be in my mouth. [2]My soul shall make her boast in the Lord: The humble shall hear thereof, and be glad. [3]O, magnify the Lord with me, and let us exalt his name together.

All this was written to encourage and stir a desire to praise and exalt the one and only true and living God of Creation. This is why Praise is what I do!!!

Remember: On a daily basis, please let us bow before the Lord God Almighty and give Him the praise and Honor that is due to Him just because He is worthy of our praise. Let us not praise him for blessings but praise Him because He alone is WORTHY of my praise. Does God not deserve this from me (personally)?

Notes: _____

_____

_____

_____

_____

_____

_____

_____

_____

_____

_____

_____

_____

_____

_____

_____

_____

_____

_____

_____

_____

_____

_____

_____

_____

Week 6

I MUST BRIDLE MY TONGUE

BIBLICAL PRINCIPLE - James 1:26 - [26]**If any man among you seem to be religious, and bridles not his tongue, but deceives his own heart, this man's religion is vain (useless).**

This is one of my favorite Scriptures! It teaches me the value of a quiet tongue and why it is so important for me to consider my words before I speak. Many times we say things that can never be retracted. Our words can help or damage, hurt or bring healing to the receiver. Whatever I choose to say can give me a friend for life or it can very well make me an enemy for life! To bridle my tongue means to be able to control or restrain my words.

In the third chapter of James the Lord speaks so much about the tongue. Why? Because even though the tongue is so very small and is located inside of our mouth, It has the power to do more damage to a human being than almost any other part of the body! The tongue has the power to hit like a whip, to cut like a knife, to punch like a fist, and to kill like a gun if used in the wrong way! It also has the ability to cut as deep as a deadly sword. I have had conversations with people that spoke about some of the harsh things people have said to them and they actually said they would have preferred the individual to hit them rather than say what was spoken to them. I can recall some harsh words spoken to me and to be honest with you it took a while for me to erase those words from my mind!!!

This week let us focus on controlling our tongue. It is a fact that if you love me, you will do all that is within you to keep from hurting me even with your words. Many have said "if you thought it, you may as well say it", this is not true. If you thought something and it will hurt someone change your mind and reconsider what you want to say. If your words are not helpful then keep them to yourself!

Let us go into some Scriptures and find out why my words really do matters.

PRACTICAL APPLICATIONS:

1. There are so many things we are able to accomplish in this life. We go to schools and colleges to obtain degrees for employment, better lives, and many other reasons. We actually succeed and make great achievements. We are able to control our lives to the point that we will not quit until we get this done. But what happens to me even if I accomplish all of this and cannot control my tongue, what have I accomplished? Should not my speech reflect the way I live? I must not take pride in a tongue that hurt others, it does not matter what accomplishments I have achieved.

   A. James 3:3-6

   > ³Behold, we put bits in the horse's mouth that they may obey us; and we turn about their whole body. ⁴Behold also the ships, which though they be so great, and are driven of fierce

winds, yet are they turned about with a very small helm, whither soever the governor desires, ⁵Even so the tongue is a little member, and boasts great things. Behold, how great a matter a little fire kindles. ⁶And the tongue is a fire, a world of iniquity: so is the tongue amongst our members, that it defiles the whole body and set on fire the course of nature; and it is set on fire of hell (I can control many things but my tongue will always need me to place a constant watch over it to prevent damages to others)!!!

2. Words spoken with my tongue can actually cripple me for life. So many times we have said things that were negative regarding ourselves and our future and when those things happened to us we blamed everyone else for our failures. Be careful of the things you say about yourself if you do not want them to happen in your life. Remember, you have what you say!!! The ability to control the tongue is a true mark of wisdom!

   A. Proverbs 18:21

      ²¹Death and life are in the power of the tongue: and they that love it shall eat the fruit thereof (you can either bless or curse yourself with your own tongue).

   B. Proverbs 13:3

      ³He who guards his mouth keeps his life: But he who opens wide his lips shall have destruction (it is not good to talk all the time, keep quiet).

3. Do not let your tongue take you into another man's matter. Learn how to keep your mouth from the business of others. In other words learn how to mind your own business and do not be a talebearer in someone else's life! Do not be a false witness.

A. Proverbs 15:4

   [4]A wholesome tongue is a tree of life: But perverseness therein is a breach in the spirit (if you cannot speak good and wise words, do not speak at all. I must train my tongue to be wholesome or healthy to bring health and life to the hearers).

B. Proverbs 11:13

   [13]A talebearer reveals secrets: But he that is of a faithful spirit conceals (to keep from being seen, found, or observed) the matter (A talebearer will always talk about everyone's downfalls to cause divisions but will never reveal his own secrets).

C. Proverbs 18:8

   [8]The words of a talebearer are as wounds, and they go down into the innermost parts of the belly (Gossip is like eating good food, it taste great while you eat it but the results can pass on for generations causing hate, pain, hurt, and sometimes death).

D. Proverbs 20:19

   [19]He that goes about as a talebearer reveals secrets: Therefore meddle not with him that flatters with his lips (A talebearer cannot be trusted he/she will always reveal your doings while never speaking of his/her own. Be careful not to do such dealings yourself. Consider how you would feel if the same thing were to happen to you)!!!

4. God is the one who gave me my tongue and He is also the one who gave me his Holy Spirit to assist me in proper usage of that same tongue. Scripture teaches me that I am to keep my tongue from evil and use my tongue to bless my God! I am to run from evil, do not speak guile, and run after peace. Just watch your TONGUE!!!

A. Psalm 34:13-14

[13]Keep your tongue from evil, and your lips from speaking guile. [14]Depart from evil, and do good; seek peace, and pursue it.

B. Psalm 35:28

[28]And my tongue shall speak of thy righteousness and of thy praise all the day long.

C. Proverbs 21:23

[23]Whoso keeps his mouth and tongue keeps his soul from troubles.

D. Proverbs 10:20a

[20a]The tongue of the just (righteous) is as choice silver.

E. James 3:8-12

[8]But the tongue no man can tame; it is an unruly evil, full of deadly poison. [9]Therewith bless we God, even the Father; and therewith curse we men, which are made in the similitude of God. [10]Out of the same mouth proceeds blessings and cursing. My brethren, these things ought not so to be. [11]Doth a fountain send forth at the same place sweet water and bitter? [12]Can a fig tree, my brethren, bear olive berries? either a vine, figs? So can no fountain both yield salt water and fresh.

The mouth of a Christian should bear the characteristics of a person who has been with the Lord! We should not have the same words and actions with our tongue as before we became a child of God. It is my responsibility to allow the Holy Spirit to transform my speech into a speech worthy of a Christian. Remember we cannot bless God and curse men with the same tongue, it should not be.

Remember: Work on bringing your tongue into subjection to the will of God! Be slow to speak but quick to listen, this will give you time to consider your words. You truly can have a tongue that will be pleasing to our God!!! Just start working on it because practice makes perfect!

Notes: _____

_____

_____

_____

_____

_____

_____

_____

_____

_____

_____

_____

_____

_____

_____

_____

_____

_____

_____

_____

_____

_____

_____

_____

_____

_____

Week 7

OBEDIENCE TO GOD IS A MUST

BIBLICAL PRINCIPLE - 1SAMUEL 15:22 - ²²And Samuel said, Hath the Lord as great delight in burnt offerings and sacrifices, as in obeying the voice of the Lord? Behold, to obey is better than sacrifice, and to hearken than the fat of rams.

In this particular Scripture the Lord had given King Saul orders to destroy everything he had found in the land (Amalek) Saul was sent to conquer. But King Saul decided to keep the so called best stuff to sacrifice unto the Lord. God sent the prophet Samuel to tell King Saul that what he had done was direct disobedience to the word of God. Because of this the Lord removed King Saul from being the King over God's people. It broke Samuel's heart because he and the King were close but even this did not change God's mind about God's decision. God wanted King Saul to know that God did not delight in sacrifices but his delight is found in obedience. There is nothing a human can give to God that God does not already own, except God requires it of me!

It is so important to God that His people learn to obey his word. Do not take unto yourself the attitude to disobey God and do what you want to do and think that God should sign off on it. We must always remember that God's word is settled in heaven and will not be changed for you or me. This leaves only one solution, I must do the changing! I must adjust my lifestyle and habits to God's will and not God adjust his will to me because I am the imperfect one. God is always PERFECT in everything and in every way. I will do well to remember this throughout this relationship!!!

All through Jesus' ministry He constantly repeated that he came to do the will of his Father in Heaven. He said not my will but thou will be done, referring to the reason He was sent to the earth. It is a great thing to obey the will of God and to place your agendas on the back burner. When I recognize that it is God who has all power in His hands and that He is the God who provides for me, then I will practice daily obeying the Word of God! The more I learn and practice to Obey God, the easier obeying and living my life becomes.

Now let us see how to practice obeying the Word of God daily!!!

PRACTICAL APPLICATIONS:

1. One of the first things I need to learn is that I need to change my mind about how I see the word of God. I must understand that the Bible is not your everyday novel or history book. The Bible is "God's Eternal Plan of Salvation". Meaning, in this book you will find God's Map to eternal life for all mankind. All through the pages you will see a roll out of God's plan to redeem mankind from the clutches of our enemy, Satan. When I began to understand this concept, I will know why I need to fully obey the entire word of God. You see if I am on a journey it would be nice to know that I

have light to show me the way. I once walked in darkness before I met Jesus but now that He, the Light of the World has come, I no longer walk in darkness but in true light!!! How awesome!

A. Psalm 119:105

[105]Thy word is a lamp unto my feet, and a light unto my path (God's word will show you the way).

B. John 1:1-5

[1]In the beginning was the Word (Jesus), and the Word (Jesus) was with God, and the Word (Jesus) was God. [2]The same was in the beginning with God. [3]All things were made by him (Jesus); and without him was not anything made that was made. [4]In Him (Jesus) was life; and the life was the light of men. [5]And the light (Jesus) shines in darkness; and the darkness did not comprehend it (the Word of God is Jesus himself and the more I eat the Word the more I become like Him).

C. John 8:12

[12]Then Jesus spoke again unto them, saying, I am the light of the world: he that follows me shall not walk in darkness, but shall have the light of life.

2. When I obey God I am known to Him as His sheep. So to be called one of His sheep, I will hear his word, obey whatever he says, and not be labeled as a stranger. I cannot use the excuse of not knowing Jesus' voice if I am his sheep or child! Since the Spirit of God abides inside of me, I must take the time to get to know everything about Him and how to obey His voice. This is one of the most important parts of my relationship with Jesus. Because if I do not know his voice or when He is speaking to me, how will I ever obey what he wants me to do. Look how personally Jesus knows me, He calls me

by my name. This alone explains why you cannot expect everyone to understand and accept what plans God has for your life because He spoke it personally to you. You obey Him and do not get caught up with other people's responses.

A. John 10:2-4

> ²But he that enters in by the door is the shepherd of the sheep (Jesus). ³To him the porter (door) opens; and the sheep hear his voice: and he calls his own sheep by name, and leads them out. ⁴And when he puts forth his own sheep, he (Jesus) goes before them, and the sheep follow him: for they know his (Jesus) voice (I will follow Jesus because I know Him).

3. Because my relationship with God is very personal, I am responsible for allowing His Holy Spirit to order my steps on a daily basis to keep iniquity (sin) away from me. This is done by reading, studying, understanding, and obeying the Word of God, also practicing everything I read. Do not just take other people word about what the Word of God means. Start becoming an active participant in learning of God! The Word of God teaches me that even though I may fall I will not be utterly cast down because God will hold me with His Hand!!!

A. Psalm 119:133

> ¹³³Order my steps in thy Word: and let not any iniquity have dominion over me (the word will teach me how to walk).

B. Psalm 37:23-24

> ²³The steps of a good man are ordered by the Lord: and he delights in his ways. ²⁴Though he fall, he shall not be utterly cast down: for the Lord upholds him with His hand (all of my steps are ordered by the Lord).

4. We all want to be blessed by God, we want Him to do so many great things for us in this life, but what am I willing to do to obtain such blessings? Am I willing to draw nigh unto Him so that He can draw nigh unto me? Am I willing to deny my- self, take up my cross and follow Him? Am I willing to obey what He commands me to do? Am I willing to delight (give) myself totally to Him for His use? If my answers are yes to these questions, then look for your blessings! If my answers are maybe, perhaps, I do not know, or no, maybe God's answers are the same to me! Scriptures teach us that God loves us and want us to love Him and draw nigh (move toward) Him. This is not asking too much from me. This is the least I can do since He Gave His life for me!!!

A. James 4:8a

[8a]Draw nigh (come close) to God, and He will draw nigh (come close) to you.

B. Matthew 16:24

[24]Then said Jesus unto His disciples, If any man will come after me, let him deny himself (forget about you, your wants, and your desires), and take up his cross (a sign of total commitment even if it causes death), and follow me (obey me).

C. Deuteronomy 28:1-2

[1]And is shall come to pass, if thou shall hearken (to listen, give heed) diligently (earnestly, giving heed to) unto the voice of the Lord your God, to observe and to do all his commandments which I command you this day, that the Lord thy God will set you on high above all nations on the earth: [2]And all these blessings shall come on you, and overtake you, if you shall

hearken unto the voice of the Lord your God (I am blessed by obeying God).

D. Psalm 37:4-5

[4]Delight thyself also in the Lord; And He shall give you the desires of your heart. [5]Commit your way unto the Lord; Trust also in him; and He shall bring it to pass.

So here we see that it is not a light thing to obey our God! We learn to obey God because it is profitable for us to be able to walk in his presence continually. Obedience proves to God that I truly love, honor, respect, and desire Him more than anything else in my life. The more I practice obeying God through his word, the more I will become transformed into his likeness. After all, this is what my relationship should produce in me daily!!

Remember: Obey God always and watch your life change from life to abundant life! Practice living in obedience to God's life changing Word, then see yourself living the ABUNDANT LIFE God intended for you. The challenge is now in your hands, what will you do?

Notes: _____

_____

_____

_____

_____

_____

_____

_____

_____

_____

_____

_____

_____

_____

_____

_____

_____

_____

_____

_____

_____

_____

_____

_____

_____

_____

Week 8

I WILL ACCEPT WHO GOD SAYS I AM

BIBLICAL PRINCIPLE - Jeremiah 1:4-5 - ⁴Then the word of the Lord came unto me saying, ⁵Before I formed thee in the belly I knew thee; and before thou came forth out of the womb I sanctified thee, and I ordained thee a prophet unto the nations.

This Scripture is so important because it allows me see myself worth, my importance to God, and how much God values me. It takes me directly to the heart of God for the purpose He has for my life. God was speaking to His prophet Jeremiah commissioning him to service. Because God knew Jeremiah so intimately and so well, He knew the plans Jeremiah was created to fulfill. God already knew how Jeremiah would respond, what he felt he could and could not do, and whatever reactions Jeremiah would present when given this commission. So being the loving and gracious God that He is, God assured Jeremiah he could get it done. HOW? By letting Jeremiah know that God's plan for him was made long before Jeremiah was placed in his mothers' womb, before he was born, and before he had a name!

This same intimate knowledge that God had for Jeremiah, is the same for you and I. Since God took the time to pursue a relationship with us do you not think that he already know what we can and cannot do. God is not like man keeping all the negative things that we do just to hold over our head when we do not obey what He wants us to do. It is for my best interest if I do obey. When we were born God placed the ability to fulfill his purpose inside of us, but it is up to me to walk before God and get it done. So whatever God say I can do, I can do it!! Whoever God say I am, that's who I am. I will accept God's knowledge of who I am above everyone else.

Many times we allow the opinions of others to direct our course in this life. We allow them to dictate what we are and are not capable of doing. So many times we feel within ourselves that I can do better than this but we keep listening to negative people who are going nowhere fast. PLEASE snap out of it!!! Wake up and look into the mirror of life and began to see that God made you the person He wanted you to be! God did not make a mistake about you so because of this He Can use you to do great things in his kingdom!! Start surrounding yourself with positive people of God and staying in the Word of God to see who you really are.

We are going to walk through the Bible to see what God has to say regarding you and I because I have to live with myself everyday:

PRACTICAL APPLICATIONS:

1. I will have confidence in the fact that I am fearfully and wonderfully made by the hand of God. No one else can take credit for who I am

except my all powerful God! He knows me as the One who formed me. Even though sometimes I cannot understand myself, God always understand me. He is not surprised at who I am, He only wants to make me much better, if I will allow Him the opportunity.

A. Psalm 139:14

[14]I will praise thee; for I am fearfully and wonderfully made: Marvelous are your works; and that my soul knows right well.

2. God knows everything about and inside of me: my thoughts, my feelings, my behavior, my flaws, and everything else that makes me who I am. Sure there are some things I need to get rid of in order to please God and those are the things He expects me to delete!!! I know you are probably thinking: if He made me like I am, why do I need to get rid of things? Well, the truth is because I was born in sin and shaped in iniquity, I picked up some things that are totally against the work and will of God. So now after becoming a child of God I need to allow the Holy Spirit to help me start the deleting process. God knows I cannot do it on my own so He sent His Spirit to assist in the process.

A. Psalm 139:15-16

[15]My substance (everything I am) was not hid from thee, when I was made in secret, and curiously wrought in the lowest parts of the earth. [16]Your eyes did see my substance, yet being imperfect; And in your book all my members (body parts)were written, Which in continuance were fashioned, when as yet there was none of them (before all my parts were fully formed).

B. Psalm 51:5-6

[5]Behold, I was shaped in iniquity; And in sin did my mother conceive me. [6]Behold, thou desirest truth in the inward parts: And in the hidden part thou shall make me to know wisdom.

C. John14:16-17

> [16]And I will pray the Father, and He shall give you another Comforter (Holy Spirit), that he may abide with you forever; [17]Even the Spirit of truth; whom the world cannot receive, because it sees him not, neither knows him: but ye know him; for he dwells with you and shall be in you (The Holy Spirit Is the power you need to change).

3. Because the Spirit of the Most High God lives in me, I now have become the righteousness of God through Christ Jesus. I receive daily the grace to be a child of God! It is such a wonderful thing to know, that I can be all that God said I am, because He loves me. The purpose I am to fulfill is attainable, God said it and I believe it. Jesus bore all of my sins and exchange it for His righteousness, all of this happened by God's Divine Grace! What would I do without God's Divine Grace?

A. 2Corinthians 5:21

> [21]For He (God) hath made Him (Jesus) to be sin for us, who knew no sin; that we might be made the righteousness of God in Him (Jesus).

B. 1John 3:1

> [1]Behold, what manner of love the Father hath bestowed upon us, that we should be called the sons of God: therefore the world knows us not, because it knew Him not.

Now I must walk as a child of God, walking in the word and promises of God. Knowing that (Romans 8:1 -There is therefore now no condemnation to them who are in Christ Jesus who walk no after the flesh, but after the Spirit). As long as I walk after the leading and directing of the Holy Spirit, no one can condemn me. I am free in Christ Jesus to be Who God said I am!

Remember: I will accept the testimony of who God says I am! I am a Child of The King!!! The rest does not matter at all because God is the one who made me!

Notes: _____

_____

_____

_____

_____

_____

_____

_____

_____

_____

_____

_____

_____

_____

_____

_____

_____

_____

_____

_____

_____

_____

_____

_____

_____

_____

_____

_____

Week 9

GIVING CONTROL
OF ME TO GOD

BIBLICAL PRINCIPLE - Romans 8:13-14 - [13]For if you live after the flesh (doing what you want to do), you shall die: but if you through the Spirit do mortify (kill, destroy) the deeds of the body, you shall live. [14]For as many as are led (controlled) by the Spirit of God, they are the sons of God.

This particular Scripture was written to the Christians regarding their walk with God! We are told that if we have been born again and filled with the Spirit of God, there is a certain way we should walk or live. We are not to continue living as we did when we were yet in our sins, but we are to walk in the newness of life. After being born again my life has changed, I am no longer the same. I have a new name, new Father, and new Sisters and brothers. The writer is confirming that if I continue to live the way I once lived, I cannot call it a new life. Once my new life and relationship with God started, old things were passed away and all things became new! God gave me a fresh start, forgetting old things and making me a new individual inside out.

I have received a new Spirit with a new way of living. I can no longer do what I want to do because now my life is not my own, I belong to God. My body has now become the Temple of God's Holy Spirit. The most wonderful thing has happened to me, my body is where the Spirit lives, He abides in me and I abide in Him. We are now one!

Because He is all knowing, all powerful, and everywhere present, I will give God the total control of my new life. He knows all about me, He knows what it takes to please Him, and He also knows how to keep me in subjection and obedience to his will.

This Scripture tells me that as long as I am led by the Spirit of God I am a son of God.

Let us go to the Word of God to learn how to give complete control of me to GOD!!!

PRACTICAL APPLICATIONS:

1. The first place to start giving God control of me is in my mind! I need to change my mind regarding the way I have always done things. This does not mean that everything I do is wrong, but I will make fewer mistakes if I allow God to lead the way. Many times we are so familiar with having our way until it becomes hard to allow God to have His way. My mind needs to agree with the way God see and want things to go. How does this happen? By going to the Word of God (Bible) and read it to get the understanding of what God is saying. To be led by God, I must know the direction he is going. Search the Word of God yourself to see what it is saying!

Start training your mind to be flexible to change. Jesus always had a mind to be led by God the Father!!

A. Acts 17:11

[11]These were more noble than those in Thessalonica, in that they received the word with all readiness of mind, and searched the Scriptures daily, whether those things were so (They had a ready mind to see what the word of God said).

B. Philippians 2:5

[5]Let this mind be in you, which was also in Christ Jesus (I cannot think like myself anymore, I really need the mind of Christ).

C. Romans 12:2

[2]And be not conformed to this world: but be ye transformed by the renewing of your mind, that you may prove what is that good, and acceptable, and perfect will of God (a change must happen in my mind).

2. It takes a very **HUMBLE** individual to allow someone else to take charge of your life. For another person to lead you, to Guide you, and to allow that person to change the course or direction you feel you should be going. It takes humility to allow this to happen. This is exactly what God requires, humility to place Him (God) at the head of my life. God wants to call the plays that goes on in my life so that He can show me a more perfect and abundant way of living!! Once my life has changed, I cannot honestly make it to the top without God's approval. Promotion comes directly from God!

A. James 4:10

> [10]Humble yourselves in the sight of the Lord, and He shall lift you up (when you submit yourself to God, He will do impossible things in your life).

B. Psalm 75:5-7

> [5]Lift not up your horn on high: Speak not with a stiff neck (do not walk in pride, walk in humility). [6]For promotion cometh neither from the east, nor from the west, nor from the south (It is God who exalts His servants). [7]But God is the judge: He puts down one, and sets up another (when God is leading the way, He will place you where you are to be placed and he does not need any man's approval, it is His decision alone).

C. Jeremiah 29:11-12

> [11]For I know the thoughts that I think towards you, says the Lord, thoughts of peace, and not of evil, to give you an expected end (God's plan for your life are already established but you need to sign off on them). [12]Then shall ye call upon me, and ye shall go and pray unto me, and I will hearken unto you (God is the ultimate source of prosperity).

3. Practice asking God daily at the start of your day, "Lord what will you have me to do?" I must get into the habit of putting God first in everything I do. It is the same process of developing other habits in my life. Habits are developed by doing things repetitiously, over and over again! So if I get into the habit of consulting God daily about my doings it will eventually become a part of my everyday life. Then God will be able (by my choice) to have control of my life. Practice, practice, practice!!! Saul in the book of Acts was persecuting the Christians, but when called into the service of the

Lord, Saul started his service by asking God "what will you have me to do?" This became the lifestyle of Saul (Paul) for the rest of his life, serving with God leading!!! It was not Paul's will that he wanted to do but God's will.

A. Acts 9:4-6

> [4]And he fell to the earth, and heard a voice saying unto him, Saul, Saul, why are you persecuting me? [5]And he said, who art thou Lord? And the Lord said, I am Jesus whom you are persecuting: it is hard for you to kick against the pricks. [6]And he trembling and astonished said, Lord, what will you have me to do? And the Lord said unto him, Arise, and go into the city, and it shall be told what you must do.

So in serving God, let us make a point of placing God first in our lives to lead and guide us into all truth and righteousness.

We have said many times that God is a lawyer who has never lost a case. If this is true then let us give God the Power of Attorney (a legal document giving someone legal authority to act in my best interest) to our lives and watch Him move in our favor!!!

Remember: God is Sovereign! This means God has absolute rights and ownership over His creations, this includes humans too. Since God has ownership, why not give him the permission to have His way in my life!!

Notes: _____

_____

_____

_____

_____

_____

_____

_____

_____

_____

_____

_____

_____

_____

_____

_____

_____

_____

_____

_____

_____

_____

_____

_____

_____

_____

_____

_____

_____

_____

_____

_____

Week 10

ALWAYS DEAL WITH MATTERS OF MY HEART

BIBLICAL PRINCIPLE - Psalm 19:14 - ¹⁴Let the words of my mouth and the meditation of my heart, be acceptable in thy sight, O Lord, my strength, and my redeemer.

This is a very familiar passage of Scripture where King David is praising God for his greatness in creation and His commandments. But he ends this psalm with a praise offering to God asking God to let the words of his mouth and the meditation of his heart be acceptable in the sight of God. David recognized that even in his praise for the creation and his praise for the commandments of God, none of this mattered if his words and his heart were not acceptable in the sight of his God!

David had walked with and before God long enough to know that God does not look on the outward appearance of a man, God looks at the heart. It does not matter what you present from the outside to an individual, all that really counts is the activities of your heart.

You can pretend to be real but the truth is always in the heart!! Your words and your thoughts come from the inner most parts of your heart, and you can say all day long you did not mean to say it, but people know your words came straight from your heart. This is one of the reasons words hurt so badly. Words from the heart speak volumes of how a person really feels regarding you and regarding things.

David wanted God to accept his offering of praise that was given in the earlier verses but he knew his heart and words needed to pass God's approval. We should be as King David and ask God to continuously keep our hearts clean and purged from all unrighteousness. My heart has everything to do with how I appear before God and man. It also has everything to do with the way I perceive things and people.

I must keep my heart right before God because he is my strength and He is the redeemer of my soul. How do I keep a prepared heart at all times? Let us go directly to God's word and find our answers.

PRACTICAL APPLICATIONS:

1. The things I allow to enter into my heart will be the things that will dictate my life. My heart is the center of my emotions, my desires, doubt, fear, evil, hatred, love, lust, obedience, pride, and many other things. This is why I cannot let any and every thing enter into my heart. I am responsible for guarding or protecting my own heart because these issues will flow from it and will relay to others what I truly feel and how I really am. In other words, my heart is the REAL ME!!! If I desire to be heard of God, I will not let any evil hide in my heart.

A. Proverbs 4:23

[23]Keep thy heart with all diligence; for out of it are the issues of life (protect your heart and keep wickedness away from you).

B. Psalm 66:18

[18]If I regard iniquity in my heart, the Lord will not hear me (if I hide sin in my heart God will not hear me. Confess it and get rid of it).

C. 1Peter 3:4

[4]But let it be the hidden man of the heart, in that which is not corruptible, even the ornament of a meek and quiet spirit, which is in the sight of God of great price (I should have a meek and quiet spirit in my hidden man, my heart , it is very valuable).

D. Matthew 15:18-19a

[18]But those things which proceed out of the mouth come forth from the heart, and they defile a man. [19a]For out of the heart proceed evil thoughts (evil comes out of the heart and it will defile the whole man, so keep evil out).

2. I must serve God with my whole heart, therefore I need to keep my entire heart clean. I have to be careful of everything I allow to enter in my heart. This refers to conversations, dealings, thoughts, gossip, feelings, and etc. When I let trash go into my heart I began to talk trashy. If I allow gossip, I become a gossiper. If I compromise with evil dealings, I develop evil intentions. So I must practice righteous talking, dealings, and intentions. The heart can be very deceptive

and if I am not careful it will deceive even me. I will have a false interpretation of what is truth and right!!

A. Ephesians 5:19-20

[19]Speaking to yourselves in psalms and hymns and spiritual songs, singing and making melody in your heart to the Lord; [20]Giving thanks always for all things unto God and the Father in the name of our Lord Jesus Christ (this is a sure way to keep a guard around my heart).

B. Romans 6:17

[17]But God be thanked, that you were the servants of sin, but you have obeyed from the heart that form of doctrine which was delivered you (The gospel you heard that saved you is the same doctrine that is able to keep your heart right before God, continue in the WORD).

C. Matthew 13:15

[15]For this people's heart is waxed gross (no sensitivity or discernment), and their ears are dull (clogged) of hearing, and their eyes they have closed; lest at any time they should see with their eyes, and hear with their ears, and should understand with their heart, and should be converted, and I should heal them (I cannot afford to lose the sensitivity and discernment from my heart).

3. I must forgive all debts as they occur to keep me in direct communication with the Almighty God. If I do not forgive others I will not be forgiven. It is so amazing how God allowed us free choice to be as close to Him as we desire. He made it possible for me to learn how and desire to forgive others. When I take into account how much God has forgiven me and how he is constantly forgiving me , I must have a heart to forgive others!!!

A. Matthew 6:14-15

   [14]For if you forgive men their trespasses, your heavenly Father will also forgive you: [15]But if you forgive not men their trespasses, neither will your heavenly Father forgive your trespasses (so there you have it, I forgive and I am forgiven).

B. Matthew 6:12

   [12]And forgive us our debts, as we forgive our debtors (if you want others to forgive you of debts or things you cannot repay, you must also forgive the debts of others by choice).

4. Do not be a busy body in other men matters!! This is one of the things that seem to keep so much confusion in other people's life. Being a talebearer and a truce breaker is awful for a Christian. If you did this in your life before you accepted Jesus as your personal Savior, be very careful that you do not engage in this type of behavior as a Christian. It is ugly and very costly to the one on the receiving end. Think about how you would feel if someone did this to you. Families have been broken up, lives have been destroyed, Churches split, and friendships destroyed forever because of talebearers and trucebreakers!! Practice breaking this yoke because this is exactly what it is. It is pure confusion and it looks bad when a Christian is wearing it!!!

   A. Leviticus 19-16-17a

      [16]Thou shall not go up and down as a talebearer (busybody, one who gossips) among your people: neither shall you stand against the blood of your neighbor: I am the Lord. [17a]You shall not hate your brother in your heart (this behavior is so awful that the Lord spoke against it after giving the Ten

Commandments, people can lose their life over this, keep your heart free from this).

B. Proverbs 11:13

    [13]A talebearer (gossiper) reveals (tell) secrets: but he that is of a faithful spirit conceals (keep it private) the matter (a talebearer cannot be trusted with any private matters because they talk too much).

C. Proverbs 18:8

    [8]The words of a talebearer are as wounds, and they go down into the innermost parts of the belly (The words of a gossiper are pleasant when spoken, but the words cause deep wounds in the life of the person they are spoken against. Sometimes the wounds carry over into generations because they are so deep)!!!

D. Proverbs 20:19

    [19]He that goes about as a talebearer reveals secrets: Therefore meddle not with him that flatters with his lips (It is dangerous to hang out with a talebearer because you become a part of the gossip).

E. 1 Timothy 5:13

    [13]And withal they learn to be idle, wandering about from house to house; and not only idle, but tattlers also and busybodies, speaking things which they ought not (avoid being idle because you can find yourself in other people business).

F. 2 Thessalonians 3:11-12

    [11]For we hear that there are some which walk among you disorderly, working not at all, but are busybodies. [12]Now them that are such we command and exhort by our Lord Jesus Christ, that with quietness they work, and eat their own bread

(sometimes being idle will allow you opportunities to interfere with other people's affairs, get busy)!

G. 1Peter 4:15

[15]But let none of you suffer as a murderer, or as a thief, or as an evildoer, or as a busybody in other men's matters (busybodies are ranked among these other sins, but most participants of this behavior do not see it as being this serious).

Please take the time to evaluate everything that may be going on in your heart. Be very particular as to what you allow to enter into your heart because it can be very detrimental to your relationship with the Almighty God!! Keep your heart clean and always ask the Lord as King David did, "to create in me a clean heart O God and renew a right spirit within me". This is how important dealing with matters of the heart is.

Remember: Practice daily dealing with all matters of your heart and avoid things that can and will make my heart SICK!!!

Notes: _____

_____

_____

_____

_____

_____

_____

_____

_____

_____

_____

_____

_____

_____

_____

_____

_____

_____

_____

_____

_____

_____

_____

_____

_____

_____

_____

_____

_____

_____

Week 11

WALKING IN THE PEACE OF GOD

BIBLICAL PRINCIPLE - Mark 9:50 - Salt is good: but if the salt have lost his saltiness, wherewith will you season it? Have salt in yourselves, and have peace one with another.

What is PEACE? According to the American Heritage College Dictionary peace is defined as: (1) The absence of war or hostilities; (2) An agreement or treaty to end hostilities; (3) Freedom from quarrels and disagreement, or harmonious relations; (4) Inner contentment; serenity; and (5) Free from strife.

Mark, the writer of this Gospel, made a point of informing the Christians of a true sign of discipleship. He compared the Christians' power in life and ability to keep peace with one another to the power of salt being able to preserve whatever it is placed upon. What a great comparison!! We should be in such loyalty with Jesus and the Gospel until we will do all the things necessary to keep peace with our fellowman.

How far are you willing to go to pursue peace with others? Many times we will not work on keeping peace because the other person is the one who broke the peace in the first place. But according to the Word of God, you and I are to go after peace and do all that is within us to make this happen. We are not to sit back and wait for the other individual to come to us if we know the peace is broken.

We have a problem with pride sometimes and taking the humble or lower seat can be very challenging, especially if we think or know that we are not wrong in the matter. Please know my brothers and sisters it is okay to take the lower seat and make it right! In fact this is what Scripture teaches us as being a servant of the Most High God!

When we take the lower seat or the humble way to correct the matter, it shows that we have a lot of salt in our life. We display the season or flavor in our character and the season in our maturity in Christ Jesus. Remember we are not doing this to prove others that we are great people. But we do this to HONOR the truth, the authority, and the power of God's Word!!!

When walking with God we must conform to His teachings! To be a Christian is to be Christ like so we must know in our heart that Jesus would make peace even if He did not break it. He came to this earth to make peace between God the Father and us, His humans!!

Let us learn how to walk in peace with one another from the instructions given throughout the Word of God:

PRACTICAL APPLICATIONS:

1. To walk in peace I must have peace within myself! I cannot walk in or offer something I do not have. As being a Christian, the peace of God should abide inside of me. I received the peace of God when

I received the Spirit of God in my life. So if I do not have peace today, what happened to disrupt the flow of my peace? How did I allow someone else the power and the authority to interrupt my peaceful lifestyle? I am responsible for keeping peace in my life at all cost. Where did I get off course? How did this happen? When did this happen? I need my peace back! Remember how God gave me peace!!!

A. Luke 8:48

[48]And he (Jesus) said unto her, Daughter be of good comfort: your faith has made you whole; go in peace (you see it is by faith that I walk in the peace of God! Reclaim your peace, yes Lord I believe).

B. Romans 5:1

[1]Therefore being justified (not guilty before God) by faith, we have peace with God through our Lord Jesus Christ (not just a feeling of peace but also peace of mind).

2. Since the Word of God has given me my peace by faith, I need to learn how to walk in peace through faith. The Bible tells me to be a peacemaker and also pursue (go) after peace. It did not say if people treat you right that you will always have peace. The bible warns me that there will be people who will not walk in peace, but this should not change my course to keep peace. As I stay on course, my peace remains in me because I will do what the Bible instructs me regarding peace keeping.

A. Matthew 5:9

[9]Blessed (the object of God's favor) are the peacemakers: for they shall be called the children of God (I am to promote peace

as far as it depends on me, this show the character of God in my life as a child of God).

B. Matthew 5:11-12

   [11]Blessed are you, when men shall revile (speak abusively of) you, and persecute (afflict, oppress, torment) you, and say all manner of evil against you falsely, for my sake. [12]Rejoice, and be exceedingly glad: for great is your reward in heaven: for so persecuted they the prophets which were before you (one of the hardest things to do when being verbally attacked by someone especially when you know they are wrong, is to be quiet and still, but if I know it is not true, I do not have to prove it to anyone else. I will trust God for the truth to come out).

C. Psalm 34:13-14

   [13]Keep your tongue from evil and your lips from speaking guile. [14]Depart from evil (remove yourself from the incident), and do good; Seek peace (hold onto your peace and let the situation go), and pursue it (keep walking and looking for peace, even in that situation).

3. Christian conduct is very important when it comes to peace. My conduct will prove to the world just what I am made of as a Christian. If I continue responding to situations the same way I responded before becoming a Christian, what changes have I made? Since I am a light to the world, a city that sits on a hill, I must proceed with caution as to how I display my light! People do not always listen to what you say but they remember what they see you do! So if you do peace and not just talk about it, you may be remembered as a peacemaker. Live peace!!!

A. 1Peter 3:8-11

> [8]Finally, be ye all of one mind, having compassion one of another, love as brethren, be pitiful, be courteous: [9]Not rendering evil for evil, or railing for railing (bitter, harsh, criticism, abusive language): but contrariwise blessing; knowing that you are thereunto called, that you should inherit a blessing. [10]For he that will love life, and see good days, let him refrain (keep) his tongue from evil, and his lips that they speak no guile (speak wise words). [11]Let him eschew (avoid, shun) evil, and do good; let him seek peace, and pursue it.

This is written to the people of God to encourage us to do the right things; to show the world that our God has changed our lives forever! Furthermore, to demonstrate that being a Christian is to reflect the life of Jesus in the earth. We have a responsibility to the lost, to the hurting, to the broken hearted, and the rest of the world, to show them Christ and the peace He can give them. This is why we are to walk in the peace of God!!!

If the world can reward people for good conduct and good behavior, how much more will God reward His children for the same! We should love the Lord so much that we are willing to give up the things that bring dishonor to his name and take unto us the things that bless His name and bring honor and glory to his name!! Remember Jesus died for us so that we could have His peace abiding inside of us, it is up to me to keep this peace active in my life. If I practice peace in all of life situations, surely I will walk victoriously in the peace of God. Practice makes perfect and the Holy Spirit has the power to make this happen, only if I want Him to and if I allow Him to rule in my life!!!

Remember: Hebrews 12:14 - Follow peace with all men, and holiness, without which no man shall see the Lord: If I want to see The Lord I must follow peace with all people, do all that is within me to make peace happen!!!

Notes: _____

_____

_____

_____

_____

_____

_____

_____

_____

_____

_____

_____

_____

_____

_____

_____

_____

_____

_____

_____

_____

_____

_____

_____

_____

_____

_____

_____

Week 12

STAY COMMITTED TO GOD'S CHARGE

BIBLICAL PRINCIPLE - Mark 16:15-16 - ¹⁵And He (Jesus) said unto them, Go ye into all the world, and preach the gospel to every creature. ¹⁶He that believeth and is baptized shall be saved; but he that believeth not shall be damned.

This Scripture teaches us that before Jesus ascended back into the heavens He left a command or charge to his disciples. He told them to go into (the entire) world and preach (teach) the Gospel to every creature. It would seem as though this was written only to the eleven men who followed Jesus, but this charge goes further into the future. After you and I became born again Christians, we entered into Jesus' family. Since Jesus' ascension this charge is passed on to all Christians throughout the ages. This, my brothers and sisters, includes you and me also!

It is so important for us to take this charge serious because the world need to hear about all that Jesus did for us. We need to get the message out that Jesus loves all of us and it does not matter what we have done in our life He still loves us and wants to give us eternal life. If we do not take the time to tell the world about Jesus, we are not staying committed to God's charge.

I know life happens! Sometimes we get very busy with other cares of this life, but we must stay committed to this charge. We need to take the time out to add up the cost of discipleship and see what we need to change in our life to stay committed to this charge. Because we are to trust God to take care of us, He will show us what we need to do to get this done if we ask Him. We must remember that our lives are not our own and if someone did not take the time out of their busy schedule we may not have heard about Jesus or His eternal plan of Salvation!!!

The end of this verse teaches us, he that believe and is baptized shall be saved but he that does not believe is damned. At least if we tell people about Jesus they will have the choice of believing or not believing, it will be their choice. Let us not make that decision for them by not informing the people about the choices they have.

What is it that keeps me from telling people about Jesus? How do I get back to my charge and tell the world about Jesus? The word of God will tell me what I need to do and why I need to do it.

PRACTICAL APPLICATIONS:

1. Sometimes we lose our courage when it comes to witnessing to other people about Jesus. We are well aware of the charge to go into (the entire) world and tell others about Him, but if it is not someone I know or feel comfortable with I will keep quiet. What do I do? I ask God for the help I need to get the work done realizing I cannot do it without the help of the Holy Spirit!

A. Acts 4:29

   [29]And now, Lord, behold their threatening: and grant unto
   your servants, that with all boldness they may speak thy
   word (Always remember it is okay to ask God to give you the
   boldness needed to fulfill his will in your life, even the disciples
   needed boldness).

B. 2Timothy 1:7

   [7]For God hath not given us the spirit of fear; but of power, and
   of love, and of a sound mind (If you lack confidence be honest
   and ask God to give you the confidence you need to complete
   the charge).

C. Philippians 1:6

   [6]Being confident of this one thing, that he which hath begun a
   good work in you will perform it until the day of Jesus Christ
   (you must be confident that not only did God save you but
   that he also placed His powerful Spirit inside of you, this alone
   gives you the power and boldness to proclaim God's word).

2. Sometimes we lose our zeal (intense enthusiasm for something) for
   what God has called us to. Maybe it was something someone said
   to you or about what you were doing in the ministry. Maybe it was
   the fact that you are just not feeling it right now. It may even be that
   you are just burnt out and need a break. Whatever the situation, we
   cannot remain in this condition. We need an encounter with God
   to stir up the gift inside of us!!

   A. 2Timothy 1:6

      [6]Wherefore I put thee in remembrance that thou stir up the
      gift of God, which is in thee by putting on of my hands (your

gift came from God and sometimes you need someone to pray for you to rekindle the gift for more production).

B. John 15:1-4

[1]I am the true vine, and my Father is the husbandman. [2]Every branch in me that bears not fruit he takes away: and every branch that bears fruit, he purges it (cut away or prune), that it may bring forth more fruit. [3]Now ye are clean through the word which I have spoken unto you. [4]Abide in me, and I in you. As the branch cannot bear fruit of itself, except it abide in the vine; no more can ye, except ye abide in me (sometimes after we have been productive in witnessing, God may need to cut away some things that may hinder my abilities to produce more fruit, so I need to ask Him to purge me Lord).

There are so many reasons why I need to ask God to help me to complete the work He started in me. I need to take the time out of my busy schedule, do some deep soul searching to see where I am, and what I need to be doing as it relates to my productivity in keeping God's charge. Telling the world about Jesus is one thing I need to keep doing for the rest of my life, so I must make a point of practicing this daily!!!

Always remember: Jesus said in Matthew 28:20 - Teaching them to observe all things whatsoever I have commanded you: and lo, I am with you always, even unto the end of the world. Amen! Keep reminding yourself that my Savior is always with me through whatever I encounter in this life.

Notes: _____

_____

_____

_____

_____

_____

_____

_____

_____

_____

_____

_____

_____

_____

_____

_____

_____

_____

_____

_____

_____

_____

_____

_____

_____

_____

_____

Week 13

LIVE TO STAY IN GOD'S PRESENCE

BIBLICAL PRINCIPLE - Romans 8:3-5 - ³For what the law could not do, in that it was weak through the flesh, God sending his own son in the likeness of sinful flesh, and for sin, condemned sin in the flesh: ⁴That the righteousness of the law might be fulfilled in us, who walk not after the flesh, but after the Spirit. ⁵For they that are after the flesh do mind the things of the flesh; but they that are after the Spirit the things after the Spirit.

In this Scripture Paul was letting the Church know that the law of God still plays a great part in the believer's life. Not as a means of salvation but as a moral and ethical guide. The Lord was saying that the law was given to make man aware of sin and the problems sin creates. He also wanted the world to see why we needed a Savior, because we are not able to stop sinning on our own. We needed the help of a Savior to come and take away our sins, not just suspend them but to remove them and give us a new nature through His Son, Jesus Christ!!! So

Jesus truly became a man like you and I, but sinless so that God could condemn (pronounce judgment of) sin in Jesus perfect flesh!

The word of God also says that once we become Christians we are not to continue living our lives as if there were no changes in our spirit. Yes, we still have the same body but there is a major spiritual change inside of us and we should live as such!!

He said the righteousness of the law was fulfilled in us. Meaning, Jesus fulfilled the law while He was on earth and now that we are born again Christians, the Spirit inside of us is empowering us to walk in the righteousness of God through Christ Jesus! This is so amazing to know that if I can believe that Jesus did everything that the law required, by faith in Him, I am accounted the righteousness of God. This being said, I am no longer to walk in the deeds of my old ways. I am now to walk by the leading and directing of the Holy Spirit everyday!

How is this done? It is done by denying what you want to do and allow God to have His rule in your life. This means admit that you do not know what is best for yourself, but you want to live the life that will please God. Constantly read and study the Word of God to learn the things that will please Him. Ask Him to teach you how to walk in this new life and how to depart from the things of your former life.

When talking about walking after the flesh many Christians do not really understand what this means. It means for me to not let my sinful nature persuade my body and mind to obey what I want to do that is against the will of God! A lack of self denial or self control is one thing that will get me out of the will of God. We must practice daily to say no to my desires until my desires are transformed into the desires that God want for my life!!

I know by now you are probably saying that is hard to do. You are so right! In your own power you cannot get it done, but in the power of the Holy Spirit, it is possible! God through His Son Jesus, have given us His powerful Spirit to live on the inside of us to make living this life happen! Now I am able to live a life that will keep me in the presence of God.

Let us see what the Word of God have to say about making this a part of who I am.

PRACTICAL APPLICATIONS:

1. Why should I want to live to stay in God's presence? In today's time there is so much confusion, distrust, hatred, and many other things going on that causes people to live in fear and anxiety. As Christians we have the assurance that in God's presence is Joy, peace, healing, deliverance, and abundant life. If this is not enough, there is eternal life, blessings, and His protection! I must pray for a desire to stay in His presence!!

   A. Psalm 16:11

   [11]Thou wilt show me the path of life: In your presence is the fullness of joy; At your right hand there are pleasures for evermore (In the presence of the Lord, He will sustain my joy, gladness of heart, and protect me).

   B. Psalm 140:13

   [13]Surely the righteous shall give thanks unto thy name: The upright shall dwell in thy presence (we stay in God's presence because this is what we do).

2. How do I stay in the presence of the Lord?

    A. Psalm 100:2-4

[2]Serve the Lord with gladness: Come before His presence with singing. [3]Know ye that the Lord he is God: It is he that hath made us, and not we ourselves; We are His people, and the sheep of His pasture. [4]Enter into his gates with thanksgiving, and into his courts with praise: Be thankful unto him, and bless his name (I should not serve God because I have to, I serve Him because he is God and by choice, he made me, I am one of his people and on a personal note, I am his sheep).

    B. Psalm 31:20

[20]Thou shall hide them in the secret of your presence from the pride of man; Thou shall keep them secretly in a pavilion from the strife of tongues (in God's presence his protection will secretly keep me from the pride of man and their evil speaking against me).

    C. John 15:1-3

[1]I am the true vine, and my Father is the husbandman. [2]Every branch in me that bears not fruit he takes away: and every branch that bears fruit, he purges it, that it may bring forth more fruit. [3]Now ye are clean through the word which I have spoken unto you (we are to abide, stay in Christ so he can constantly cut away everything from me that can pull me from Him also we must read, study, and obey the Word of God).

3. What must I do to stay in the presence of the Lord?

    A. Deuteronomy 6:5

> [5]And thou shall love the Lord thy God with all your heart, and with all your soul, and with all your might (to be in the presence of the Lord, I must love Him with my entire being).

    B. John 14:23

> [23]Jesus answered and said unto them, if a man love me, he will keep my words: and my Father will love him, and we will come unto him, and make our abode with him (when we obey God's words Jesus and His Father will come and live in us).

To walk in the presence of the Lord is such an honor! When we think of all the great things God has done in creation and in our lives and who He really is, we should want to be in His presence. God could have chosen anyone else to serve him but He chose you. This is the greatest honor to be conferred upon a human being!!!

Remember: To know how Great God is, should make me stand in total AWE of his glory and shout out "What a Mighty God We Serve and O How I Love Jesus".

Notes: _____

_____

_____

_____

_____

_____

_____

_____

_____

_____

_____

_____

_____

_____

_____

_____

_____

_____

_____

_____

_____

_____

_____

_____

_____

Week 14

KEEPING MY VESSEL (BODY) PURE

BIBLICAL PRINCIPLE - 1Corinthians 6:19-20 - ¹⁹What? know you not that your body is the temple of the Holy Ghost which is in you. Which you have of God, and you are not your own? ²⁰For you are bought with a price: therefore glorify God in your body, and in your spirit, which are God's.

The Apostle Paul was writing to the Corinthian Church reminding them that their bodies belonged to the Almighty God! He wanted them to know how to possess their bodies as temples of the Living God. When you and I received the Holy Spirit, our bodies became the property of God. We no longer own our bodies (not that we ever did), but now we have become the temple of God!

What does all of this mean? Well, it simply means that I cannot just do what I want with my body and think that it is alright. I am responsible for keeping my body in such a pure, holy, and clean way because the Spirit of God now abides inside of me, how Awesome!!!

Every Christian should value his/her body as a sacred place where God dwells and that by the power and presence of the Holy Spirit their bodies can be kept from the impurities of sin! We are instructed by God to keep our bodies clean.

This is truly something that can be achieved but not against our will. We must allow the Holy Spirit to work inside of us producing control outside. After all self control is a fruit of the spirit. If I cannot control my own vessel, how can I expect or tell anyone else to do it. I must care enough for God and for myself that I do not want anything that is not related to my walk with Christ to abide inside of me!!!

Because God is so holy and so righteous, I should make it top priority to keep my vessel as clean as possible so the Holy Spirit would not mind living and walking inside of me! I must take pride in the fact that this Holy God wants to live in this earthly vessel. This is enough to keep me up in the Spirit and allowing the Holy Spirit to be as strong as he desires to be in me. Have your way in my life Holy Spirit, should be my daily cry.

How do I make this become a reality in my life? Let us see what the word of God has to say about this!!

PRACTICAL APPLICATIONS:

1. Now that I am a Christian there are some things I need to make a priority in my new life. One of the first things I need to do is recognize that I am a new creature! Meaning I cannot continue to sin as I did before I accepted Christ as my personal Savior!

A. Romans 6:1-4

   [1]What shall we say then? Shall we continue in sin, that grace may abound? [2]God forbid. How shall we, that are dead to sin, live any longer therein? [3]Know you not, that so many of us as were baptized into Jesus Christ were baptized into his death? [4]Therefore we are buried with him by baptism into death: that like as Christ was raised up from the dead by the glory of the Father, even so we should also walk in newness of life (even though we are saved by grace, it does not give us the permission to continue to sin. We died to sin and rose to righteousness in our new life).

B. Romans 12:1-2

   [1]I beseech you therefore, brethren, by the mercies of God, that you present your bodies a living sacrifice, holy, acceptable unto God, which is your reasonable service. [2]And be not conformed to this world: but be transformed by the renewing of your mind, that you may prove what is that good, and acceptable, and perfect will of God (we do not have to offer up dead animals to God anymore for our sins, now God want me to give him my entire body, soul, and spirit renewed and holy walking in this new life).

C. Romans 6:12-14

   [12]Let not sin therefore reign in your mortal body, that you should obey it in the lusts thereof. [13]Neither yield your members as instruments of unrighteousness unto sin: but yield yourselves unto God, as those who are alive from the dead, and your members as instruments of righteousness unto God. [14]For sin shall not have dominion over you: for ye are not under the

law, but under grace (when you have the urge to sin resist it, get into the word of God and began to pray).

2. When it comes to fornication (sexual relations among the unmarried), do not put yourself in the line of fire, trying to prove to someone else that you can endure the temptation. If you know this is a problem or a snare for you, please remove yourself from the situation until you have allowed the Holy Spirit to deliver you from the problem! You as a Christian must learn how to resist the desire instead of giving into it. You must develop Self-Control!!!

   A.   1Corithians 6:13b

   [13b]Now the body is not for fornication, but for the Lord; and the Lord for the body (this Scripture teaches the dignity of the human body, so to engage in unmarried sexual activity is to deny the dignity of your body and disobey God's word).

3. I must see how important my walk and living for the Lord really is! There are some things that are specifically called out in Scripture that God loudly say NO!!! He will not compromise His word for my lack of self-control. When I continue in the things that God says no to, I am saying Lord your Holy Spirit is not powerful enough to keep me from the acts of my flesh.

   A.   Galatians 5:18-21

   [18]But if you are led by the Spirit, you are not under the law. [19]Now the works of the flesh are manifest, which are these; Adultery, fornication, uncleanness, lasciviousness, [20]Idolatry, hatred, variance, emulations, wrath, strife, seditions, heresies, [21]Envyings, murders, drunkenness, revellings, and such like: of the which I tell you before, as I have also told you in time past, that they which do such things shall not inherit the

kingdom of God (these are a list of the sins of the flesh which are forbidden by God for Christians to commit).

Also it is very important to know what each of these acts are because if I do not understand what they are, I will continue to commit the works of the flesh!!

Definition of these acts:

1. Adultery - sexual unfaithfulness to husband or wife, looking on a woman or man to lust after. (Matthew 5:28)

2. Fornication - including all forms of immoral and sexual acts, premarital sex, adultery, abnormal sex, all kinds of sexual vices. (Ephesians 5:3; 1Corithians 6:18)

3. Uncleanness - moral impurities, doing all kinds of dirty things that pollute life. (Ephesians 5:3; Colossians 3:5)

4. Lasciviousness - filthiness, indecency, shamelessness, unrestrained evil thoughts and behavior; having brutish and lustful desires. (Ephesians 4:19)

5. Idolatry - the worship of idols, giving your primary time and energy to something other than God; More than just a stature. (Galatians 5:19-21)

6. Witchcraft - sorcery, the use of evil spirits or drugs to gain control over your life or someone else's life. Astrology, palm reading, etc. (Isaiah 8:19-20)

7. Hatred - hostility, enmity, animosity, a hate that continues on and on embedded deep within the heart. (1John 4:20)

8. Variance - fighting, struggling, quarreling, discord, strife, fighting against others to gain what you want. (Proverbs 26:21)

9. Emulations - jealousy, wanting and desiring what others have, material things, honor, position, etc. (Proverbs 6:34)

10. Wrath - explosive temper, burst of anger, indignation, quick tempered, anger that arise and fades away quickly. (James1:19-20)

11. Strife - conflicts, fight, a party spirit, a cliquish spirit, struggle, and contention. (Philippians 2:3)

12. Seditions - standing against others, divisions, rebellion, splitting off from others. (2Peter 2:10)

13. Heresies - rejecting the beliefs of God, Christ, Scriptures, the Church, and holding to doctrine that is not the truth. (1Timothy 4:11)

14. Envying - this is more than jealousy, more than wanting what others have but also begrudges the fact that they have them. They want things to be taken from the person and the person to suffer through the loss of the things, (Galatians 5:26; Romans 13:13)

15. Murders - to kill or take the life of another. (1 Peter 4:15; Matthew 19:18)

16. Drunkenness - taking drugs or drinking to affect the senses for lust or pleasure, intoxication, seeking to loosen moral restraints for fleshly pleasures. (Ephesians 5:18; 1Corinthians 6:10)

17. revellings - uncontrolled indulgence, pleasure, taking part in wild or drinking parties, lying around indulging in feeding the lusts of the flesh, orgies. (1Peter 4:3; 2Peter 2:13-14)

I must remember that my body belongs to God and God alone! I must live the life I talk so much about if I want to please God. Nothing else will do because to be a Christian means to be like Jesus Christ and He lived a Holy life.

Remember: So Live like you want the Holy Spirit to Stay in Your House, since your body is the house of God!!!

Notes: _____

_____

_____

_____

_____

_____

_____

_____

_____

_____

_____

_____

_____

_____

_____

_____

_____

_____

_____

_____

_____

_____

_____

_____

_____

_____

_____

_____

_____

52 weeks of practical application to biblical principles

Week 15

WALKING IN THE JOY OF THE LORD

BIBLICAL PRINCIPLE - Psalm 16:11 - ¹¹Thou wilt show me the path of life: in thy presence is fullness of joy; at thy right hand there are pleasures for evermore.

What is Joy? Joy is gladness of heart. It is a deep inner gladness and pleasure inside the heart. Joy is an assurance and a confidence so deep in God that whether I see my way or not, I know that God will handle things on my behalf. It is not like happiness which is based upon whether things are going well or not. Joy is one of the fruit of the Spirit and remains in you even through times of testing, disappointments, when you have, and when you have not. True joy does not change because your situations changed, it still remains the same!!! Spiritual Joy also produces a spiritual change in my behavior that will radiate to an outward display that others will notice.

King David is teaching in this particular Scripture that God will show us the path of life. In the presence of the Lord is the fullness of Joy!

To walk in the joy of the Lord one must truly know and trust in him, because joy comes from the Lord!

David knew that God was his provider; his Keeper, his King, and everything he needed to survive in this life. He had suffered through so many things and knew that if it had not been for the Lord who was on his side, he would not have made it. Yes some things he brought on himself and some things others did to him, but nevertheless David found out for himself that if He placed his trust in God, he would have joy in his life.

David also had to realize that joy was more than just laughing when thing were fine. He knew that when he trusted God and walked in God's presence he had gladness of heart which was not dictated by bitterness of circumstances!

When understanding that even in the midst of trials, disappointments, mistreatment, and whatever hand you are given in life, you can still have JOY! Even when you are not in the presence of others, you can have joy. You can have joy when it seems like everything that can go wrong goes wrong; because your joy is located in your heart and no one can take it from you.

How do I get joy? Where does this joy come from? How do I keep joy on a daily basic?

There are things that I must do to walk in the joy of the Lord, but am I willing to do what is necessary to obtain it? Let us search the Scriptures to find the answers to the questions above.

PRACTICAL APPLICATIONS:

1. Now you know what joy is, but where does it come from? Joy is listed as one of the fruit of the Spirit and since this is true it must

come from the Holy Spirit. So if you have the Holy Spirit, should not you have joy? The answer is yes, but it must be matured so that it will remain unchangeable!

A. Galatians 5:22a

[22a]But the fruit of the Spirit is love, joy, peace (this is one of the fruit that is only produced through the indwelling of the Holy Spirit; you cannot produce this on your own).

2. What must you do to obtain this joy? To have anything in this life one must know how to work for it. Salvation is different, it is a gift from God, but grooming and maturing the fruit of joy will cost some extra applications. You must encounter different types of tests, trials, and experiences to obtain a level of trust that will give you the type of joy you need in times of crisis. You will only know how much joy you have during the time of testing. You must always remember that the joy of the Lord is your strength. So, no joy, no strength, little joy, little strength, much joy, much strength, more joy, more strength!!! It is entirely up to you to have the level of joy and strength you desire.

A. Nehemiah 8:10b

[10b]For this day is holy unto our Lord: neither be ye sorry; for the joy of the Lord is your strength (the people of God had forgotten his laws and sinned against God. But after the reading of God's words they began to weep and repent of their sins then their leader instructed them to rejoice now because the Lord's joy is their strength).

3. Why is it important to have joy? It is important to have joy to keep the right perspective on things in your life as they occur whether good or bad. Joy will also help you to be able to do things for others

without being selfish because you will see their needs through the Spirit of God. You will also recognize that you can help others regardless of how much or how little you have. You need joy to receive the word of God correctly in your heart.

A. 2Corinthians 8:2

   ²How that in great trial of affliction the abundance of their joy and deep poverty abounded unto the riches of their liberality (the Philippians Church was a very poor Church but because of their joy and love for the Gospel, they often sent offerings to other Churches in their time of needs).

B. Philippians 1:4

   ⁴Always in every prayer of mine for you all making request with joy (the apostle Paul prayed for this congregation with his heart of joy making requests to God for them even though Paul himself was suffering great afflictions).

4. Can I really have joy every day? Yes! Jesus said in His word that the words he spoke unto us will remain and that our joy would be full. There is a condition connected to this promise and that is we must love one another. So if you find that your joy is not full I advise you to check on your level of love for your brothers and sisters. When the Christians come together, there will be great joy in the city because we are responsible for the outcome of the world!

A. John 15:11-12

   ¹¹These things I have spoken unto you, that, my joy might remain in you, and that your joy might be full. ¹²This is my commandment that you love one another, as I have loved you (Jesus was saying that if we keep his words, obey his

commandments, and love one another as he loves us, our joy would be full and it will remain).

B. Acts - 8:5-6, 8

⁵Then Phillip went down to the city of Samaria, and preached Christ unto them. ⁶And the people with one accord gave heed unto those things which Phillip spoke, hearing and seeing the miracles which he did. ⁸And there was great joy in that city (when we have real joy in our hearts, we can do the work of God and this will bring great joy in that city).

5. How can you walk in the joy of the Lord? The first thing to note as a Christian is the fact that the Holy Spirit is joy and he abides in you, so you must abide in Him. This is a mutual agreement between both parties. The more the Holy Spirit abides in you and you in Him, he will be able to help you produce fruit. This includes the fruit of joy. We must know that there are four stages of fruit production and they are: 1) no fruit, 2) fruit, 3) more fruit, and 4) much fruit. The closer you are attached to the true vine (Jesus) the closer you are to the nutrients inside of the vine. With this you are guaranteed to produce fruit at any level. Now you will find yourself walking in joy without even thinking about it. I will come naturally because joy is now in you!!!

A. John 15:1-5

¹I am the true vine (JESUS), and my Father is the Husbandman (caregiver). ²Every branch (us) in me that bears not fruit He (Jesus) takes away: and every branch (us) that bears fruit, He (Jesus) purges it, that it may bring forth more fruit. ³Now you are clean through the word which I have spoken unto you. ⁴Abide in me, and I in you. As the branch cannot bear fruit

of itself, except it abide in the vine; no more can you except you abide in me. [5]I am the vine, you are the branches: He that abides in me, and I in him, the same brings forth much fruit: for without me you can do nothing.

Yes, you can walk in the joy of the Lord every day of your life if you abide (stay, continue, be steadfast) in Jesus. To abide in Him means I must obey, love, honor, and commit all my ways unto Him and He will direct my path!

Remember: Proverbs 3:6 - In all your ways acknowledge Him, and he SHALL direct your paths. As you allow God to direct your path He will integrate your joy into your daily walk. Just trust Him to do so!!!

Notes: _____

_____

_____

_____

_____

_____

_____

_____

_____

_____

_____

_____

_____

_____

_____

_____

_____

_____

_____

_____

_____

_____

_____

_____

_____

_____

Week 16

STAYING ENCOURAGED IN THE LORD

BIBLICAL PRINCIPLE - Deuteronomy 31:6 - ⁶Be strong and of a good courage, fear not, nor be afraid of them: for the Lord your God, He it is that will go with you; He will not fail you, nor forsake you.

What does it mean to be encouraged in the Lord? It means to inspire (stimulate to action; motivate) with hope, courage, and confidence by Divine influence.

The Lord instructed Moses to speak to the children of Israel and let them know that Moses was not going with them into the Promised Land. God had chosen Joshua, Moses' minister to replace Moses as the new leader and Joshua would be the one to take the people into the land of promise. Joshua knew the people had great respect and honor for Moses but now they were to expect the same movement of God in Joshua's life as how God moved in Moses.

I am so sure that Moses understood how Joshua must be feeling right about now! So the Lord told Moses to go before the people and let them know that it was God who had chosen Joshua and not Moses. Moses was also instructed to encourage Joshua and the people so that the transition would be easy.

In this Scripture I can very well understand how insecure Joshua must have felt. Joshua had walked very closely with Moses and he heard, saw, and remembered so many things Moses suffered at the hands of the people. Now God is saying to Joshua, it is your time to step up and lead this great congregation of people. What a challenge, what fear must have fallen upon him, and there must have been some level of anxiety in the mind of Joshua. But even in this, God did not change his mind about his leader!!

So Moses tells Joshua before the congregation to: 1) Be strong, because God does not want you to be a weak leader. 2) Be of good courage, God wanted Joshua to be fearless in the face of danger because on this journey danger would happen. 3) Fear not, do not be afraid of anything or anyone. 4) The Lord your God will go with you, because Joshua had seen the Hand of God move with Moses, God was assuring Joshua that He, God, would be with him also! 5) God would not fail Joshua, the same way He did not fail Moses, God knew that Joshua needed that same trust and confidence in Him to get the mission done. 6) God would not forsake Joshua, it does not matter how rough the road gets, or how tough the mission seems, God is saying, I your Lord and God will never leave you alone!!!

This encouragement coming from God to His servant leader had to have eased all of Joshua's feelings of inabilities, insecurities, and doubt. Now Joshua could focus on the mission ahead and not on his own abilities.

This should make all of us be encouraged because these same words apply to us as Christians today. God has not sent us out without His presence going with us to get the job done. It does not matter what the job or mission may be, God has already made all the provisions that will be necessary. What a Mighty God we serve!!!

Some of our discouragements comes from trying to be like someone else or trying to do things the same way everyone is doing it. You must understand that when God gives you an assignment to do, allow Him to instruct you on the way God wants it done. This will help to relieve some of your pressure.

I would like to give you some Scriptures to read and study so that you can stay encouraged in the Lord and in the power of His might! Your power and might will never be sufficient to accomplish the things of God.

PRACTICAL APPLICATIONS:

1. Deuteronomy 31:8

   [8]And the Lord, he it is that will go before you; he will be with you, he will not fail you, neither forsake you: fear not, neither be dismayed.

   A. Always know without a doubt that God is true to His word. If He said he will be with you, then He will be with you always. You may leave but God will not leave you!!!

2. Isaiah 41:10

   [10]Fear thou not, for I am with you: Be not dismayed; for I am your God: I will strengthen you; yes, I will help you; Yes I will uphold you with the right hand of my righteousness.

A. The Lord does not want you to allow fear to cloud your mind or judgment. Neither does he want you to lose your strength, because since God called you He will hold you up in his right hand, which signifies power and salvation. You are truly taken care of by the Almighty Himself!!

3. 1Samuel 30:6

   6And David was greatly distressed; for the people spoke of stoning him, because the soul of all the people was grieved, every man for his sons and for his daughters: but David encouraged himself in the Lord his God.

   A. David had just finish fighting a great battle away from home, when he returned home another army had come in and destroyed the city and taken all of their families captive. The people that were with David blamed him for their loss. They were angry enough to stone David, not realizing that His family was taken too. David did not get angry but he had to encourage himself in the Lord. David went directly to his God for the comfort he so badly needed.

   B. Always keep your relationship with God in a way that you can call on him at all times and expect answers. DO NOT put your trust and confidence in humans because they can let you down when the way for them is hard!!!

4. 1Corinthians 10:13

   13There has no temptation taken you but such as is common to man: but God is faithful, who will not suffer you to be tempted above that you are able; but will with the temptation also make a way to escape, that you may be to bear it.

A. To stay encouraged you need to know and remember that when you are tempted, God will not allow you to be tempted above that which you are able to endure. So take comfort in the fact that God will make a way for you to escape, but you must utilize the escape route. So when the load is heavy, encourage yourself in the Lord knowing you can make it!!!

5. 2Corinthians 4:16-18

> [16]For this cause we faint not; but though our outward man perish, yet the inward man is renewed day by day. [17]For our light affliction, which is but for a moment, works for us a far more exceeding and eternal weight of glory. [18]While we look not at the things which are seen, but at the things which are not seen: for the things which are seen are temporal; but the things which are not seen are eternal.

A. When your life is dealt a hard hand and it seems as though you are going under, please do not faint or give up. What you see with the natural eyes is not the whole story because God is working on things in the spirit realm. So what you see is giving you more strength and you are gaining more eternal glory.

B. Also remember what you see is not always what you get. When God is moving in your favor, things are subject to change!

6. Psalm 9:9

> [9]The Lord also will be a refuge for the oppressed, a refuse in times of trouble.

A. God is your shelter in the time of storms and your provider! God will take care of you just put it all in His hands!

7. Psalm 55:22

> ²²Cast your burdens upon the Lord, and He shall sustain thee: He shall never suffer the righteous to be moved.

A. The Lord delights in His children casting all their cares upon Him, this is how great his love and concern is for his people. God will keep you and will not allow you to be moved!

8. Psalm 23:4

> ⁴Yea, though I walk through the valley of the shadow of death, I will not fear evil: for you are with me; your rod and your staff they comfort me.

A. You are His sheep and may walk through some very dark valleys but you will not have to fear any evil because God is with you . With the staff and rod of a Shepherd, God will lead, guide, protect, and rescue you from the danger!

9. Matthew 11:28-29

> ²⁸Come unto me, all of you who labor and are heavy laden, and I will give you rest. ²⁹Take my yoke upon you, and learn of me; for I am meek and lowly in heart: and you shall find rest unto your souls.

A. Jesus is extending an invitation for you to come if you are tired and heavy with burdens and he will give you the rest you need in the time you need it!!

Remember: It is important to stay encouraged in the Lord so that you will not neglect the will of the Lord. If you are encouraged in the Lord you will be able to tell the Lord thank you in all things! Please know that God will take care of you all the time. Trust in Him totally!!!

Notes: _____

_____

_____

_____

_____

_____

_____

_____

_____

_____

_____

_____

_____

_____

_____

_____

_____

_____

_____

_____

_____

_____

_____

_____

_____

_____

_____

_____

_____

Week 17

READING AND STUDYING THE WORD OF GOD DAILY

BIBLICAL PRINCIPLES - 2Timothy 2:15 - ¹⁵Study to show yourself approved unto God, a workman who does not need to be ashamed, rightly dividing the word of truth.

In this Scripture the apostle Paul is giving his young pastor Timothy some valuable reminders as to how Timothy should remain effective in the call of God. As we all know there is a tendency to get comfortable or too relaxed in the work of the Lord. Not only is this a problem but it is also a truth!

Paul began his instructions with the importance of studying the word of God. To be effective in teaching or preaching anything, you must possess knowledge of the contents. Not only a head knowledge but also a conviction in your heart about what you are doing (that is in anything). As you are studying the word of God, there should be a change in you through the power of the word. Your results of studying must present you approved unto God. It does not matter what others are thinking but the main point is: are you approved unto God. If you do not change by what you are studying other will not change either.

Studying the word of God should stir up a desire inside of the reader to want more and more of what you are getting on a daily basis. The more you study, the more you will desire to study. It is of utmost importance to give abundant time to the study of God's word. So what if you are not a preacher or a leader, will you still need to commit to abundant study time? Yes, yes, yes! Because you are called to the field of a servant of the Lord, and to serve Him you should desire to increase your knowledge of everything about your God. Do not take what everyone else is saying as the Gospel. Read and study for yourself so you can develop a sensitive ear to the voice of God and His perfect will for your life.

We all must understand that this relationship is very personal between yourself and God, so personally, you need to invest as much time as possible to enhance this union. You must understand that if you study and get God's approval on your life, you will not be ashamed to spread this Gospel to the rest of the world.

Now you have become a skilled workman able to rightly divide the word of truth whenever needed. You will not take the Word of God and use it to your own advantage to prove or argue with others. Being a skilled workman will teach you that the word of God is for the use of God's will not your agenda!! In the study of God's word you will learn the way to execute what you have learned. You will understand that without controversy, debating, or contention your witness is much greater!

Please allow the Holy Spirit and the Word of God to defend Himself! Studying help and enhance me to do a great work for the Lord, but

God's Word and His Holy Spirit is more than able to do just what He said He would do.

Let us look at some Scriptures that will encourage me to study the Bible on a daily basis.

PRACTICAL APPLICATIONS:

1. Why must you study the word of God daily? The word of God will teach you to have a proper attitude toward God and the things of God.

   A. Psalm 119:161b

      161bBut my heart stand in AWE of your Word (studying the word will cause you to stand in the utmost respect to the Word of God).

   B. Jeremiah 23:28a

      28aThe prophet that have a dream, let him tell a dream; and he that have my word, let him speak my word faithfully (as you grow in your study of the word, you will speak the word faithfully).

   C. Acts 17:11

      11These were more noble than those in Thessalonica, in that they received the word with all readiness of mind, and searched the Scriptures daily, whether those things were so (it is very important to receive the Word of God with a ready mind, but do not stop there, go home and search the Scriptures to see for yourself if what was said is there).

   D. Acts 11:1

¹And the apostles and brethren that were in Judea heard that the Gentiles had also received the word of God (studying the word of God makes me more receptive to the word).

E. Acts 13:48

⁴⁸And when the Gentiles heard this, they were glad, and glorified the word of the Lord: and as many as were ordained to eternal life believed (as you continue to study the word you will find yourself glorifying the word of God).

F. James 1:22-24

²²But you be doers of the word, and not hearers only, deceiving your own selves. ²³For if any be a hearer of the word, and not a doer, he is like unto a man beholding his natural face in a glass: ²⁴For this man beholds himself, and straightway forgets what type of man he was (We are not to just read and study, but take what we have read and start applying it to our everyday life, DO the word).

2. In the Christian's life the word of God is:

A. A Restraint

Psalm 119:9,11 - ⁹Wherewithal shall a young man cleanse his ways? By taking heed thereto according to your word. ¹¹Your word have I hid in my heart, that I might not sin against you.

B. A Guide

Psalm 119:133 - ¹³³Order my steps in your word: and let not any iniquity have dominion over me.

C. Source of Joy

Psalm 119:47, 97-98, 162 - [47]And I will delight myself in your commandments, which I have loved. [97]O how I love your law! It is my meditation all the day. [98]You through your commandments have made me wiser than my enemies: For they (your commandments) are ever with me. [162]I rejoice at your word, as one who finds great spoils (riches).

D. Standard of Conduct

Titus 2:5 - [5]To be discreet, chaste, keepers at home, good, obedient to their own husbands, that the word of God be not blasphemed.

E. Source of New Life

1Peter 1:23 - [23]Being born again, not of corruptible seed, but of incorruptible, by the word of God, which lives and abides forever.

F. Spiritual Food

1Peter 2:2 - [2]As newborn babies, desire the sincere milk if the word, that you may grow thereby.

3. What will the word do for me?

A. Heal and Deliver

Psalm 107:20 - [20]He sent His word, and healed them, and delivered them from their destructions.

B. Make You Free

John 8:32 - [32]And you shall know the truth, and the truth shall make you free.

C. Illuminate

Psalm 119:130 - [130]The entrance of your words gives light; It gives understanding unto the simple.

A. Produce Faith

Romans 10:17 - [17]So then faith comes by hearing, and hearing by the word of God.

B. Rejoice the Heart

Jeremiah 15:16 - [16]Your words were found, and I did eat them; and your word was unto me the joy and rejoicing of my heart: for I am called by your name, O Lord God of Host.

C. Reprove, Rebuke, and Exhort

2Timothy 4:2 - [2]Preach the word; be instant in season and out of season; reprove, rebuke, exhort with all longsuffering and doctrine.

D. Regenerate

James 1:18 - [18]Of His (God) own will He brought us forth by the word of truth, that we might be a kind of first fruits of His creatures.

Since you see that reading and studying the Word of God can and will do so many positive things in your life, I know you are now more than persuaded to start studying. Get into the habit of reading and studying everyday because you will only get out what you put in!!!

Remember: If you walk in the Word of God, You will reflect the life of Jesus Christ because Jesus is the Word!!!

Notes: _____

_____

_____

_____

_____

_____

_____

_____

_____

_____

_____

_____

_____

_____

_____

_____

_____

_____

_____

_____

_____

_____

_____

_____

_____

52 weeks of practical application to biblical principles

Week 18

HOW TO BE STEADFAST IN GOD

BIBLICAL PRINCIPLES - 1Corinthians 15:58 - **[58]Therefore, my beloved brethren, you be steadfast, unmovable, always abounding in the work of the Lord, for as much as you know that your labor is not in vain in the Lord.**

First of all we must note that in this Scripture the Lord refers to us as my beloved brethren before he gives us anymore instructions. Why would this be of any importance? Because the Lord is letting us know that we are loved very much by Him. Beloved is a title of endearment, meaning act of affection. Before encouraging us to be steadfast, we are told that we are loved. We must understand that as life happens to all of us, it is very reassuring to know we have a God who is very personal and cares for you and me. More than we will ever know.

Because of the resurrection of Christ, we are not working for empty promises. Jesus is faithful and when He promises something it is going to happen regardless of your deadline or circumstances. I am so glad that God is not surprised when we have situations that are disappointing! Because of His Eternal and Sovereign nature, he is always in total control. We get in an uproar but it is good to know our God never sweats or lose his cool!!!

So when the Lord tells us to be steadfast, He means for us to be firm, persistent, and determined in our endeavors. God does not want us to start something and never complete the task. We must keep on moving forward so that we will experience the feeling of completion and pleasing God. To God be the glory should be our desire!

To be unmovable is to be emotionally unaffected, not able or intended to be moved. It is almost impossible to stay on task if your mind is constantly roaming. To be unmovable is to keep your mind on the things of God. Keep your focus on the assignment given to you and spend less time worrying about what someone else is doing. Many times we become anxious because we do not trust God to guide us in the path of His will, so we get busy telling others how to complete their assignment. Stay on task, keep your mind free, and allow God to order your steps. Determine in your own heart, you are in Christ Jesus to stay forever.

Always abounding or increasing greatly in the work of the Lord. We should always want to produce fruit in the Lord! In fact the Bible informs us that if we abide in the vine (Jesus), we will be able to bear fruit, then more fruit, and finally much fruit. In this process we are to always remain abounding in God's work. A Christian should never be content to just be saved; we must always move toward perfection and always strive to bring glory to the name of our God.

Finishing up He lets us know that our labor is not in vain. Everything you do for the Lord will be rewarded by Jesus Himself. Our hearts must be in everything we do for our Savior or we would be better off not doing anything. God desire faithfulness to Him from our heart, not lip service and empty promised.

Can you imagine living a steadfast, unmovable, and greatly increasing life for Christ? This can really be achieved and we will go into the Word of God to see how to walk this out.

PRACTICAL APPLICATIONS:

1. Let me start with being steadfast in the Lord, when the Lord commands us to be steadfast, meaning to be firm, persistent, and determined in our endeavors. You must realize that it is up to you to do the things that will give you a steadfast life in Christ. In this life everyone will go through trials, tribulations, discouragement, failures, persecutions (inside and outside your family and church), and many other things. But your key to survival is to remain steadfast in the Lord! I will give you some Scriptures to study, place in your heart, and apply to your daily walk for growth in this area. Giving up is not an option for you!!!

    A. Enduring Chastisement

        Hebrews 12:7 - 7If you endure chastening, God deals with you as with sons; for what son is he whom the father does not chastise?

    B. Bearing Persecution

        Romans 8:35-37 - 35Who shall separate us from the love of Christ? Shall tribulation, or distress, or persecution, or famine, or nakedness, or peril, or sword? 36As it is written, for Christ sake we are killed all day long; we are accounted as sheep for the slaughter. [37]No, in all these things we are more than conquerors through Christ who loved us.

C. Maintaining Perseverance

Hebrews 3:6, 14 - [6]But Christ as a Son over His own house; Whose house we are, if we hold fast the confidence and the rejoicing of the hope firm unto the end. [14]For we are made partakers of Christ, if we hold the beginning of our confidence steadfast unto the end.

D. Stability of Faith

Colossians 2:5-6 - [5]For though I (Pau l) be absent in the flesh, yet I am with you in the spirit, having joy and beholding your order, and the steadfastness of your faith in Christ. [6]As you have therefore received Christ Jesus the Lord, so you continue walking in Him.

E. Persevering in Service

1Corinthians 15:58 - [58]Therefore, my beloved brethren, you be steadfast, unmovable, always abounding in the work of the Lord, for as much as you know that your labor is not in vain in tie Lord.

F. Defending Christian Liberty

Galatians 5:1 - [1]Stand fast therefore in the liberty wherewith Christ has made us free, and be not entangled again with the yoke of bondage.

2. To be unmovable is to be emotionally unaffected, not able or intended to be moved in your whole walk with the Lord. There are days when you do not feel like staying focus, doing the things of God, or being involved in things pertaining to the Church, that's okay, just do not be moved. Take time to rest your mind, your

emotions, and get back into the ring. I am sure all Christians get tired at some point in this walk, but we cannot give up or give in to what we are feeling. When you have counted up the cost, you realize that your life belongs entirely to The Lord Jesus Christ and Jesus has never quit. Take the time to study these Scriptures and let them sink deep within your heart, soul, and spirit so that you will not be moved!!!

A. Psalm 55:22

[22]Cast your burden upon the Lord, and he shall sustain you: He shall never suffer the righteous to be moved.

B. Psalm 66:8-9

[8]O bless our God, you people, and make the voice of His praise be heard: [9]Which holds our soul in life, and will not suffer our feet to be moved.

C. Psalm 112:5-6

[5]A good man shows favor, and lends; He will guide his affairs with discretion. [6]Surely he shall not be moved forever: the righteous shall be in everlasting remembrance.

D. Psalm 121:1-3

[1]I will lift up my eyes unto the hills, from whence comes my help. [2]My help comes from the Lord, which made heaven and earth. [3]He will not suffer my foot to be moved: He that keeps me will not slumber.

E. Psalm 125:1

[1]They who trust in the Lord shall be as mount Zion, which cannot be removed, but abides forever.

F. Proverbs 10:30

³⁰The righteous shall never be removed: but the wicked shall not inhabit the earth.

G. Psalm 62:6

⁶He only is my rock and my salvation: He is my defense; I shall not be moved.

3. Christians must always be abounding or increasing greatly in the work of the Lord. Scripture teaches us that as we abide in Jesus and He abides in us we will produce fruit, more fruit, and much fruit. This alone tells us that we are to be active in our work for God. We must never become unproductive even in times of testing. Testing should produce character in us and leave us with experience that will help someone else alone the way. We must always know that we are not here for ourselves but for the benefit of others. We are lights in dark places to illuminate the path for others.

A. **In Edifying Others**

1Corinthians 14:12 - ¹²Even so you, for as much as you are zealous (intense enthusiasm for something) of spiritual gifts, seek that you may excel to the edifying of the Church.

B. **In Giving**

2Corinthians 8:2 - ²How that in great trial of affliction the abundance of their joy and their deep poverty abounded unto the riches of their liberality.

2Corinthians 8:7 - ⁷Therefore, as you abound in everything, in faith, and utterance, and knowledge, and in all diligence, and in your love to us, see that you abound in this grace also.

C. **In Every Good Work**

2Corinthians 9:8 - [8]And God is able to make all grace abound towards you: that you, always having sufficiency in all things, may abound to every good work.

D. In Love

Philippians 1:9 - [9]And this I pray, that your love may abound yet more and more in knowledge and in all judgment.

1Thessalonians 4:9-10 - [9]But as touching brotherly love you need not that I write unto you: for you yourselves are taught of God to love one another. [10]And indeed you do it towards all the brethren which are in Macedonia: but we beseech (call to) you, brethren that you increase more and more.

1Thessalonians 3:12 - And the Lord make you to increase and abound in love one towards another, and towards all men, even as we do towards you.

E. In Joy

Philippians 1:26 - [26]That your rejoicing may be more abundant in Jesus Christ for me by my coming to you again.

F. In Thanksgiving

Colossians 2:7 - [7]Rooted and built up in him, and established in the faith, as you have been taught, abounding therein with thanksgiving.

G. A Life That Pleases God

1Thessalonians 4:1 - 1Furthermore then we beseech (call to) you, brethren, and exhort you by the Lord Jesus, that as you have received of us how you ought to walk and to please God, so you would abound more and more.

4. Your labor is not in vain in the Lord. Your God is always faithful, but there are things we must do. We must abide in the vine and allow the vine to abide in us because we need nutrients from the vine. Without the vine we cease to exist and there will be no fruit. There are 4 stages of fruit bearing (1)-no fruit, (2)-fruit, (3)-more fruit, and (4)-much fruit, it is up to me what level or stage of fruit bearing I will produce. We should desire excellence, MUCH FRUIT!!!

   A. John 15:1-5 - ¹I am the true vine, and my Father is the husbandman, ²Every branch in me that does not bear fruit he takes away: and every branch that bears fruit, he purges it, that it may bring forth more fruit. ³Now you are clean through the word I have spoken unto you. ⁴Abide in me, and I in you. As the branch cannot bear fruit of itself, except it abide in the vine; no more can you, except you abide in me. ⁵I am the vine, you are the branches: He that abides in me, and I in him, the same brings forth much fruit: for without me you can do nothing.

Let us practice every word these Scripture are teaching, work on each area until you see change. Make up in your mind that you are changing even if you start off with small steps, at least you are moving.

Remember: Giving up, quitting, and throwing in the towel is never an option. You will become and remain steadfast, unmovable, and always abounding in the work of the LORD because you love Him and desire to please Him in all things!!!

Notes: _____

_____

_____

_____

_____

_____

_____

_____

_____

_____

_____

_____

_____

_____

_____

_____

_____

_____

_____

_____

_____

_____

_____

_____

_____

_____

_____

_____

_____

_____

Week 19

GETTING RID OF STINKING THINKING

BIBLICAL PRINCIPLES - Romans 12:2-3 - ²And be not conformed to this world: but you be transformed by the renewing of your mind, that you may prove what is that good, and acceptable, and perfect, will of God. ³For I say, through the grace given unto me, to every man that is among you, not to think of himself more highly than he ought to think; but to think soberly, according as God has dealt to every man the measure of faith.

Here we are instructed not to think as the world think with its evil thoughts and doings. Christians are to live an entirely different way, but it can only happen if we change our minds. The way we once thought, felt, lived, and acted cannot come into my new life. We must forbid our old ways of thinking and habits to be in control of the life we live.

I call this stinking thinking because if you do not get rid of it, it will get rid of you!! We must be transformed, meaning to change the nature, the function, and the condition of, also to convert our minds! When understanding this, you have a responsibility to yourself to start the process of change in your mind. It will not happen all at once, because it is a process! As you began to change your process of thinking, your thoughts on morality (principles of right conduct) will change also. This is how you start walking upright. A mind change means a life change!!!

This process is also known as mind renewal. When you change your mind to do what is right, you will be able to prove through your new lifestyle what is that good, acceptable, and perfect will of God. Please understand the proof is not just in words but also in the way you live. The world needs to know that you have truly been changed from the inside out. This is the transformation spoken of in this Scripture.

As you began to change your mind you will start a process called spiritual and moral growth or maturity. This is when you began to be acceptable unto God. Sometimes man may not see or recognize your growth but God will because He knows your heart!

With maturity comes sobriety, meaning you will not think too highly of yourself. You will think with a clear honest view of your life. You will only see yourself through God by the true measure of faith given unto you. Because you now understand that all power comes from God, and the ministry you have been placed into, is given to you by Him, therefore there can be no superior attitude or self righteousness on your part. What do you have that has not been given unto you from God? Why should you boast and how can you brag?

Every believer was given by God, the power to fulfill God's ministries in His Church. So no more stinking thinking of how great you are, but think about how great God is in you!!!

We must see what Scripture teaches about your thinking!

PRACTICAL APPLICATIONS:

1. There are so many areas of stinking thinking that can prevent your spiritual growth. I know we cannot deal with all of them but I will give you Scriptures that will alert you to what can happen when you allow yourself to walk in stinking thinking. Your mind is a very powerful tool and weapon in your walk with Christ, therefore you need to have the mind of Christ.

   A. 1Corinthians 2:16

      [16]For who has known the mind of the Lord, that he may instruct Him? But we have the mind of Christ (we cannot instruct Christ, but with the mind of Christ I can obey and live for Him, I cannot do what I want to do).

   B. Philippians 2:5

      [5]Let this mind be in you which was also in Christ Jesus (Jesus always kept His Father's will top priority, he came to obey God and we are to obey Jesus, not an option but a command).

2. One of the greatest downfalls of Christians is always wanting someone to esteem them higher than others. This is not why you became a Christian. You became a Christian to lift up Jesus, not for you to be lifted up. In fact Scripture encourages you to lift others up higher than yourself. Practicing this will keep you from always thinking about yourself! If you have any intimate personal

relationship with Christ and any fruit of the Spirit in you, start putting others first.

A. Philippians 2:1-4

> [1]If there be therefore any consolation in Christ, if any comfort of love, if any fellowship of the Spirit, if any bowels and mercies, [2]Fulfill you my joy, that you will be like minded, having the same love, being of one accord, of one mind. [3]Let nothing be done through strife or vainglory: but in lowliness of mind let each esteem other better than themselves. [4]Look not every man on his own things, but every man on the things of others (we must live in such unity that we want the best for others, not always just for myself).

B. Philippians 4:13

> [13]I can do all things through Christ who strengthens me (when I walk in unity with Christ and the body of Christ, I can do all things because Christ is my strength).

3. Positive thinking is always a must. To create this type of thinking for yourself there are things to do. Let me recommend that you start giving your mind some healthy food for thought. You cannot put any and everything into your mind and expect to have godly thoughts. Remember it has always been said, you are what you eat. The way you think is the way you will live. Speak the truth, be honest in your heart, treat people right and fair, and keep your mind pure. You will be surprised at how much you will grow in Christ!!

A. Philippians 4:8

> [8]Finally brethrens, whatsoever things are true, whatsoever things are honest, whatsoever things are just, whatsoever

things are pure, whatsoever things are lovely, whatsoever things are of good report: if there is any virtue, and if there is any praise, think on these things (these are the right things you need to think on daily, put good stuff in and get good stuff out).

B. Proverbs 23:7a

[7a]For as he thinks in his heart, so is he (your heart speaks the truth about your mind and how you think).

4. There are some dangerous places that the Christian's mind must be protected against. If you practice what the Scripture teaches, you will avoid these pit holes. You will not walk with your head down because you lost your focus. My advice to you is to stay FOCUSED and stay away from worry, doubt, disunity, growing weary, mental disturbances, and spiritual disturbance!!! You do not need these in your Christian walk!

A. Worry

Luke 12:29 - [29]And do not seek (worry about) what you shall eat, or what you shall drink, neither be of a doubtful mind (Do not worry about things you cannot change).

B. Doubt

Matthew 21:21 - [21]Jesus answered and said unto them, verily I say unto you, if you have faith, and doubt not, you shall not only do this which is done to the fig tree, but also if you shall say unto this mountain, you be removed, and be cast in the sea; it shall be done (doubt will stop you from progress).

C. Disunity

> 1Corinthians 1:10 - [10]Now I beseech you, brethren, by the name of our Lord Jesus Christ, that ye all speak the same thing, and that there be no divisions among you; but that you be perfectly joined together in the same mind and in the same judgment (disunity will destroy a relationship, church, and you).

D. Grow Weary

> Hebrews 12:3 - [3]For consider Him that endured such contradiction of sinners against himself lest you be wearied and faint in your minds (whenever you feel weary, think about the things Jesus suffered for you and I and count it an honor to suffer for Christ).

E. Mental and Spiritual Disturbances

> 2Thessalonians 2:2 - [2]That you be not soon shaken in mind, or be troubled, neither by spirit, nor by word, nor by letter as from us, as that the day of Christ is at hand (do not let anything upset your mind or your spirit, stand on what you know is true).

If you can practice realigning your mind daily to the will of God, and really get rid of stinking thinking you can become everything the Lord desires for you in this life. Start today working on changing your mind to the mind of Christ.

Remember: The time you waste on stinking thinking will be the time you could trust, obey, glorified God and give him praise. Do not waste you valuable time anymore!!!

Notes: _____

_____

_____

_____

_____

_____

_____

_____

_____

_____

_____

_____

_____

_____

_____

_____

_____

_____

_____

_____

_____

_____

_____

_____

_____

_____

Week 20

I AM NOT A VICTIM BUT A VICTOR

BIBLICAL PRINCIPLE - Romans 8:27-28 - ²⁷And he that searches the hearts knows what is the mind of the Spirit, because he makes intercessions for the saints according to the will of God. ²⁸And we know that all things work together for good to them that love God, to them who are the called according to His purpose.

First of all please scream with me, I am not a victim but a victor! These Scriptures are so great, they tell us that God searches our hearts and God also knows the mind of the Holy Spirit because they are one. The Holy Spirit inside of us makes intercessions which are prayers offered in our behalf, according to what God's will is for me! Because God the Father and the Holy Spirit are so close and united, when the Holy Spirit prays for me he does not have to speak out loud, His thoughts are always known to God!!

There are times when we do not know what we should pray for, but I am so glad the Holy Spirit knows what is best for us and what is needed for us at the proper time. He knows when we need to be tested, when we need correction, and the type of testing needed for my good! He lives inside of us for a reason. The Holy Spirit was sent to help us fulfill the purpose and plans that God have for our life. Moreover, the Holy Spirit is the Spirit of the Living God; who better to take all of our needs directly than God himself? This is the main reason we need to allow the Spirit of God to have complete control of every area of our life. Do not practice trying to do what you want to do; you do not know what is truly best for you!!!

If you walk in the Spirit of God and not in the desires of your flesh, you will understand why you are no longer a victim but a victor. Your flesh will always remind you that your way is so hard because the flesh have a way of not forgetting your past. In your life before you became a Christian you were a victim, Satan held you captive and abused you as much as he desired, because he was you master! But God, after sending His Spirit to live inside of you, have made you not just a conqueror, but now you are more than a conqueror through Christ Jesus our Lord!!! Because of this you are no longer a victim and you cannot cry victim anymore. If you continue to act, live, or cry as a victim, you are testifying that God's Spirit is not able to heal you and your broken pieces. We know that our God is a healer and a deliverer in every area!!!

But you must walk in the Spirit so you will not fulfill the lusts of your flesh. When you do this, the rest of this Scripture will pertain to you. Now God is saying to you: And we know that all things work together for good to them that love God, to them who are the called according to His purpose. It does not matter to God how bad your life was. It does not matter to God how long your life was that way. It does not matter to God who made your life that way. All that matters to God now is that you belong to Him and all things will work together for your good, regardless of the bad broken baggage that made you appear to be nothing. God can and will take all of that and present it in your ministry package!!!

Why would God do this for you? Because he loves you and now you love Him. It is that simple. Our God is so AWESOME and POWERFUL that he can make greatness in you out of what you have been through. This is when you look back and say, the devil meant it for your bad but God meant it unto good!!

Now you will fulfill your purpose and in Christ Jesus, because you are called according to God's purpose and you are not a victim but a VICTOR!! Let us see what the Word of God has to say about these things!

PRACTICAL APPLICATIONS:

1. When you think of the Word Conqueror and add it to who you are as a Christian, you should experience an enormous amount of joy on the inside. Because a conqueror is one who overcomes by physical, mental, or moral force, also conquers fear. Now do you see why you must rise above your feelings and start walking in the Spirit and the authority given to you as a Child of the most High God!!! Stop looking at how hard things are and began to use the power given to you to overcome. You will make it, this is a given!

   A. Romans 8:36-37

      [36]As it is written, for Christ sake we are killed all the day long, we are accounted as sheep for the slaughter. [37]No, in all these

things we are more than conquerors through Him (Christ) that loved us.

2. Pull you body together and tell it to obey the word of God. Pull your mind together and start thinking with the mind of Christ. It is your responsibility to fast and pray (if needed) to bring your flesh into alignment to the perfect will of God. Jesus had the mind to humble Himself to do whatever His Father desired of Him and you can have the same mind. Practice makes perfect; you must start at some point to condition your body and mind to change to God way of thinking.

   A. Philippians 2:5-6

   ⁵Let this mind be in you which was also in Christ Jesus: ⁶who being in the form of God, thought it not robbery to be equal with God (even though Jesus knew He was equal with God his Father, He did not consider His high position to be something he could not give up).

3. You are walking in a new life now and you must forgive yourself for what you have done wrong and forget it just as God has forgotten it. When changing your mind you must not allow your thoughts to keep going down memory lane, just let it all go. There is so much life ahead of you to live, without bringing your past with you. Throw that old baggage away, pick up your bright new future, and began to live again, only this time in Christ Jesus our Lord!!! You can do this, that is why it is called Born Again!!

   A. Philippians 3:13-15

   ¹³Brethren, I count not myself to have apprehended (taken hold of): but this one thing I do, forgetting those things

which are behind, and reaching forth unto those things which are before. [14]I press toward the mark for the prize of the high calling of God in Christ Jesus. [15]Let us therefore, as many as be perfect, be thus minded: and if in anything you be otherwise minded, God shall reveal even this unto you (after you become a child of God, you have a brand new life and the old life is not important anymore).

B. Philippians 4:13

[13]I can do all things through Christ who strengthens me (it is not by your power that you will accomplish this, but by the power of Jesus Christ our Lord).

4. Look in the mirror and see the new individual God have made you to become and start telling Him thank you every day for this new creature. The old you is gone and hopefully never to return again, that is up to you. The devil meant for people to see you at your worst but God wants to show them your better, if you will allow Him. What was meant for bad, God made it good.

A. Genesis 50:20

[20]But as for you, you thought evil against me; but God meant it unto good, to bring to pass, as it is this day, to save much people (only God knows how to bring all the pieces of your life together and make your future brighter than you could ever imagine).

B. 2Corinthians 5:17

[17]Therefore if any man be in Christ, he is a new creature: old things are passed away; behold all things are become new (you

can serve your eviction notice to your old man because the new you is here and active).

Do not waste any more of your time living as a victim. Start today walking as the Victor you are in Christ Jesus our Lord!!

Remember: God does not sit down and hold your old life in His hands, He is too busy giving you life, more abundantly! All you have to do is accept it and LIVE!

Notes: _____

_____

_____

_____

_____

_____

_____

_____

_____

_____

_____

_____

_____

_____

_____

_____

_____

_____

_____

_____

_____

_____

_____

_____

_____

_____

_____

_____

_____

_____

_____

Week 21

I WILL TRUST YOU LORD

BIBLICAL PRINCIPLES - Proverbs 3:5-6 - ⁵Trust in the Lord with all your heart; and lean not unto your own understanding. ⁶In all your ways acknowledge Him, and He shall direct your paths.

What does trust mean? Trust means to have firm reliance on the integrity, ability, or character of a person or thing. Trust is something committed into the care of another. Finally, trust also means to place your confidence in something or someone.

In this Scripture we are instructed or commanded first, to trust in the Lord with all of our heart and not to lean on our own understanding. God is saying to us, have complete confidence in Him, knowing that God is the one and only faithful God! He wants us to rely on or be dependent on Him for support, for help, and to supply all of our needs. We are to do it with our whole heart, not half heartedly or not thinking in our heart that he may not come through for us (doubt). Even when we cannot see our way or if it seems like there is no way for this to happen, we must stand still and wait for God's response.

Stop leaning to your own understanding! You do not know how or when God will work it out, but you must know in your heart that he will do it. Your God is so faithful all the time!!!

Sometimes we are so busy trying to figure things out while God is already working on the far end of the situation. We are humans, meaning we can only see so far into the situation, but because God is everywhere present, He sees and know the entire situation. God have all the resources needed and available for His usage that you do not know of. God can move things, people, and whatever else is needed to change your situations and bring you to your expected end. Many times we are looking for God to move one way when in fact He will move in an entirely different way working it out for your good!!

We want right now relief and are only concerned with right now results. God looks into the future because He is eternal meaning, God exist outside of time, there is no beginning or ending to Him! Therefore what he does with your situation will last longer than right now and He will not rush because He knows how long you have on this earth and what needs to happen in your life time. His solution to the problem will be the best and carry you the farthest in life. God has access to your future and He knows things regarding your life that you do not have a clue is going to happen. Would you not agree with me that because of this major future knowledge possessed by the Almighty God, He is the one to put your confidence in. I often say that my God is working on my situation even if I do not know what He is doing with it.

This brings me to the rest of the story "In all your ways acknowledge Him, and He shall direct your paths". You are to always acknowledge God in everything you do whether small or great. I think our problem is that we think God is not interested in my small life and the small things that are going on in it. This, my brothers and sisters could not be farther from the truth. In all reality, your God is so concerned about your life that He sent His only Son to the Cross to die just for you, yes that is right, just for you! Now, you tell me why God wouldn't be interested in the affairs of your life. With this kind of LOVE for you, why can't you trust Him with your entire life?

I think too, we are afraid that what God do may not be what you want done, but it is best for you. Your understanding is limited and His is not. Let us get into the habit of consulting with God before we make our move in all things. See what God has to say about your decisions and how to truly trust in the Lord!

PRACTICAL APPLICATIONS:

1. You are to put your trust in God's name His Word and His Son. To trust God is to trust His Word. Everything written in the word of God is to be walked out daily in your life. When you say you trust what God is saying the evidence is you walking it out. The word of God is all about His Son, Jesus the Christ. To have a personal relationship with Jesus is to walk out everything He commands you to do. It takes self- control and daily practice to get into the habit of trusting God. You need to start out by putting your trust in:

   A. Trust in God's Name

      Psalm 33:21 - [21]For our hearts shall rejoice in Him, because we have trusted in his holy name.

   B. Trust in God's Word

      Psalm 119:42 - [42]So shall I have wherewith to answer him that reproaches (criticize, disapprove, disappointed in) me: For I trust in your Word.

C. Trust in the Lord

>   Matthew 12:18,21 - [18]Behold my servant, whom I have chosen; my beloved in whom my soul is well pleased: I will put my Spirit upon Him, and He shall show judgment to the Gentiles. [21]And in His name shall the Gentiles trust.

>   Proverbs 22:19 - [19]That your trust may be in the Lord, I have made known to you this day, even to you.

2. There are certain things and people we are forbidden to place our trust in. We are not to trust in weapons, wealth, leaders, man, works, and our own righteousness because they will fail us. Things and people are only temporal and can very easily be removed or can let us down. So it is important to put all my trust in the Lord who made the heavens and the earth. Trust in the God who has all power in His hands. Do not put your trust in:

A. **Weapons**

>   Psalm 44:6-7 - [6]For I will not trust in my bow, neither shall my sword save me. [7]But you have saved us from our enemies, and has put them to shame that hated us.

B. **Wealth**

>   Psalm 49:6-7 - [6]They that trust in their wealth, and boast themselves in the multitude of their riches; [7]None of them can by any means redeem his brother, nor give to God a ransom for him.

C. **Leaders**

>   Psalm 146:3-5 - [3]Put not your trust in Princes, nor in the son of man, in whom there is no help. [4]His breath goes forth, he

returns to his earth: and that very day his thoughts perish. [5]Happy is he that have the God of Jacob for his help, whose hope is in the Lord his God.

D. Man

Jeremiah 17:5-6 - [5]Thus says the Lord: cursed be the man that trusts in man, and makes flesh his arm, and whose heart departs from the Lord. [6]For he shall be like the heath (destitute) in the desert, and shall not see when good comes, but shall inhabit the parched places in the wilderness, in a salt land (an evidence of God's curse) and not inhabited.

E. Works

Jeremiah 48:7a – [7a]For because you have trusted in your works and in your treasures, you shall also be taken.

F. Ourselves

2Corinthians 1:9-10 - [9]But we had the sentence of death in ourselves that we should not trust in ourselves, but in God which raises the dead: [10]Who delivered us from so great a death, and does deliver: in whom we trust that he will deliver us.

3. There are so many benefits for trusting in the Lord! These are just a few:

A. Joy

Psalm 5:11-12 - [11]But let all those who put their trust in you rejoice: Let them ever shout for joy, because you defend them: Let them also that love your name be joyful in you. [12]For you,

Lord, will bless the righteous; With favor will you compass his as with a shield.

B. Deliverance

Psalm 22:4-5 - [4]Our fathers trusted in you: They trusted, and you did deliver them. [5]They cried unto you, and were delivered: They trusted in you and were not confounded.

C. Triumph

Psalm 25:2-4 - [2]O my God, I trust in you: let me not be ashamed, Let not my enemies triumph over me. [3]Yes, let none that wait on you be ashamed: Let them be ashamed which transgress without a cause. [4]Show me your ways, O Lord.

D. God's Goodness

Psalm 31:19-20 - [19]O how great is your goodness, which you have laid up for them that fear you; Which you have prepared for those who trust in you. [20]You shall hide them in the secret of your presence from the pride of man: You shall keep them secretly in a pavilion from the strife of tongues.

E. Mercy

Psalm 32:10 - [10]Many sorrows shall be to the wicked: But he that trusts in the Lord, mercy shall compass him about.

F. Provisions

Psalm 37:3,5 - [3]Trust in the Lord and do good; So shall you dwell in the land, and verily you shall be fed. [5]Commit your ways unto the Lord; Trust also in Him; and He shall bring it to pass.

G. Blessedness

Psalm 40:4 - [4]Blessed is that man who makes the Lord his trust, and respects not the proud, nor such as turn aside to lies.

H. Guidance

Proverbs 3:5-6 - [5]Trust in the Lord with all your heart; and lean not unto your own understanding. [6]In all your ways acknowledge Him, and He shall direct your paths.

I. Safety

Psalm 56:3-4,11 - [3]Whenever I am afraid, I will trust in thee. [4]In God I will praise His word, In God I have put my trust; I will not fear what flesh can do unto me. [11]In God have I put my trust: I will not be afraid what man can do unto me.

J. Usefulness

Psalm 73:28 - [28]But it is good for me to draw near to God: I have put my trust in the Lord God, that I may declare all thy works.

It is very important that you learn to trust in the God. Your salvation is dependent upon your trust in Jesus the Son of God so, if you cannot trust in God the father how can you trust in God the Son? Make it a priority to trust God.

Remember: Trusting God is all about the level of confidence you have in God's integrity, ability, and character! When you trust Him, daily obedience and walking in His word will come natural. All you need to do is "Just do it".

Notes: _____

_____

_____

_____

_____

_____

_____

_____

_____

_____

_____

_____

_____

_____

_____

_____

_____

_____

_____

_____

_____

_____

_____

_____

_____

_____

_____

_____

_____

_____

Week 22

WALKING IN THE SPIRIT

BIBLICAL PRINCIPLES - Romans 8:12-15 - [12]Therefore, brethren, we are debtors, not to the flesh, to live after the flesh. [13]For if you live after the flesh, you shall die: but if you through the Spirit do mortify the deeds of the body, you shall live. [14]For as many as are led by the Spirit of God, they are the sons of God. [15]For you have not received the spirit of bondage again to fear; but you have received the Spirit of adoption, whereby we cry Abba, Father.

What does it mean to walk in the Spirit? The only way to conquering the works of the flesh is by the power of the Holy Spirit. All believers are to walk daily in the power and presence of the Holy Spirit. No human has the power within himself to control the lusts of the flesh. The human flesh fights or wars against the desires of the Spirit and if you do not allow the Holy Spirit to overrule the flesh you will find yourself doing everything the flesh desires. As Christians we are to mortify (kill) the works of the flesh but not kill the flesh. Every believer is to stay in the word of God, submit to the will of God, and walk away from the pressures and urges of the flesh then call upon the Lord for strength and deliverance from the lusts that is pulling at him/her. This is walking in the Spirit!

Scripture teaches us that as Christians, we no longer have to live after the desires of the flesh. We have been given freedom and deliverance by the death and resurrection of Jesus Christ from all control of fleshly desires. Jesus sent His Holy Spirit to indwell every believer with the power needed to walk in the desires of the Lord.

We all know what it is to have strong urges and desires of the flesh pulling and tugging at us, but this is not an excuse to give in to the struggle. This is when you go into that secret place with the Almighty God and cry out to him in faith for him to deliver you. If it is something you are able to walk away from, please walk away. We know that if you walk after the flesh (fulfilling the lust of the flesh) you will die. Fulfilling the desires of the flesh will prevent you from doing the will of God and eventually you will find yourself walking away from the very God who delivered you.

If you on the other hand, walk after the Spirit of God and kill the works of your flesh, you will live. Many times we want to walk in the Spirit but will not stay before the Lord long enough to develop the fruit of Self-Control. You have self- control within you but as anything else it must be developed and matured. This may cause for some trials where you learn resistance to yielding! When you confess that you are a Christian and filled with the Spirit of God, if you do not exhibit self-control in your living, no one believes you are a Christian. The presence of the Holy Spirit is evidenced by a Spirit controlled life. This is when you ask yourself am I living a life of self-control.

For you to be called a son of God, you must be led by the Spirit. This may sound like a hard way to live but it is not. Being led by the Spirit of God is the best life you will ever live. As you develop into this person God desires you to become, you will find yourself with the peace, love, forgiveness, and blessings of God. If you allow the Holy Spirit to develop your godly character and all the fruit that goes with it, you will one day look in the mirror and see the new and transformed you!! Do not be afraid to take whatever testing needed to make the transition happen. We all have had to make changes and adjustments in every phase of life to get to where we are now. It is no different in the Christian way of living. You must change and adjust your life to giving the Holy Spirit total control of leading and guiding you through the will of God.

You must avoid the works of the flesh and cling to the fruit of the Spirit. You have not been given the Spirit of bondage again to fear but the Spirit of adoption as children of the most High God. Now you can call Him Abba, father meaning, you now have an exceptionally close Father and Son relationship with God your Father through His Son Jesus Christ!! Since you are now a son or child of God, you are required to live like it. You cannot live in your old sinful ways any longer because the Spirit of God abides in you, and is in you to stay!

I will list some of the works of the Flesh so you will know what to avoid and the fruit of the Spirit for you to know what needs to be developed:

PRACTICAL APPLICATIONS:

1. Let us take a look at the works of the flesh to find out what they are, so you will be able to identify them. Each of these acts has a very broad meaning and is not limited to just one thing. You have the power in you through the Holy Spirit to resist that desire. Do not give in.

A. Galatians 5:18-21

> [18]But if you be led by the Spirit, you are not under the law. [19]Now the works of the flesh are manifest, which are these; Adultery, fornication, uncleanness, lasciviousness, [20]Idolatry, witchcraft, hatred, variance, emulations, wrath strife, seditions, heresies, [21]Envyings, murders, drunkenness, revellings, and such like: of the which I tell you before, as I have also told you in time past, that they which do such things shall not inherit the kingdom of God.

Works of the Flesh Meaning:

- Adultery-sexual unfaithfulness to husband or wife, looking on a woman or man to lust after. (Matthew 5:28)

- Fornication-including all forms of immoral and sexual acts, premarital sex, adultery, abnormal sex, all kinds of sexual vices. (Ephesians 5:3; 1Corithians 6:18)

- Uncleanness-moral impurities, doing all kinds of dirty things that pollute life. (Ephesians 5:3; Colossians 3:5)

- Lasciviousness-Filthiness, indecency, shamelessness, unrestrained evil thoughts and behavior. Having brutish and lustful desires. (Ephesians 4:19)

- Idolatry-the worship of idols, giving your primary time and energy to something other than God. More than just a stature. (Galatians 5:19-21)

- Witchcraft-sorcery, the use of evil spirits or drugs to gain control over your life or someone else's life. Astrology, palm reading, etc. (Isaiah 8:19-20)

- Hatred-Hostility, enmity, animosity, a hate that continues on and on embedded deep within the heart. (1John 4:20)

- Variance-fighting, struggling, quarreling, discord, strife, fighting against others to gain what you want. (Proverbs 26:21)

- Emulations-jealousy, wanting and desiring what others have, material things, honor, position, etc. (Proverbs 6:34)

- Wrath-explosive temper, burst of anger, indignation, quick tempered, anger that arise and fades away quickly. (James1:19-20)

- Strife-conflicts, fight, a party spirit, a cliquish spirit, struggle, and contention. (Philippians 2:3)

- Seditions-standing against others, divisions, rebellion, splitting off from others. (2Peter 2:10)

- Heresies-Rejecting the beliefs of God, Christ, Scriptures, the Church, and holding to doctrine that is not the truth. (1Timothy 4:11)

- Envying-this is more than jealousy, it is not just wanting what others have but also begrudges the fact that they have them. They want things to be taken from the person and the person to suffer through the loss of the things, (Galatians 5:26; Romans 13:13)

- Murders-to kill or take the life of another. (1 Peter 4:15; Matthew 19:18)

- Drunkenness-taking drugs or drinking to affect the senses for lust or pleasure, intoxication, seeking to loosen moral restraints for fleshly pleasures. (Ephesians 5:18; 1Corinthians 6:10)

- Revellings-uncontrolled indulgence, pleasure, taking part in wild or drinking parties, lying around indulging in feeding the lusts of the flesh, orgies. (1Peter 4:3; 2Peter 2:13-14)

2. When your flesh begins to pull at you, trying to get you to commit such acts, if you have studied in the Word of God and fed the Spirit, you will feel the constraint (force or restriction) and pressure between the Holy Spirit and your flesh. As this happens, the Holy Spirit is giving you the power to overcome the flesh (this is when you resist your fleshly urge). Resisting the flesh enough will give you the control you need to overcome the next episode should it happen again, until you gain the fruit of Self-Control. The flesh will keep you from doing what you should, because it is contrary to the Spirit and fights the Spirit constantly.

A. Romans 8:2-4

²For the law of the Spirit of life in Christ Jesus has made me free from the law of sin and death. ³For what the law could not do, in that it was weak through the flesh, God sending his own Son in the likeness of sinful flesh, and for sin, condemned sin in the flesh. ⁴That the righteousness of the law might be fulfilled in us, who walk not after the flesh, but after the Spirit.

B. John 16:13-14

¹³Howbeit when he, the Spirit of truth, is come, He will guide you into all truth: for he shall not speak of himself; but whatsoever he shall hear, that shall he speak: and he will show you things to come. ¹⁴He shall glorify me: for he shall receive of mine, and shall show it unto you.

3. After learning the works of the flesh, it is imperative that I introduce to you the fruit of the Spirit. You are required by God to mature the fruit of the Spirit in your life. If the Fruit of the Spirit is actively moving in your life as it should be, you will not have to spend much time on the works of the flesh. This depends on you and how well you mature in Christ. If you allow the Holy Spirit to have His way in producing His fruit in you and your life, growth is inevitable, it must happen!!!

   A. Galatians 5:22-26

> [22]But the fruit of the Spirit is love, joy, peace, longsuffering, gentleness, goodness, faith, [23]Meekness, temperance: against such there is no law. [24]And they that are Christ's have crucified the flesh with the affections and lusts. [25]If we live in the Spirit, let us also walk in the Spirit. [26]Let us not be desirous of vain glory, provoking one another, envying one another.

Fruit of the Spirit Meaning:

- Love - (agape)- Is the love of the mind, of reason, and of will. It is selfless, unconditional, and is the kind of love Jesus has for us. This love can only be experienced through a personal relationship with Jesus. (Romans 5:5)

- Joy - Is an inner gladness, deep seated assurance and confidence which produce a cheerful heart with cheerful behavior. This joy is not affected by circumstances. (Philippians 1:4)

- Peace - This is when you are so united together with God that it produces an inner soundness, wholeness, harmonious relationship between you and others, and to be reconciled. (John16:33).

- Longsuffering - This is patience, bearing and suffering a long time, perseverance, being constant, steadfast, and enduring without striking back or retaliating. (1Timothy 1:16)

- Gentleness - It is being good, kind, helpful, useful, considerate, gracious, sweet, and gentle through situations. (Ephesians 2:4-7)

- Goodness - Must be full of virtue, excellence, peace, consideration, kindness, helpfulness. When you are full of good you will do good things. (Romans 15:14)

- Faith - To be faithful, trustworthy, loyal standing firm in devotion, constant, and will deny and sacrifice self for others. He will believe God and trust Him to work all things out for his good. (1Corinthians 4:2)

- Meekness - To be gentle, humble, mild, tender, considerate, but strongly. In meekness you have the strength to control and discipline but you will do it at the right time. Meekness is a strong state of mind and it has self- control. (Galatians 6:1)

- Temperance - To be able to master and control the body or the flesh with all of its lusts. Means self- control, the master of desires, appetite, and passions, and especially sensual urges and cravings. Taking the stand against the works of the flesh, the lust of the eye, and the pride of life. (1John 2:15-16)

To walk in the Spirit is to take a strong stand against the works of the flesh. Not to allow your flesh to control you but you control your flesh. Most of us hate to be called weak, but if I allow my flesh to control my Spirit as a Christian that is not strength. This can be avoided if I let go and let God have his way in my life.

Remember: If you want to live, walk in the Spirit, but if you want to die, walk in the flesh. The choice is entirely up to you!!!

Notes: _____

_____

_____

_____

_____

_____

_____

_____

_____

_____

_____

_____

_____

_____

_____

_____

_____

_____

_____

_____

_____

_____

_____

_____

_____

_____

_____

_____

Week 23

KEEPING UNITY WITH OTHERS, NO MATTER WHAT

BIBLICAL PRINCIPLES - Ephesians 4:1-3 - [1]I therefore, the prisoner of the Lord, beseech you that you walk worthy of the vocation wherewith you are called, [2]With all lowliness and meekness, with longsuffering, forbearing one another in love; [3]Endeavoring to keep the unity of the Spirit in the bond of peace.

What is unity? Unity is the state or quality of being one; singleness. It is also harmony; being in accord.

This is such a powerful Scripture because it tells us to walk worthy of the calling to which we have been called of God. To do this we must be able to work and walk together in oneness that is unbreakable by the world or the cares of this life. We are to:

- Walk in humility (lowliness), meaning not one of us should think that we are more important than our brothers and sisters. We must never assume or act as if God loves us more than anyone else. This will break our unity at a fast speed and before you know it there is major damage to the body of Christ. We are to humble ourselves as long as it takes to keep the unity steadfast, without mumbling, grumbling, or striking back at others.

- Walk in meekness with longsuffering, we are to practice in a strong manner being gentle, kind, tender, and considerate, with a gentle state of mind. Yes we are to mean what we say but say what we mean in a kind manner. It is so important that I love people and love keeping peace with people. Longsuffering is required because everybody does not mature at the same rate and some may never mature.

- We are to forbear one another in love, not talking about them to others and judging them. It is good to consider yourself in the situation and think how would you want to be treated. You never know when you may need mercy!

- Endeavoring (an earnest attempt) to keep the unity of the Spirit in the bond of peace. We must strive with all that is within us to keep the oneness of the Spirit in peace. We may be very different from each other but this should not affect the way we work and walk in the Spirit. We should always remember that we were called by God and given a gift from God, which is to be respected by the body of Christ. Since the Holy Spirit gives the gift to whomever he pleases, why should there be disunity between each member. We must mature enough to allow the Spirit to move in unity and peace.

It is the heavy responsibility of Christians to keep that unity from being disturbed or broken. God through Jesus Christ has made it possible by sending the Holy Spirit to live inside each believer. Now it is up to us to make or allow this to happen.

We will use the authority of Scripture to help us get it done.

PRACTICAL APPLICATIONS:

1. First you must understand how important unity is for the Christians. Unity is so important that Jesus prayed to his Father to make His disciples one as He and His Father are one. Jesus knew the power of unity because the unity between Him and God kept him doing God's will. Unity will keep you encouraged to complete the work that you have been call to do. Jesus knew the divisiveness of this world and how cruel the world would be to the future Church.

    A. John 17:11

> [11]And now I am no more in the world, but these are in the world, and I come to thee, Holy Father, keep through your own name those whom you have given me, that they may be one, as we are.

2. Unity is important and needed to keep the cohesiveness of the body of Christ! When the Church walks together as one complete body, there is nothing she cannot do. Scripture speaks of a group of people that were so unified that God had to change their language to stop their building of a temple directed to heaven. Now just imagine if the people of the Most High God would come together on one accord, all the things we would be able to accomplish! Please work on unity.

    A. Genesis 11:4-8

> [4]And they said, go to, let us build us a city and a tower, whose top may reach unto heaven; and let us make us a name, lest

we be scattered abroad upon the face of the whole earth. [5]And the Lord came down to see the city and the tower, which the children of men built. [6]And the Lord said, behold, the people is one (unified), and they have all one language; and this they begin to do: and now nothing will be restrained from them, which they have imagined to do. [7]Go to, let us go down, and there confound their language, that they may not understand one another's speech. [8]So the Lord scattered them abroad from thence upon the face of all the earth: and they left off to build the city.

3. Unity builds up love between people. When we can get alone with one another, understanding of the individuals you are with will play a large role on the way you will treat them. You will learn the person and their behavior, character, and the way they think about things. This alone will cause you to have love for your brothers and sisters. Yes I must admit, this will take some time to develop and it will require developing patience, longsuffering, and forgiveness on both parties' behalf. You will have to commit to doing your part and not worry about how the other individual is coming alone. You must stay focus on your commitment and do it as unto God. Stay committed, do not falter because you do not see any changes, remember Changes will take time, you just continue to build unity!!

   A. 2Peter 1:5-8

      [5]And besides this, giving all diligence (earnest, persistence), add to your faith virtue; and to virtue knowledge; [6]and to knowledge temperance; and to temperance patience; and to patience godliness; [7]and to godliness brotherly kindness; and to brotherly kindness charity (love). [8]For if these things be in you (personally), and abound, they make you that you shall

neither be barren nor unfruitful in the knowledge of our Lord Jesus Christ.

4. All of this means that you as a Christian are to live and walk in unity with other believers. You are not to allow the divisive spirit of the world to come into and take over your life. You are to avoid at all cost grumbling, griping, complaining, criticizing others, envying, gossiping, opposing one another, overlooking others, ignoring, and isolating yourself. This is called living soberly and godly in this present world. Because you are a new creature in Christ Jesus it is a must that you walk in unity. Do not let the problems and the disunity in the body of Christ be accounted to you, you have better things to do.

A. Titus 2:11-13

[11]For the grace of God that brings salvation has appeared to all men, [12]Teaching us that denying ungodliness and worldly lusts we should live soberly, righteously, and godly in this present world; [13]Looking for that blessed hope, and the glorious appearing of the great God and our Savior Jesus Christ.

You must walk in the unity that Jesus prayed to His Father for all Christians! We know this had to be very important to Jesus because he included this subject in His prayer. You must strive with all that is within you to be sure that the unity is never broken among the people of God because of you.

Remember: Psalm 133:1 - Behold, how good and how pleasant it is for brethren to dwell together in unity! Life will be pleasant when you walk in unity with God's people.

Notes: _____

_____

_____

_____

_____

_____

_____

_____

_____

_____

_____

_____

_____

_____

_____

_____

_____

_____

_____

_____

_____

_____

_____

_____

_____

_____

_____

Week 24

I CHOOSE TO BE POWERFUL IN THE LORD

BIBLICAL PRINCIPLES - Acts 1:8 - ⁸But you shall receive power, After that the Holy Ghost is come upon you: and you shall be witnesses unto me both in Jerusalem, and in all Judea, and in Samaria, and unto the uttermost part of the earth.

This Scripture teaches us that after we receive the Holy Spirit, we shall also receive power to be witnesses of Jesus Christ. Why do we need power to witness about Jesus Christ? To witness means to give firsthand account of something, one who furnishes evidence or something that serves as evidence, a sign.

For you to give firsthand evidence you must have or know something regarding the subject to which you are to bear witness. How will you be able to witness about Jesus and all that He did except you have some type of sign or evidence? What evidence or sign must I present to a people to convince them of the resurrection power of our Lord and

Savior Jesus Christ? What did He do for you that gave you the ability and the authority to tell others about Him?

This is where you need power to witness, and this power comes directly from the indwelling of the Holy Spirit. Since the Holy Spirit lives inside of you, He has given you the power and the authority from Jesus Christ our Lord to witness about Him to others. The Holy Spirit comes with power and He is inside of you to equip you with whatever you need to do the will of God. He is the administrator of the Trinity, sent to fulfill the will of God in the believer's life.

There are some things you must do to activate this power. You must chose to give your life and affairs over to the charge of Holy Spirit to have His way. The Spirit of God will not man handle you and make you subject to his leading. You have the option to allow or not allow him total control of your life. Now you can either choose to be powerful or you can choose to walk in your own way. The choice is totally up to you.

When Jesus told His disciples to go and wait for the Holy Spirit to come upon them, He knew they could not start the New Testament Church without some spiritual power. So He gave them power from on high to be able to carry out His commands. The same is true for you and I, we cannot carry out the will of God without this same power the disciples needed, because we are responsible for the Church of today. The disciples had a choice to obey the Words of Jesus to go and wait until they received the Spirit of God or they could have chosen to move on and do what they wanted to do. They choose to receive the Holy Spirit and fulfill the will of God. What will you chose to do? The Church is still responsible for making new disciples and we cannot make them without the help and power of the Holy Spirit leading and guiding us to His will. Only the Holy Spirit knows the perfect will of God, He knows just what God requires from each of us.

Imagine what the world would be like if all the Christians would choose to be powerful in the Lord! Can you even imagine all the changes that would take place on this earth all because you and I chose to be powerful in the Lord? Let us not wait any longer, do it today and choose to be powerful in the Lord.

We will go to the Word of God to see why it is so important to choose to be powerful in the Lord.

PRACTICAL APPLICATIONS:

1. When thinking of how much Jesus loves us and the exceedingly high price He paid for our salvation, is it not only proper that we give him the rights to our life. Not only did he give us salvation but he sent the Holy Spirit to assure us that if we would just let him live and move freely inside of us, He would open our spiritual eyes and allow us to see the exceeding greatness of his power toward us.

    A. Ephesians 1:17-19

> [17]That the God of our Lord Jesus Christ, the Father of glory, may give unto you the spirit of wisdom and revelation in the knowledge of Christ. [18]The eyes of your understanding being enlightened; that you may know what is the hope of his calling, and what the riches of the glory of his inheritance in the Saints. [19]And what is the exceedingly greatness of his power to us who believe, according to the working of his mighty powers.

2. The Holy Spirit comes in the Power of God but you must continue to read, study, and live by the Word of God, to stay in line with the will of God, through the Spirit. The Word of God is so sharp and powerful, that if you practice doing what it says on a daily basis, the Spirit will change you and remove things that are against the will of God, so you will fit the call of Christ in your life. You will also develop a desire for the Holy Spirit to lead you. This is when you know you made the right choice to be powerful in the Lord. The word is described as a living power that judges us with all seeing eyes that penetrates all through our soul, heart, and every part of us keeping us filtered from unrighteousness.

   A. Hebrews 4:12

   [12]For the word of God is quick, and powerful, and sharper than any two edged sword, piercing even to the dividing asunder of soul and spirit, and of the joints and marrow, and is a discerner of the thoughts and intents of the heart.

   B. Hebrews 4:15-16

   [15]For we have not a high priest who cannot be touched with the feelings of our infirmities; but was in all points tempted like as we are, yet without sin. [16]Let us therefore come boldly unto the throne of grace, that we may obtain mercy, and find grace to help in time of need.

3. To have an effective ministry the power of God must be flowing freely through us. I love Jesus so much because He did not leave us to carry out His will without sending us the power needed to do the job. His love is still flowing freely to give us our expected end by the power of the Holy Spirit. Just as Jesus told His disciples to go and wait for the promise of His Spirit and the power that accompanies

the Spirit, He is tell you and I the same thing. Do not attempt to do the work of God without the Spirit of God because you cannot do it on your own. Choose to accept the power of God to do the work of God! Do not go out on the mission field until you have received inner power from on high.

A. Luke 24:48-49

> [48]And you are witnesses of these things. [49]And behold, I send the promise of my Father upon you: but tarry (remain) in the city of Jerusalem, until you be endued (to be provided with a quality or trait) with power from on high.

B. Romans 1:16a

> [16a]For I am not ashamed of the gospel of Christ: for it is the power of God unto salvation to everyone that believes.

4. So in all reality, you need the power of God to be able to serve Him as He requires. You and only you can choose to be powerful in the Lord. It does not matter how bad someone else may want this for you, only you can activate the power of the Almighty God in your life. Get busy, stir up the gift that is in you through the Holy Spirit, because this is spiritual war and you are no match in your powerless flesh for the battle that belongs to the Spirit. Your human effort is inadequate for this battle, but God's power is invincible! Only He is able to defeat the tricks of the enemy.

A. 2Timothy 1:6

> [6]Wherefore I put you in remembrance that you stir up the gift of God, which is in you by the putting on of my hands.

B. Ephesians 6:10-12

> [10]Finally, my brethren, be strong in the Lord, and in the power of His might. [11]Put on the whole armor of God, that you may be able to stand against the wiles of the devil. [12]For we wrestle not against flesh and blood, but against principalities, against powers, against the rulers of the darkness of this world, against spiritual wickedness in high places.

To be successful in God you must arm yourself with the power He has so freely made available to every Christian. There is no reason for any Christian to fail in God, not with all of the resources and authority placed in our reach. Tell your mind that you choose to be powerful in the Lord right now and that you will not wait another minute to activate you God given powers.

Remember: You are only as powerful as you choose to be in the Lord. Words alone will not produce this power, but as you remain in Jesus and Jesus remains in you, living in the power of His word will become what you do!!!

Notes: _____

_____

_____

_____

_____

_____

_____

_____

_____

_____

_____

_____

_____

_____

_____

_____

_____

_____

_____

_____

_____

_____

_____

_____

_____

_____

_____

_____

_____

Week 25

I MUST CHANGE ME TO FIT GOD'S WILL

BIBLICAL PRINCIPLES - 2Corinthians 5:16-18 - [16]Wherefore, henceforth (from now on) know we no man after the flesh: yes, though we have known Christ after the flesh, yet now henceforth know we him no more. [17]Therefore if any man be in Christ, he is a new creature: old things are passed away; behold, all things are become new. [18]And all things are of God, who has reconciled us to himself by Jesus Christ, and has given to us the ministry of reconciliation.

This is one of my favorite Scriptures because it reminds me of the fact that Jesus really walked upon the earth and many people knew Him in the flesh. But today we no longer see Him in the flesh but through the Spirit. Now we are to see and know Him by faith. It takes faith to believe that I cannot see him but I know without doubt that my Savior lives. Not only does he live but He has made it possible for you and I to live also! I know you are probably saying, I already live, this is very true, in the flesh or body. But do you live in the Spirit of God?

You have a spirit man who needs life just as much as your natural man. You cannot see him but, he lives inside of your body, whether good or bad, he is in there. Once you become a born again Christian, you have a new Spirit, and must make the necessary adjustments to accommodate His needs.

Everything that was a part of your old spirit man is gone, passed away, and no longer present. Now you must start living by the new needs of your new Spirit man. As this Scripture states, old things are passed away and behold all things become new. The new Spirit of Christ inside of you has no need to use the old things of your past. You are new and the Spirit is sent to bring all new things into your life. Now the transformation starts, this is where you change all of you to fit all of Christ. The old you was an enemy to God because of your sins, but after being forgiven and receiving Christ as your personal Savior, your entire past has been forgiven and now you start your brand new life as a child of the Most High God. How wonderful this new life can be if you will allow the Holy Spirit to bring into your life all of the good things God has prepared just for you.

You have been given a new purpose in life and the ministry of reconciliation by Jesus Christ, the Son of God! You are now to go to the world and tell them all about this Savior you have living on the inside. But please note: people will not listen to you if the old you appears to still be in control. This is the reason you must renew your mind to match your new Spirit. Talking and speaking about Jesus is great, but living the life that resembles Him is even greater!

As you know change is difficult, most people would agree, but it is not impossible. If you had to produce this change by your own powers, I would be the first to tell you it will not happen. But I would also tell you that this is the work of the Holy Spirit. Only He can help you produce such great changes in your life.

Now the question to ask is: will you trust the Holy Spirit to work inside of you removing, adding, adjusting, and perfecting whatever is in need of change? Will you take your hands off and place yourself entirely in His care and not interfere while He is working? Can you really cast all your cares upon the Holy Spirit because He cares for you? Will you do your part in making this change happen? Whatever it takes to get you to your expected end, will you allow the Spirit of the Most High God to have his way and do the navigating to get you there.

If you cannot answer yes to all of the questions above, you have a problem and are not willing to change you to fit God's will.

We will go to the bible to see what needs to happen in you to prepare for change.

PRACTICAL APPLICATIONS:

1. What is it that prohibits you from allowing the Holy Spirit to have His way in your life? Many times we are familiar with doing things our way but with God things are different. You must deny yourself, take up your cross, and follow the Lord. In walking with Jesus, your way will only cause you hardship because you are required to surrender yourself totally to God. When you give up control change will happen. Self-denial is one of the hardest things a Christian will do to surrender to the Spirit. Giving up your control over you will

probably make you feel as though you have lost control of life, but you have not. You have only signed off for God to do what is best for you.

A. Matthew 16:24-25

> [24]Then said Jesus to his disciples, if any man will come after me, let him deny himself, and take up his cross, and follow me. [25]For whosoever will save his life shall lose it: and whosoever shall lose his life for my sake, shall find it.

2. Taking up your cross is another issue to be discussed. The cross represents an instrument of death and it symbolizes the necessity of totally surrendering unto God even unto death. This is the reason you must get into the habit of allowing the Spirit to lead and guide you into all truth and righteousness. God has not asked you to die for Him but he does require that you do his will and not the lust of your flesh. Most of the time you desire to follow Christ but sometimes you will allow the flesh to dictate your response rather than the Spirit. At some point you must tell your flesh NO, NO, NO!!!

A. Matthew 10:38-39

> [38]And he that takes not his cross, and follow after me, is not worthy of me. [39]He that finds his life shall lose it: and he that loses his life for my sake shall find it.

B. Psalm 37:5-6

> [5]Commit your way unto the Lord; Trust also in him; and he shall bring it to pass. [6]And he shall bring forth your righteousness as the light, And your judgment as the noonday.

C. 1Peter 4:19

> [19]Wherefore let them that suffer according to the will of God commit the keeping of their souls to him in well doing, as unto a faithful Creator.

3. You will never get to follow the Lord if you cannot deny yourself and take up your cross. Sufferings will happen to everyone at some point in this life, but Christians should not be afraid to suffer some things because it produces the character and mind of Christ in you. The pruning process must happen if you are to bear fruit in the Lord. This is painful because useless branches must be removed so new branches will began to grow. Let God Prune you and watch yourself blossom into this new changed for the better you.

A. John 15:1-3

> [1]I am the true vine, and my Father is the Husbandman. [2]Every branch in me that bears not fruit he takes away; and every branch that bears fruit, he purges it, that it may bring forth more fruit. [3]Now you are clean through the word which I have spoken unto you.

Make up in your mind today that you will change you to fit God's will, even if it is a little painful. He will grace you to get it done if only you commit to the change.

Remember: Change is inevitable, but when you submit to the Holy Spirit and let Him have his way, the results will be a better you!

Notes: _____

_____

_____

_____

_____

_____

_____

_____

_____

_____

_____

_____

_____

_____

_____

_____

_____

_____

_____

_____

_____

_____

_____

_____

_____

_____

_____

_____

_____

Week 26

BEING EFFECTIVE IN THE WORK OF GOD

BIBLICAL PRINCIPLES - Hebrews 12:1-2 - ¹Wherefore seeing we also are compassed about with so great a cloud of witnesses, let us lay aside every weight, and the sin which does so easily beset (ensnares, to attack from all sides) us, and let us run with patience the race that is set before us, ²Looking unto Jesus the author and finisher of our faith; who for the joy that was set before him endured the cross, despising the shame, and is set down at the right hand of the throne of God.

In this Scripture, we are to take notice of the fact that there have been so many other Christians before us who ran this same race and completed the entire course without failing. They walked with God, obeyed his word, and stayed in the entire race for salvation until the end. Sure they faced many hardships, disappointments, trials, and tribulations, but they stayed in the race. Not only did they stay in the race, but according to the word of God, they have the testimony that they pleased God.

Now that you and I are presently running in this same race, we also are expected to endure hardship as a good soldier, obey, and stay faithful to our God. The only way to do this is to lay aside every weight and sin that so easily attacks us from all sides. Being a Christian does not stop us from having trouble in our lives, but with the power and presence of the Holy Spirit we will be able to overcome whatever comes our way.

In this Scripture the Christian journey is pictured as a long distance race with many runners participating in the event. We are instructed to lay aside or pull off everything that will prohibit us from winning this race. Now on a more personal note, because there are many runners in the race, I must prepare myself to win.

I must not look at any one else participating in this race but focus completely on what I must do to win. Some of the things I must pull off may not be a sin but it may be heavy enough to prevent me from winning, so I need to pull it all off. Believe it or not, if I continue to carry extra baggage it may cause me to lose the contest. There are things that God specifically tells me in His word to remove from my life, but if I allow it to stay then it produces disobedience and may cause me to be disqualified while in the race. This is when I will look unto Jesus the author and the finisher of my faith to keep me qualified to run this race. Jesus is the one who started me in this race and the one who is able to keep me from falling and present me faultless before my God.

We must realize that this is not an everyday race that if you lose today, you can compete on next week. In this race you must remain a qualified participant for the rest of your life because the rules are stated that you must remain until death. So to be effective in the work of the Lord, you must not become faint hearted, unfaithful, weary in well doing, shame of God or the Gospel, and start looking back while trying to run forward.

It is so important that you do a spiritual, honest, heartfelt evaluation, and allow the Holy Spirit the opportunity to remove everything out of you, that may cause disqualification for your competition in this Christian race. Only you know what is preventing you from full participation in the eternal Christian race. You must be concern enough about your very own salvation that you are willing to make all the necessary changes to become an effective Christian in the work of God.

Why is being effective in the work of God so important? What is expected of me to be effective? Does it really matter to God if I am effective?

Let us look into the Word of God and find out the answers to these questions.

PRACTICAL APPLICATIONS:

1. The reason it is so important to be effective in the work of God is because God demands this. When you are effective in God's work you become a light to the world enabling them to see the way to Christ. It is very hard to see in the dark except there is light. Will you be that light to help others walk out of darkness? You are to let your light shine so that others will see your good works and glorify God. These are the words of Jesus as he spoke to his disciples and these same words apply to you and I today!

   A. Matthew 5:14-16

   [14]You are the light of the world. A city that is set on a hill cannot be hid. [15]Neither do men light a candle, and put it under a bushel, but on a candlestick; and it gives light unto all

that are in the house. [16]Let your light so shine before men, that they may see your good works, and glorify your Father which is in heaven.

2. What is expected of me to be effective? You must walk in a way that others will desire to be like you and inquire of the reasons you live the way you live. People are always searching for a direction that will have great returns in their lives, so why not offer them Jesus the Christ, the Son of the Living God! This is where laying aside every weight and sin that keeps on pulling at you becomes a reality, let it all go. The Holy Spirit inside of you should mean more to you than holding on to things that will eventually cripple you. This is when you decide that you really want to be effective in the work of God. If you continue to walk in the things that dim your spiritual light, people may not see exactly who Jesus is in you. Do you want them to associate you with Christ?

A. John 8:12

[12]Then spoke Jesus again unto them, saying, I am the light of the world: he that follows me shall not walk in darkness, but shall have the light of life.

B. John 15:16

[16]You have not chosen me, but I have chosen you, and ordained you, that you should go and bring forth fruit, and that your fruit should remain: that whatsoever you shall ask of the Father in my name, He may give it to you.

3. Does it really matter to God if I am effective? Yes! God sent his son Jesus into the world to set the example of how we are to walk, and that is like Him. Jesus spent years showing his disciples what was

required of them to please God. He taught them that everything he did was always about pleasing his Father. Jesus spoke many times about us being productive in bearing fruit, more fruit, and much fruit. He also said that we must stay connected to Him to produce the required fruit. If we are not bearing fruit or being effective, the Scriptures teach that we are taken away. But if we produce fruit, then God will purge us so that we will bear more fruit. If it did not matter, why would he spend time teaching about abiding in the vine and producing fruit?

A. John 15:1-5

> [1]I am the true vine, and my Father is the husbandman. [2]Every branch in me that bears not fruit he takes away: and every branch that bears fruit, he purges it, that it may bring forth more fruit. [3]Now you are clean through the word which I have spoken unto you. [4]Abide in me, and I in you. As the branch cannot bear fruit of itself, except it abide in the vine; no more can you except you abide in me. [5]I am the vine, you are the branches: He that abides in me, and I in him, the same brings forth much fruit: for without me you can do nothing.

B. John 15:8-9

> [8]Herein is my Father glorified, that you bear much fruit; so shall you be my disciples. [9]As the Father has loved me, so have I loved you: continue in my love.

So my brothers and sisters to be effective in the work of God, you and I must stay qualified and do the things that are pleasing in His sight. This is to be done on a daily basis, not just when you feel like doing it but even when you do not feel like it!

Remember: God is looking for someone who will not mind laying aside every weight and the sin which does so easily best us, and run this Christian race faithfully, whole heartedly, and with a willing mind to please Him!! Will this person be YOU?

Notes: _____

_____

_____

_____

_____

_____

_____

_____

_____

_____

_____

_____

_____

_____

_____

_____

_____

_____

_____

_____

_____

_____

_____

_____

_____

_____

_____

_____

Week 27

WHAT AM I DOING WITH MY TALENTS?

BIBLICAL PRINCIPLES - MATTHEW 25:14-30 - [14]For the kingdom of heaven is as a man travelling into a far country, who called his own servants, and delivered unto them his goods. [15]And unto one he gave five talents, to another two, and to another one; to every man according to his several ability; and straightway took his journey. [16]Then he that had received the five talents went and traded with the same, and made them other five talents. [17]And likewise he that had received two, he also gained other two. [18]But he that had received one went and dug in the earth, and hid his lord's money. [19]After a long time the Lord of those servants came and reckoned with them. [20]And so he that had received five talents came and brought other five talents, saying, Lord you delivered unto me five talents: behold, I have gained besides them five talents more. [21]His Lord said unto him, Well done, you good and faithful servant: you have been faithful over a few things, I will make you ruler over many things: enter you into the joy of your Lord. ²²He also that had received two talents came and said, Lord you delivered unto to me two talents: behold, I have gained two other talents besides them. ²³His Lord said unto him, Well done good and faithful servant; you have been faithful over a few things, I will make you ruler over many things: enter you into the joy of your lord. ²⁴Then he which had received the one talent came and said, Lord, I knew you that you are a hard man, reaping where you have not sown, and gathering where you have not scattered seeds: ²⁵and I was afraid, and went and hid your talent in the earth: lo, there you have what is yours. ²⁶His lord answered and said unto him, you wicked and slothful servant, you knew that I reaped where I had not planted, and gathered where I have not scattered seeds: ²⁷You therefore should have put my money to the exchangers, and then at my coming I should have received my own with usury (interest). ²⁸Take therefore the talent from him, and give it unto him which have ten talents. ²⁹For unto everyone that have shall be given, and he shall have abundance: but from him that have not shall be taken away even that which he have. ³⁰And cast the unprofitable servant into outer darkness: there shall be weep and gnashing of teeth.

I took the time to give you this entire passage of Scripture to show how important it is to be active with your God given talents. Notice, I said God given talents! In this Scripture we see that the Lord gave talents to each of His servant according to each servant's ability. This shows that the Lord knows exactly what you and I are capable of doing, so He will not give us any job that we cannot perform. In saying this, we will not have any excuse that will stand before God as to why we did nothing with His talents that were placed in our care. We are to work until Jesus return!

In this Scripture the Lord was preparing to go on a long journey, but before he left he made sure all of his servants received gifts or talents to keep them busy while he was away. Notice he did not give everyone the same assignment or the same amount to do because he knew what each person was capable of accomplishing. Sometimes in the Church we are so caught up in what everyone else is doing until we lose sight on what we have been charged to do.

The servant with five talents went to work, minding his own affairs, being very thankful and responsible regarding his assignments, and doubled the talents that were given to him. He knew what the Lord required of him so he did not waste any of his time worrying about what the other servants were doing with their talents. This also shows that he was mindful and respectful of the will of his Lord and wanted to please his master upon the master's return. This servant worked from his heart and got the job done!

The servant with two talents performed just as the servant with the five talents. He did not look at the servant with five talents and wanted what that servant had. Instead, he was thankful for what was entrusted to his care and went to work pleasing his Lord. This servant went out with his two talents and was very productive in the Lords work and doubled what he was given. He now possesses four talents.

Look at the attitude and the responsibility of these two servants as to how much they loved their Lord. They could have said the Lord is gone now so we can work or do whatever we feel like doing because no one is watching us. But they loved the Lord from their hearts and pleasing

God was all they were living to do. Procrastination was not an option! What about you, do you procrastinate when it comes to doing the Lord's work?

The servant with one talent was very slothful or lazy and made excuses why he could not, or shall I say, would not do anything with his talent. He dug a hole and put the Lord's talent in it and did nothing while his master was gone. Does this sound like you? Are you just holding on to your talent and doing nothing with it? What are you doing with the Lord's talent(s) that was left to your care?

You see the Master or Lord returned one day when no one was expecting him. The two servants that had been productive were very excited when the Lord returned because they occupied and produced while they were waiting for him. They were ready to give a full report of how they worked with the talents of the Master and the amount of fruitfulness that was produced. They did not come complaining about how hard the job was, or how no one else would help them. They gave a report of what they did with the talents because they knew the Lord left the talents in each individual's care. This means that you are responsible for your very own talents. No one else can make you be productive in the work of God, this is something you must purpose to do from your heart.

As you operate in the talents God has placed in your care, you will become productive and the fruit of the Spirit will become mature in your life. You become more concerned about others and their need of Salvation. Not only this but you will hear the Lord say well done my good and faithful servant, you have been faithful over a few things now I will make you rulers over many things, enter into the JOY of your Lord. This is not just at the Christian's death but it is right now!! You can enter into the joy of the Lord daily and can be promoted by God while you are here on this earth, if you are productive and faithful in the Lord's work.

Please do not be as the slothful servant, because he felt that he was only given one talent so why work. It does not matter how many talents you are given. What does matter is what you are doing with your God given talent. Occupy and love God so much that you desire to please Him by doing what is required of you with your talent(s). Believe it or not, as you work in your talent(s) you will began to experience a joy that no one can take from you and a peace that will last throughout anything you will encounter in this life.

Let us go straight to the word of God and see why I must be productive with my God given talent(s).

PRACTICAL APPLICATIONS:

1. First of all, you must know that your talent(s) were given to you directly from God that you must please him and give an account of how you handled your talents. Sometime you can get caught up in the doings of others and forget that they were not the giver of your talents. So it really does not matter if people approve of what God is doing in and through you because God is the one in control of you and your talents. Seek to please God and everything else will fall in place, just do you!

    A. 1Corinthians 12:4-7

    > [4]Now there are diversities (various kinds) of gifts, but the same Spirit. [5]And there are differences of administrations, but the same Lord. [6]And there are diversities of operations, but it is the same God which works all in all. [7]But the manifestation of the Spirit is given to every man to profit withal.

B. James 1:17

> [17]Every good gift and every perfect gift is from above, and
> comes down from the Father of lights, with whom is no
> variableness, neither shadow of turning (God does not
> change).

2. You must recognize that your Spiritual gifts or talents are given by
the Spirit of God for the accomplishment of God's purpose in this
world, the Church, and the home. It is also given for the edification
of the Church which is the body of Christ. Your talent (gift) is to
bring the body of Christ to unity and maturity or perfection!

A. Ephesians 4:11-13

> [11]And he gave some, apostles; and some, prophets; and
> some, evangelists; and some, pastors and teachers; [12]For the
> perfecting of the saints for the work of the ministry, for the
> edifying of the body of Christ: [13]Till we all come in the unity
> of the faith, and of the knowledge of the Son of God, unto a
> perfect man, unto the measure of the stature of the fullness
> of Christ.

3. Every believer has been given spiritual gifts but always remember
all of the gifts or talents belong to God, not you or me. We cannot
use God's talents as we desire, they must be used to the Glory of
God. When using our talents, we must show good hospitality, speak
as mouth pieces for God, and always give God the praise for what
he has done through your talent.

A. 1Peter 4:9-11

> [9]Use hospitality one to another without grudging. [10]As every
> man has received the gift, even so minister the same one to

another, as good stewards of the manifold grace of God. [11]If any man speak, let him speak as the oracles of God; if any man minister, let him do it as of the ability which God gives: that God in all things may be glorified through Jesus Christ, to whom be praise and dominion forever and ever. Amen.

4. Because we as humans are not the same, we must respect the fact that our talents (gifts) are not the same. If God meant for everyone's talent to be operating the same, why would he give us different talents? If everyone would stay in their own lane, there would be fewer problems in life and in the Church. No one should think that his/her gift is more superior to anyone else, because the power is given by God to each believer to perform the ministries!!

   A.   Romans 12:3-5

> [3]For I say, through the grace given unto me, to every man that is among you, not to think of himself more highly than he ought to think; but to think soberly, according as God has dealt to every man the measure of faith. [4]For as we have many members in one body, and all members have not the same office: [5]So we being many, are one body in Christ, and every one members one of another.

Practice using your talents (gifts) in humility, love, and respecting one another so that God will be glorified in all that we do as Christians. Let us learn to walk in unity and get about our Father's business. As we do this we will see positive changes in our lives, the Church, and the world.

Remember: As Jesus said in John 9:4- I must work the works of him that sent me, while it is day: the night comes, when no man can work. GET BUSY, BUSY, BUSY!!!

Notes: _____

_____

_____

_____

_____

_____

_____

_____

_____

_____

_____

_____

_____

_____

_____

_____

_____

_____

_____

_____

_____

_____

_____

_____

_____

_____

_____

_____

52 weeks of practical application to biblical principles

Week 28

HERE AM I LORD, SEND ME

BIBLICAL PRINCIPLES - Isaiah 6:5-8 - ⁵Then said I, Woe (deep distress or misery as from grief) is me! for I am undone; because I am a man of unclean lips, and I dwell in the midst of a people of unclean lips: for mine eyes have seen the King, the Lord of Hosts. ⁶Then flew one of the seraphims (angelic beings meaning burning ones) unto me, having a live coal in his hand, which he had taken with the tongs from off the altar: ⁷And he laid it upon my mouth, and said, Lo, this has touched your lips; and your iniquity is taken away, and your sins purged. ⁸Also I heard the voice of the Lord, saying, Whom shall I send, and who will go for us? Then said I, Here am I; send me.

This Scripture describes how God commissioned Isaiah to the work of the Ministry. It describes the holiness of God, how great God is, and how the angelic host worship, honor, and work constantly for God. It is so important to take notice of these elements in the Scripture.

Before you can work for God, you must be commissioned by Him to go into his vineyard to do the job. You cannot just take upon yourself to do God's work without being qualified by Him. Because it is the work of God, you must be empowered by his grace to get the job done.

We see in this Scripture Isaiah saw the holiness of God and it made him see the true picture of how unclean he was. It is so important to see how unclean we are so that we will appreciate how Holy God is. You will never be able to complete anything in God's ministry without being filled with his Holy Spirit!!! So the first thing that needs to happen in an individual's life before starting any level of ministry, is to accept Jesus as your personal Savior and receive the Holy Spirit then you can start moving forward into the call.

God sent the seraphims with a live coal to touch Isaiah's lips and purge him of his sins. The live coal represented the Holy Spirit's fire to burn away his sins, making him qualified to be used by God. After our sins have been removed and we have the proper relationship with our God, we are now ready to enter into the work of God. So the first call is the call to a right relationship with Jesus Christ our Savior.

Now in verse eight, Isaiah said also I heard the voice of the Lord saying, "Whom shall I send, and who will go for us?" This tells us that after the cleansing process took place the Lord went further into His will for Isaiah. God asked the questions, "Whom shall I send and who will go for us?" He gave Isaiah a choice and a chance to respond to the call. God did not make Isaiah say yes, Isaiah chose to accept the call for his life willingly. God knows that if we serve him with a willing heart, we will do a better service for him. If we serve him because we feel that we must, the service is not so great. Isaiah responded "here am I; send me", informing God that he was completely available and ready to serve at any level and at any time.

Are you serving God willingly or are you doing it because you feel you have to? Are you making yourself totally available to God for His use? Is your response of "Here I am Lord, send me", of a desire to please God or is it because you think this is what churching is all about?

Let us go into the Scriptures to see why it is so important to tell God "Here am I Lord, Send Me" with a willing heart and a positive attitude.

PRACTICAL APPLICATIONS:

1. The first thing that is necessary for a servant to do is be committed and humbled before God. This will only happen if you recognize that God is not like man neither is man equal to God. This means there is a certain respect that should be given to our God and the line should never be crossed. Out of respect you should always commit your ways unto him, and let him know that it is from your heart. Also respect for God produces faithfulness in his servants.

    A. Colossians 3:12-13a

       [12]Put on therefore, as the elect of God, holy and beloved, bowels of mercies, kindness, humbleness of mind, meekness, longsuffering; [13a]Forbearing one another, and forgiving one another.

    B. 1Peter 5:5-6

       [5]Likewise, ye younger, submit yourselves unto the elder. Yes all of you be subject one to another, and be clothed with humility: for God resists the proud, and gives grace to the humble. [6]Humble yourselves therefore under the mighty hand of God, that he may exalt you in due time.

C. Proverbs 16:2-3

²All the ways of a man are clean in his own eyes; But the Lord weighs the spirits. ³Commit your works unto the Lord, and your thoughts shall be established.

D. 1Corinthians 4:2

²Moreover it is required in stewards, that a man be found faithful.

2. Stop everything you are doing and examine yourself as a Christian to see why you are doing what you do for God? Take the time to search your heart to make certain that your motives are right in serving God. Are you really saying with your heart, Here am I Lord, send me? Are you walking in your integrity before the Lord?

A. 2Corinthians 13:5

⁵Examine yourselves, whether you are in the faith; prove your own selves. Know you not your own selves, how that Jesus Christ is in you, except you be reprobates.

B. Psalm 26:1-3

¹Judge me O Lord; for I have walked in mine integrity: I have trusted also in the Lord; therefore I shall not slide. ²Examine me, O Lord, and prove me; Try my reins and my heart. ³For your loving kindness is before mine eyes: And I have walked in your truth.

3. Are you totally available to be used by God at all times? Can God really depend on you for humble service? These are the things that you must be certain of when it comes to doing the will of God. God is truly interested in using you, but you must be willing to be used.

Not only to be used but also to be used in the way God desires to use you. You do not pick the service you are assigned to do, it is given by God.

A. Proverbs 3:5-6

> [5]Trust in the Lord with all your heart; and lean not unto your own understanding. [6]In all your ways acknowledge him, and he shall direct your paths.

B. 1Samuel 3:9-10

> [9]Therefore Eli said unto Samuel, go, lie down: and it shall be, if he call you, that you shall say, speak, Lord; for your servant hears. So Samuel went and lay down in his place. [10]And the Lord came, and stood, and called as at other times, Samuel, Samuel. Then Samuel answered, speak for your servant hears.

C. John 15:16a

> [16a]You have not chosen me, but I have chosen you, and ordained you, that you should go and bring forth fruit, and that your fruit should remain.

D. 1Corinthians 12:18-19

> [18]But now has God set the members every one of them in the body, as it has pleased him. [19]And if they were all one member, where were the body.

4. Now you are ready to answer the call of God by saying, here am I lord, send me, with a new perspective on the service you give to your God. You must realize that it was nothing good that you could have done to make God call you into his presence to accept your assignment. It was all about God and nothing about you.

A. Galatians 1:15-16

> [15]But when it pleased God, who separated me from my mother's womb, and called me by his grace. [16]To reveal his Son in me, that I might preach him among the heathens.

B. Acts 9:4-6a

> [4]And he fell to the earth, and heard a voice saying unto him, Saul, Saul, why do you persecute me? [5]And he said, who are you, Lord? And the Lord said, I am Jesus whom you persecute: it is hard for you to kick against the pricks. [6a]And he trembling and astonished said, Lord, what will you have me to do.

If you really are serious about your relationship with God and would like to take it to the next level, practice being available to God at all times. Whenever God speaks to you take the time out to hear him and say, "Here am I Lord Send Me!"

REMEMBER: When you prepare your heart, mind, and body to really serve God, just say, "Here am I Lord, send me." If it is done in faith from your heart, just trust God and watch him move in your favor!!!

Notes: _____

_____

_____

_____

_____

_____

_____

_____

_____

_____

_____

_____

_____

_____

_____

_____

_____

_____

_____

_____

_____

_____

_____

_____

_____

_____

_____

_____

_____

Week 29

MY DIVINE ASSIGNMENT IS STILL DUE

BIBLICAL PRINCIPLE - Acts 13:2-3 - [2]As they ministered to the Lord, and fasted, the Holy Ghost said, Separate me Barnabas and Saul for the work where unto I have called them. [3]And when they had fasted and prayed, and laid their hands on them, they sent them away.

In this Scripture we see that while in church services, Saul and Barnabas was fasting and praying with the rest of the congregation. Then the Holy Ghost spoke and instructed the leaders to separate the two of them for the work God had called them to do. Please notice that Saul and Barnabas did not pick out the work they wanted to do, but the Holy Ghost separated them to do a work that God chose for them. They were not the only ones to know that this was the work given to them by God, it was made known to the leaders as well that God sent them out.

We see that Saul and Barnabas were fasting and praying while in the Church with the rest of the congregation. This is very important to notice in Scripture because the people were giving themselves to God in worship. Even if you are not sure of your assignment, giving yourself to God in fasting, prayer, and worship can help you silence your flesh. This will also allow the Holy Spirit freedom to move and speak the will of God for your life. No, I am not saying that you have to fast all the time for God to move, but there are times when it is necessary to fast for answers. Also praying is a very important component needed to receive instructions from God on what and how to do your assignment.

You cannot select what you want to be in God and expect him to endorse your choice. It does not matter who tells you that you look like you should be doing this or that, always make sure you have the appointment and approval from God. We all have been given a divine assignment to complete and it comes directly from God. We spend much time doing everything except what God told us to do, which is fine but do not neglect your God given assignment. The bible teaches us that Saul (who later became Paul) did many things while serving God but his main focus was on the work or shall I say assignment God sent him out to do. Sometimes Paul worked with Barnabas and sometimes he worked alone, nevertheless, Paul did his divine assignment.

Your assignment may be totally different from what everyone else is doing but as long as you know this is what God has called you to do, complete the work. Do not get caught up in trying to be like everyone else or trying to do your assignment the way others tell you to do it. You must remember that God gave you the assignments so, get caught up in obeying the voice of God. There will always be outside influence and advice on how to complete your assignment but make sure you have clarity with God's instructions.

You cannot spend time on being a people pleaser when it comes to your assignment! Even if you spend most of your time pleasing others, your divine assignment is still due. Get busy, get in a hurry, and be faithful in completing your divine assignment.

Look at your divine assignment as the greatest work you will ever do in this life, because it was given to you by the Almighty God. With this perception of your divine assignment, you should feel so privileged, and do it with great honor, in excellence, in the spirit of humility, and with the upmost respect to our Great God!!! You must realize that God could have chosen someone else to do this but He chose you. All you have to do is just get it done!

We will now look at Scriptures to encourage you to practice doing your Divine Assignment daily!!!

PRACTICAL APPLICATIONS:

1. The Lord told Jeremiah the prophet that before Jeremiah was formed in his mother's belly or born, God already knew him. God had already sanctified and ordained him to be a prophet unto the nations. You must understand that you were made for the call and the call was not made for you. The Lord already knows what you are able to do, that is why you were created. You are different from everyone else so your assignment is different from all other assignments. God do not want to hear why you cannot complete your assignment because he knows you can. So the question is, will you do your work that is assigned to you?

    A. Jeremiah 1:4-5

    ⁴Then the word of the Lord came unto me saying, ⁵Before I formed you in the belly I knew you; and before you came

forth out of the womb I sanctified you, and I ordained you a prophet unto the nations.

B. Jeremiah 1:6-7

[6]Then said I (Jeremiah), Ah Lord God, behold, I cannot speak: for I am a child. [7]But the Lord said unto me, Say not I am a child: for you shall go to all that I shall send you, and whatsoever I command you, you shall speak.

C. Philippians 4:13

[13]I can do all things through Christ who strengthens me.

2. You are unique, one of a kind! Since this is true, why not complete your unique assignment. If everyone was meant to do the same things in life, nothing would be different about life. Allow God to make you the vessel you were meant to be and bring glory to his name. This is really what your divine assignment is all about, bringing glory to the name of The Lord. When you do your good works, people will see this and give God all the glory.

A. Matthew 5:16

[16]Let your light so shine before men, that they may see your good works, and glorify your Father which is in heaven.

B. Philippians 2:12b-13

[12b]Work out your own salvation with fear and trembling. [13]For it is God which works in you both to will and to do of his good pleasure.

C. 1Corinthians 12:4-6

[4]Now there are diversities of gifts, but the same Spirit. [5]And there are differences of administrations, but the same Lord.

⁶And there are diversities of operations, but it is the same God which works all in all.

3. Never allow your assignment to bring problems in the body of Christ. You must recognize that every assignment carries the same importance in the sight of God. The same price was paid for each person and the assignment. If you allow yourself to become puffed up because you think your work is more important, you will fail the work. Avoid murmuring, and complaining at all cost. You will be rewarded by God if you complete your divine assignment.

A. Philippians 2:3-4

³Let nothing be done through strife or vainglory; but in lowliness of mind let each esteem others better than themselves. ⁴Look not every man on his own things, but every man also on the things of others.

B. 1Corinthians 3:13-15

¹³Every man's work shall be made manifest: for the day shall declare it, because it shall be revealed by fire; and the fire shall try every man's work of what sort it is. ¹⁴If any man's work abide which he has built thereon, he shall receive a reward. ¹⁵If any man's work shall be burnt, he shall suffer loss: but he himself shall be saved; yet so as by fire.

C. Philippians 2:14-15

¹⁴Do all things without murmurings and disputings: ¹⁵That you may be blameless and harmless, the sons of God without rebuke, in the midst of a crooked and perverse nation, among whom you shine as lights in the world.

You must keep in mind that your divine assignment is still due and one day God will call you into account as to whether you completed your assignment or not and the way it was performed.

Remember: We are to give God the Glory in everything we do! So are you doing your Divine Assignment?

Notes:

52 weeks of practical application to biblical principles

Week 30

MY ATTITUDE AND CONDUCT REALLY DOES MATTER

BIBLICAL PRINCIPLES - Philippians 1:27 - [27]Only let your conversation (conduct) be as it becomes the Gospel of Christ: that whether I come and see you, or else be absent, I may hear of your affairs, that you stand fast in one spirit, with one mind striving together for the faith of the Gospel.

This is one of the Scriptures that actually speak on Christian conduct or attitude! It would be so wonderful if every Christians' attitude and conduct would be like that of Jesus Christ. Can you imagine what wonderful things would take place in your homes, on jobs, in your communities, at schools, and in your Churches? We must note that the people, who are members of your Church, are the same people you come into contact with daily in all walks of life. So your attitude and conduct really does matter!

Yes it matters if you speak one thing and live another. It matters if you confess Christ with your mouth as your personal Savior, then display a bad or nasty attitude and conduct toward others. This Scripture truly says for Christians to let your conversation, meaning your conduct, be that of a representative of the Gospel. You have been sent out as God's ambassadors to a world of people who need to see a difference in your standard of conduct and the way you treat others.

Paul, being the writer, was speaking to the Christians saying, whether I am present with you or whether I am absent, please conduct yourselves as if Christ Himself was standing or sitting in your presence at all times. Paul understood as all Christians should understand, that the Spirit of Christ is inside of you therefore He really is present at all times, seeing, hearing, and knowing what type of conduct and attitude you are displaying. This alone should prompt you to be careful of the way you carry yourself in and out of the presence of others. It should also matter to you how you respect yourself. If you cannot respect yourself, how can you respect anyone else? Yes when you display bad attitudes and conducts to others it speaks volumes of how bad you treat yourself. People cannot expect you to do more for them than you would do for yourself.

Also in this Scripture Paul was making an earnest appeal to the Christians. That if he should hear of their affairs, let the report be that of a group standing fast or firmly, being unified in the Spirit with one mind, working hard together for the faith of the Gospel. If for no other reason, do it because of your love, honor, and respect for the Gospel. God expects each of us to always respect and appreciate the sacrifices that his Son made on the cross for our eternal life. This was a great price that Jesus paid for you and I to reap the benefits. Now we should honor Christ by the way we display to this world, "The Mighty God We Serve".

People will hear what you say but they will pay more attention to the way you lived before them. So you decide, what will people remember the most about you? Will it be all the things you told them or will it be the way you walked before them, treated them, and allowed them to experience hands on, what true Christianity is all about?

I would like to give you some supportive Scriptures to read, study, and practice daily. These Scriptures should help you produce whatever changes needed for you to have the type of attitude and conduct God requires of us as Christians!

PRACTICAL APPLICATIONS:

1. Sometimes life will get hard and things can happen that will cause a shift in your attitude. It is during these times that you should be able to display the attitude and conduct of Christ. You must realize that life will happen but the Holy Spirit is living inside of you to keep you with hope, letting you know that this too will pass. Do not pick up the attitude of grumbling as the world do, because this shows discontentment with God's will for you. It also expresses unbelief in God and will prevent you from pleasing Him. Always give thanks because of your trust in God.

   A. Philippians 2:14-15

      [14]Do all things without murmurings and disputing: [15]That you may be blameless and harmless, the sons of God without rebuke, in the midst of a crooked and perverse nation, among whom you shine as lights in the world.

   B. Colossians 3:23-24

      [23]And whatever you do, do it heartily (with your whole heart), as to the Lord, and not unto men; [24]Knowing that of the Lord

you shall receive the reward of the inheritance: for you serve the Lord Christ.

C. Colossians 3:17

   [17]And whatsoever you do in word or deed, do all in the name of the Lord Jesus, giving thanks to God and the Father by him.

2. There are certain things that God speaks of in Scripture that will keep you with a pleasant and joyful attitude, also help you walk in the proper conduct that will please Him. So yes, your attitude and conduct does matter to God and to your fellow man. It should also matter to you as well because it can affect the way others perceive Christ as Lord and Savior!!! It is important that you continue to learn, do, and receive the correct things of God so that you will be able to live it.

   A. Philippians 4:8-9

   [8]Finally, brethren, whatsoever things are true, whatsoever things are honest, whatsoever things are just, whatsoever things are pure, whatsoever things are lovely, whatsoever things are of good report; if there be any virtue, and if there be any praise, think on these things. [9]Those things, which you have both learned, and received, and heard, and seen in me, do: and the God of peace shall be with you.

   B. Colossians 3:9-10

   [9]Lie not one to another, seeing that you have put off the old man (sinful man) with his deeds; [10]And have put on the new man (born again man), which is renewed in knowledge after the image of him (God) that created him.

C. Galatians 5:22-23

> [22]But the fruit of the Spirit is love, joy, peace, longsuffering, gentleness, goodness, faith, [23]Meekness, temperance: against such there is no law.

3. As you began to change your attitude to God's standard for you, you will see a great difference in the way you handle life in general. You must have the mind of Christ in order to display his character and perform his will. You must humble yourself and resist the urge to be proud and arrogant, you cannot do this on your own. This is the reason Jesus sent his Holy Spirit to dwell inside of you and I. The power to do the will of God is produced through the presence of his Spirit. Allow the Holy Spirit the chance to positively move in your life so that the world will see all the good things inside of you and give glory to your Great God.

A. Philippians 2:3-7

> [3]Let nothing be done through strife or vainglory (boastful, unwarranted pride in you accomplishment or qualities); but in lowliness of mind let each esteem other better than themselves. [4]Look not every man on his own things, but every man also on the things of others. [5]Let this mind be in you, which was also in Christ Jesus: [6]Who, being in the form of God, thought it not robbery to be equal with God: [7]But made of himself no reputation, and took upon him the form of a servant, and was made a servant in the likeness of men.

B. James 4:10

> [10]Humble yourselves in the sight of the Lord, and he will lift you up (exalt you).

4. Our attitude and conduct is so important to Jesus that he took the time to sit on a mountain to teach his disciples how to be blessed. He explained it so very carefully and deeply so that there would be no misunderstanding of what type of mindset we as Christians must display. These are both moral and ethical issues towards one another and God. Many times we want to be blessed but somehow fail to realize that our attitude plays an important part in being blessed. We need humility, a clean heart, to hunger and thirst for righteousness, show mercy to others, keep peace with others, forgive, and have a joyful spirit.

A. Matthew 5:1-12

> [1]And seeing the multitudes, he (Jesus) went up into a mountain: and when he was set, his disciples came unto him: [2]And he opened his mouth, and taught them saying, [3]Blessed are the poor in spirit: for theirs is the kingdom of heaven. [4]Blessed are they that mourn: for they shall be comforted. [5]Blessed art the meek: for they shall inherit the earth. [6]Blessed are they which do hunger and thirst after righteousness: for they shall be filled. [7]Blessed are the merciful: for they shall obtain mercy. [8]Blessed are the pure in heart: for they shall see God. [9]Blessed are the peacemakers: for they shall be called the children of God. [10]Blessed are they which are persecuted for righteousness' sake: for theirs id the kingdom of heaven. [11]Blessed are you, when men shall revile you, and persecute you, and shall say all manners of evil against you falsely, for my sake. [12]Rejoice, and be exceedingly glad: for great is your reward in heaven: for so persecuted they the prophets which were before you.

You must change your attitude and conduct to fit the requirements of God in order to experience the rewards that come from a life that is well surrendered unto Him. If your attitude or conduct is not as God requires, please take the time you need to fix this because it is a problem. Whether you think so or not, you will prosper more when you get it right and so will those around you.

Remember: Romans 12:2 - ²Be not conformed to this world, but be transformed by the renewing of your mind that you might prove what is that good and acceptable, and perfect will of God.

You have everything you need living inside of you to make this change of attitude and conduct happen. Just utilize the help that the Holy Spirit is offering to you and you will not go wrong!

Notes: _____

_____

_____

_____

_____

_____

_____

_____

_____

_____

_____

_____

_____

_____

_____

_____

_____

_____

_____

_____

_____

_____

_____

_____

_____

_____

_____

Week 31

I DO NOT WANT TO WALK AROUND IN GRAVE CLOTHES

BIBLICAL PRINCIPLES - John 11:43-44 - 43And when he thus had spoken, He cried with a loud voice, Lazarus, come forth. 44And he that was dead came forth, bound hand and foot with grave clothes: and his face was bound about with a napkin. Jesus said unto them, Loose him, and let him go.

We all have heard the amazing teaching of Lazarus, raised by Jesus after being dead for four days. But there is a part of this story I would like for us to focus our attention. This part is that after being raised from the dead, Jesus calls Lazarus out of the grave and Lazarus comes forth, but he is still wrapped in grave clothes. He is walking but he is also still bound in the clothes that were used in the grave. He was alive and many people saw what happened but Jesus took special notice of the fact that he was still wearing grave clothing, so Jesus commanded someone to lose Lazarus and let him go.

Lazarus was still wrapped up in a dead man's dressing but he was no longer dead. Even his face was still covered with the napkin that was used for a dead man but he needed to be able to see through the eyes of the living. What I am saying is, many times after we have been delivered, we keep trying to walk in the things that had us bound before Christ. We have been forgiven by Jesus and our sins have been removed but, if we continue trying to do what we once did before salvation, we start returning to our grave clothes.

This happens when we stop reading and studying the word of God (Bible) on a regular basis. We get so busy doing everything but enhancing our relationship with our Savior. Jesus said for us to render unto Him what is due to him. Somewhere in our busy schedules we must give God the time that is due unto Him. Many times we are told to find time for God but I am saying find time for you and give God his time daily. When we confess that God is first in our lives, we must truly mean just that. For God to be first in our lives, our doings must come second to the will and purposes of God.

Who told you that God will accept whatever you give to Him? Who said that anything will please God? When reading the Holy Scriptures, I found that God said for us to love Him with all our heart, mind, soul, and might, meaning that God wants it all. That's right He wants all of you, not just the parts you are willing to give up but also the parts that you try to hold onto. Whenever you start holding back on God you began to allow your flesh to rise up again. Remember we were told to crucify our flesh so that it would not have the power to over rule our spirit man. When your flesh start to take over you will find yourself dressing up in the old grave clothing (your old will) and your face wrapped in the grave napkin (unable to see truth). Do not let this happen to you, rise up and come forth pulling off all the old things that are against the perfect will of God.

Walking in grave clothes will rob you of your fruit of the Spirit and your ability to walk with God as he desires. God really does want a great flourishing personal relationship with all of his Children but he gives us the choice to build upon that relationship. Your relationship with God can be as great or as pitiful as you make it. You are responsible for making sure you stay away from your old grave clothes, old habits, old fleshy cravings that got you in all kinds of trouble before. But if you choose, you can put them back on and pay less attention to what God desires for you, it is all your choice.

Now let us go into the word of God and see what he says regarding our relationship with him and staying away from yokes of bondage or grave clothes!

PRACTICAL APPLICATIONS:

1. To keep yourself away from old issues you must not become entangled again with the yokes of bondage. You must stay free in Christ walking in the newness of life. Engage in serious Bible studies, challenge your mind to make changes, and keep your heart pure before God. This should be one of your first lines of defense in walking before Christ. Be careful of the things that come forth out of your mouth because the Scriptures teach they were first conceived in your heart.

   A. Galatians 5:1

      [1]Stand fast therefore in the liberty wherewith Christ has made us free, and be not entangled again with the yoke of bondage.

B. Matthew 15:18-20

> ¹⁸But those things which proceed out of the mouth come forth from the heart; and they defile a man. ¹⁹For out of the heart proceed evil thoughts, murders, adulterers, fornications, thefts, false witnesses, blasphemies; ²⁰These are the things which defile a man: But to eat with unwashed hands defiles not a man.

2. If you allow yourself to start leaning toward the demands of your flesh, you will become weak and consumed with lust. This will put you in a bad place and have you doing the things you thought you would not do, especially as a Christian. Yes you are a Christian but you must stay delivered from your craving flesh. When you give in to fleshly lust or cravings, it will bring forth sin, and when sin is finished it will bring forth death! You cannot say that God is testing you by putting you through these types of cravings. Lust comes from your very own selfish desires, not from God.

A. James 1:13-16

> ¹³Let no man say when he is tempted, I am tempted of God: for God cannot be tempted with evil, neither tempts he any man: ¹⁴But every man is tempted, when he is drawn away of his own lust, and enticed. ¹⁵Then when lust has conceived, it brings forth sin: and sin, when it is finished, brings forth death. ¹⁶Do not err, my beloved brethren.

B. Romans 7:18-22

> ¹⁸For I know that in me (that is, in my flesh,) dwells no good thing: for the will is present with me; but how to perform that which is good I find not. ¹⁹For the good that I would I do not:

but the evil which I would not, that I do. [20]Now if I do that I would not, it is no more I that do it, but sin that dwells in me. [21]I find then a law, that, when I would do good, evil is present with me. [22]For I delight in the law of God after the inward man.

A. Galatians 5:24-26

[24]And they that are Christ's have crucified the flesh with the affections and lusts. [25]If we live in the Spirit, let us also walk in the Spirit (keep in step with the Spirit). [26]Let us not be desirous of vain glory, provoking one another, envying one another.

3. When you pull off the works of the flesh (grave clothes), No one can condemn you because you are walking or being led by the Holy Spirit. The Spirit of Christ gives the believers life, and more abundant life. Without the Holy Spirit you and I cannot control our flesh. This is the reason it takes the eternal power of the Holy Spirit to bring your flesh into subjection, if you will allow Him to do his job, which is to keep you from temptations.

A. Romans 8:1-4

[1]There is therefore now no condemnation to them which are in Christ Jesus who walk not after the flesh, but after the Spirit. [2]For the law of the Spirit of life in Christ Jesus hath made me free form the law of sin and death. [3]For what the law could not do, in that it was weak through the flesh, God sending his own Son in the likeness of sinful flesh, and for sin, condemned sin in the flesh: [4]That the righteousness of the law might be fulfilled in us, who walk not after the flesh, but after the Spirit.

B. Romans 8:12-14

[12]Therefore, brethren, we are debtors, not to the flesh, to live after the flesh. [13]For if you live after the flesh, you shall die: but if you through the Spirit do mortify (kill) the deeds of the body, you shall live. [14]For as many as are led by the Spirit of God, they are the sons of God.

C. Romans 13:14

[14]But put you on the Lord Jesus Christ, and make no provisions for the flesh, to fulfill the lusts thereof.

Please take much time to study and practice doing these Scriptures. When your flesh began to crave things that are against the will of God, tell it NO!! Do not give in to those desires, even if you have to fast and pray for strength. The Holy Spirit is constantly waiting to help you in these times of need.

Remember: Graves clothes can be many things in your life but you do not have to wear them. You have been set apart for God's use; now dress the part in your Spiritual attire!!!

Notes: _____

_____

_____

_____

_____

_____

_____

_____

_____

_____

_____

_____

_____

_____

_____

_____

_____

_____

_____

_____

_____

_____

_____

_____

_____

_____

_____

_____

_____

_____

_____

_____

Week 32

I WILL WORSHIP YOU LORD

BIBLICAL PRINCIPLES - Matthew 4:10-11 - [10]Then said Jesus unto him, Get thee hence, Satan: for it is written, Thou shall worship the Lord thy God, and Him only shall thou serve. [11]Then the devil left him, and behold, angels came and ministered unto him.

If you are not familiar with this particular passage of Scripture, let me tell you how Jesus responded to the temptations or testing of the devil. Jesus was led up into the wilderness to be tempted of the devil after fasting for forty days and forty nights. He was very hungry and Satan came to Jesus wanting him to turn stones into bread. Jesus refused him quoting the Word of God to him saying, man shall not live by bread alone, but by every word that proceeds out of the mouth of God.

Then the devil tried to tempt Jesus by saying if you are the Son of God, cast yourself off the pinnacle of the temple (a high place) because God said that he would give his angels charge over you, lest at anytime you dash your feet against a stone. Jesus responded with the Word again saying, "It is written again, you shall not tempt the Lord your God."

The devil began to show Jesus all of the kingdoms of the world, and the glory of those kingdoms. The devil said unto Jesus, all of these things will I give you, if you fall down and worship me. This is where our biblical principles start.

Because Jesus is the Living Word, he used the word to put the devil in his place. We see Jesus the Son of God (whom the devil tried to temp), let Satan know who is in charge of Him. Jesus knew what his purpose was and why he came to this earth. So Jesus tells Satan, get thee hence, Satan: for it is written, you shall worship the Lord your God, and Him only shall you serve. This is so awesome to see the Son of God tell Satan that he will only worship his Father. Jesus at this time set the standard for all Christians to worship God and Him only we must serve. Before Jesus started His ministry, He let the enemy know that his top priority was to worship and serve God and God alone. There would be no mixing loyalties when it came to his God. We must always have the same type of loyalty and devotion for God.

Through all of his testing, Jesus carefully spoke the word of God to his enemy as his responses. He did not tell him things which carried no value, Jesus spoke with authority, the written word of God and Satan had to leave him alone. Jesus also said that it is written that you shall worship the Lord your God and him only shall you serve. We are commanded to worship and serve only the Lord God. Your worship and service belongs only to God and no one else.

If Jesus, the Son of God was required to worship God the Father, use the word of God to resist temptations, and to put Satan in his place, what do you think is required of us? Because we are to have the mind of Christ, we must know how to use the word of God properly to bring us closer to God. We must get a clear understanding of what it means to worship God and know that not everyone can worship Him.

Worship is very personal between you and your God. It is when you express feelings of reverence and adoration for God. Worship brings you closer to God. This is when your heart, mind and everything else within you develop a very close and personal relationship with God. You begin to reverence who God is, Honor His majestic being, respect His holiness, and give adoration to God for His greatness. Worship also brings you to a place of obedience from your heart and faithfulness in the service of your God. Others may worship along with you, but your worship is between you and God alone!

Worship involves giving yourself totally to God in such an unselfish way, that only what God wants for you is all that matters. When you are truly in worship, you sense a close proximity to God. You realize that the presence of the Almighty God is overpowering and God's will at that moment is all you want. You become totally involved in what is happening between you and God, no one else is important at that moment. He is the Lord God Almighty!!! This is when you decide "I will worship you Lord".

Every Christian should desire to have the type of relationship with God, which will prompt worship and faithful service to Him. There should be a desire within you to take your relationship to the highest level possible for the rest of your life and declare to God, I will worship you Lord!!!

Let us look at the word of God and see what the Scripture is saying regarding worship and what is expected of you and I in this process.

PRACTICAL APPLICATIONS:

1. One of the first things you must notice is, Jesus said in the Scripture that the time would come when people must worship God in Spirit and in truth. He knew that everyone and everything that have breath could praise the Lord, but not everyone would be able to worship God. Because worship comes from the heart, a personal relationship is required.

    A. John 4:22-24

    [22]You worship you know not what: we know what we worship: for salvation is of the Jews. [23]But the hour comes, and now is, when the true worshippers shall worship the Father in spirit and in truth: for the Father seeks such to worship him. [24]God is a Spirit: and they that worship him must worship him in spirit and in truth.

    B. Psalm 150:6

    [6]Let everything that hath breath praise the Lord. Praise ye the Lord.

2. To worship God you must believe that he is God and that all that is written in the Holy Scriptures are true regarding Him and His Son. You cannot worship a God you do not truly believe in.

    A. Acts 24:14

    [14]But this I confess unto you, that after the way which they called heresy, so worship I the God of my fathers, believing all things which are written in the law and the prophets.

3. We often look for reasons to worship God. We must worship and give God the glory due unto his name, for his mighty acts,

for his greatness, and just because he is God! We must know that he is worthy of all our worship because of his presence in all the earth. God must be acknowledged as the divine King and Ruler of everything! Humbly bring yourself as an offering unto him and give him your all.

A. Psalm 29:1-2

> [1]Give unto the Lord, O you mighty, give unto the Lord glory and strength. [2]Give unto the Lord the glory due unto his name; worship the Lord in the beauty of holiness (the state of being consecrated to God or to his worship; sacredness).

B. Psalm 96:4-9

> [4]For the Lord is great, and greatly to be praised: He is to be feared above all gods. [5]For all the gods of the nations are idols: But the Lord made the heavens. [6]Honor and majesty are before him: Strength and beauty are in his sanctuary. [7]Give unto the Lord, O you kindred of the people, Give unto the Lord glory and strength. [8]Give unto the Lord the glory due unto his name: Bring an offering, and come into his courts. [9]O worship the Lord in the beauty of holiness: Fear before him, all the earth.

C. Psalm 99:5

> [5]Exalt ye the Lord our God, and worship at his footstool; For he is holy.

It is a wonderful honor and privilege to come before the presence of our Holy God, humble ourselves, bow down, and worship Him. Worshipping God is so private and personal that you must give him your whole consecrated heart and the time he requires to inhabit your worship. Always be ready to tell the Lord "I will worship you Lord", and be sincere from your heart.

Remember: Everybody can praise the Lord, but not everyone can worship Him. You must have a personal relationship to worship the Lord God Almighty!!!

Notes: _____

_____

_____

_____

_____

_____

_____

_____

_____

_____

_____

_____

_____

_____

_____

_____

_____

_____

_____

_____

_____

_____

_____

_____

_____

_____

_____

_____

Week 33

I SHALL LIVE AND NOT DIE

BIBLICAL PRINCIPLES - Psalm 118:16-17 - ¹⁶The right hand of the Lord is exalted: The right hand of the Lord does valiantly. ¹⁷I shall not die, but live, and declare the works of the Lord.

In this particular Psalm, King David was leading his nation into a praise of thanksgiving to God for God's deliverance form the hands of their enemies. They had fought the battle and God had mercy on them and delivered them for the arrows of death. The people and the king kept saying that God's mercy endures forever.

Can you imagine how dismayed and fearful these people must have been to see the enemies coming against them to destroy their lives? Even in the midst of the fear and other emotions, someone needed to stand up and bring back to their remembrance the faithfulness of the God who had fought for them so many times before. Someone needed to tell these people that, your God is able to do exceedingly more than you can ever expect or imagine. God never gets worried or loses control of anything that is happening in this earth or in your life.

This is the same attitude we as the people of God must have when facing life most difficult challenges. Yes, life does get hard at times, yes, people sometimes misunderstand you, and yes, sometimes you feel as if no one cares for you or about the things that troubles you. But my advice to you is to read this particular Psalm daily until you find the peace you need in your situations.

I only wrote this part of the Psalm because I truly wanted to inform you that the right hand of the Lord represents the Strength and the Power of the Most High God!! When you are going through rough or tough times always know that God's right hand is exalted, meaning that the Right Hand of God is elevated, exaggerated, inflated, enlarged to increase to an abnormal degree just to fight for you! What a profound revelation to have and to know in your time of need.

This same Scripture goes on to say that the right hand of God does valiantly; which, also means that God's right hand will fight for you with courage, boldness, bravery, and strength. So when you add all of this together regarding how much and how deep God's love for you is displayed in his fatherly protection, I know you will declare as the psalmist, "I shall not die, but live".

There is a reason why you should declare "I shall not die, but live". Because you are here in this earth and in this time to declare the works of the Lord. Do not sit down and allow the challenges, the cares, the disappointments, the misfortunes, and whatever life throws your way, remove your desire to live and declare the works of the Lord. Allow God to fight for you while you declare His works!

It is time for the people of the most high God to take the stand in faith knowing that He who promises to deliver His people is the Almighty, everlasting, eternal, all wise, everywhere present, faithful God!! He is the God that has never lost a case, never failed to keep a promise, and always delight in taking care of His people. So now, whose report will you believe, what you see or what you know about your great God? Stand firm on the promises of God and know what the will of God is for your life.

Never allow the things and happenings of your life cheat you out of the life that God has given unto you to live abundantly. God already knew these things would happen, so the escape route has already been established. All you need to do is keep on trusting God and declaring His word that he spoke into your life, to live and not die and declare the works of the Lord. You keep on declaring it until you believe what you are declaring.

I would like for you to take a look with me into the word of Scripture and see why you can always trust your God to come through for you.

PRACTICAL APPLICATIONS:

1. First of all let us look at who you are depending on. You are placing your trust and confidence in the God of Creation, the Sustainer of Life, the Great I Am, and the God Who Knows Everything! With this being His reputation, you must feel quite confident that whatever you need to have done, God is more than capable to get it done.

    A. Psalm 121:1-3

       [1]I will lift up mine eyes unto the hills, from whence comes my help. [2]My help comes from the Lord, which made heaven and earth. [3]He will not suffer my foot to be moved: He that keeps you will not slumber.

B. Psalm 27:1-3

> [1]The Lord is my light and my salvation; whom shall I fear? The Lord is the strength of my life; of whom shall I be afraid? [2]When the wicked, even mine enemies and my foes, came upon me to eat up my flesh, they stumbled and fell. [3]Though a host should encamp against me, my heart shall not fear: though wars should rise against me, in this will I be confident.

C. Psalm 27:5-6

> [5]For in the time of trouble he shall hide me in his pavilion (A covered place): In the secret of his tabernacle shall he hide me; He shall set me upon a rock (solid place). [6]And now shall my head be lifted up above mine enemies round about me: Therefore will I offer in his tabernacle (Church) sacrifices of joy; I will sing, yes, I will sing praises unto the Lord.

2. It is the will of God that you and I become strong in Him. Sometimes the things that happen in your life are not for defeat, but to develop you as a steadfast and unmovable Christian. Do not misunderstand when God is pruning (to cut back plants for the purpose of producing more growth) you of unwanted or unneeded things in your life. Remember He knows everything, therefore he sees so far ahead of you and knows what must be deleted from your life. Trust Him to make all the cuts that are necessary for your benefit, because some things will just have to happen to enhance your growth.

A. John 15:2-3

> [2]Every branch in me that bears not fruit he (God) takes away; and every branch that bears fruit, he purges it that it may

bring forth more fruit. ³Now you are clean through the word which I have spoken unto you.

B. 1Corinthians 15:57-58

⁵⁷But thanks be to God, which gives us the victory through our Lord Jesus Christ. ⁵⁸Therefore, my beloved brethren, you be steadfast, unmovable, always abounding in the work of the Lord, for as much as you know that your labor is not in vain in the Lord.

3. When life seems to become unbearable or just plain hard, think about the facts regarding God. Facts are always needed and are very important to calculate any types of results. The results of how much God loves you and how important you are to him are without comprehension. God loves you so much that he gave his only begotten Son to die for you to have eternal life. God also said that you are the apple of his eye. With these facts, you should without doubt know that God will deliver you, but you must trust and obey whatever he tells you to do. Your deliverance is also dependent on how you obey God's directions.

A. John 3:15-17

¹⁵That whosoever believeth in him should not perish, but have eternal life. ¹⁶For God so loved the world, that he gave his only begotten Son, that whosoever believeth in him should not perish, but have everlasting life. ¹⁷For God sent not his Son into the world to condemn the world; but that the world through Him might be saved.

B. Psalm 17:8-9

⁸Keep me as the apple of the eye, hide me under the shadow of thy wings, ⁹from the wicked that oppress me, from my deadly enemies, who compass me about.

C. Zechariah 2:8

8For thus said the Lord of Hosts; after the glory has he sent me unto the nations which spoiled you: For he that toucheth you toucheth the apple of his eye (someone small that needed to be protected at all cost).

D. Deuteronomy 32:10B

32bHe (the Lord) led him about, He instructed him, He kept him as the apple of His eye.

4. Now that you see how important you really are to the Great God of the universe, start declaring that you shall live and not die, to declare the works of the Lord. Jesus said in the Scripture, he came that you might have life and have it more abundantly, all you need to do is believe what Jesus said and live it out. Also you must know that God is able to do more than you will ever be able to understand.

A. John 10:10-11

10The thief comes not, but for to steal, and to kill, and to destroy: I (Jesus) am come that they might have life, and that they might have it more abundantly. 11I am the good shepherd: the good shepherd gives his life for the sheep.

B. Ephesians 3:17-20

17That Christ may dwell in your hearts by faith; that you, being rooted and grounded in love, 18May be able to comprehend with all saints what is the breadth, and length, and depth, and height; 19And to know the love of Christ, which passes knowledge, that you might be filled with all the fullness of God. 20Now unto him that is able to do exceeding abundantly above all that we ask or think, according to the power that works in us.

Study all of these Scriptures daily until you have digested them inside your soul and spirit. Never stop studying what you are in need of until you faith has come to the level needed for God's divine intervention. God is always ready to care for us in whatever situation we may need him, but following His instructions and being attentive to his voice will be the determining factor of how God moves in your life.

Remember: It is important that you make the declaration into your own life that you shall not die, but live, to declare the work of the Lord!!! It is your choice to look up and live or be defeated and die.

Notes: _____

_____

_____

_____

_____

_____

_____

_____

_____

_____

_____

_____

_____

_____

_____

_____

_____

_____

_____

_____

_____

_____

_____

_____

_____

_____

_____

Week 34

FIRST GIVING HONOR TO GOD

BIBLICAL PRINCIPLES - 1Timothy 1:12-17 - ^{12}And I thank Christ Jesus our Lord, who hath enabled me, for that he counted me faithful, putting me into the ministry; ^{13}Who was before a blasphemer, and a persecutor, and injurious: but I obtained mercy, because I did it ignorantly in unbelief. ^{14}And the grace of our Lord was exceeding abundant with faith and love which is in Christ Jesus. ^{15}This is a faithful saying, and worthy of all acceptation, that Christ Jesus came into the world to save sinners; of whom I am chief. ^{16}Howbeit for this cause I obtained mercy, that in me first Jesus Christ might show forth all longsuffering, for a pattern to them which should hereafter believe on him to life everlasting. ^{17}Now unto the King eternal, immortal, invisible, the only wise God, be honor and glory forever and ever. Amen.

This Scripture is where Paul is giving his testimony of how merciful, gracious, and longsuffering our eternal God is and was to him. He realized how bad a sinner he was and all he could do was first give honor to God!! He realized that he had done nothing to deserve the goodness and mercies of God. He knew he was not worthy to even stand before the presence of this holy God, but God allowed and called him to work in the ministry.

Paul was well aware of the fact that he was nothing and no one without the love, forgiveness, grace, and mercies of God. Therefore he was first giving Honor and glory to this Great God who forgave him of so much and called him to do a great work in the ministry. Paul also referred to himself as being the chief sinner, one who was worse than any other sinner. But he also realized that because he obtained mercies from God, and he wanted to be the first example to this world to show forth the pattern of longsuffering to every Christian who would come after him for eternal life.

You and I can agree that Paul did just that! He proved himself faithful, thankful, loyal, humble, and grateful to his God for all the kindness God showered upon him. All through the Scriptures we see Paul honoring, praising, and thanking God for all he did for him and for everything Paul suffered for the sake of the ministry of God.

Until we recognize how sinful we really were and how much love and forgiveness God bestowed upon us, we will never first give honor unto God. When you see yourself as not such a bad sinner, or that you were not as bad as others were, you still do not understand how much you were forgiven. Many times we compare our past life to others and see the other person as awful and some as so repulsive. But when we think of the fact that if we were not forgiven, we would still be labeled as sinners and therefore Hell would be our destination.

You see, failure to realize our true sinful state would be the reason we fail to realize that we should give honor to God first. Every blood bought Christian must have the true understanding that God did more for you than you were ever able to do for yourself. Your sin was categorized in the eyes of God as sin, not small or great, but SIN just as everyone else. This makes us all the chief of sinners! I know this is probably very hard to digest but the truth is that we all were sinners, much was forgiven of us, and only God's love, grace and mercy placed us in God's holy ministry.

You are probably saying that you are not a minster, but the truth is you really are. Every Christian is called to go into the entire world and preach this Gospel to every creature, meaning we are all servants of the Most High God. Ministers are servants sent out to serve the people of God everywhere, so this makes all of us ministers of the gospel.

It is time for all Christians to place the honor of God back in the rightful place, first! God must be honored first in everything you and I do. He must be honored as who he is, God, for what He has done, so much, for what He is doing, everyday for you and I, and because of whom He has given to be Savior, his only Son Jesus Christ. Can God depend on you to bring back the glory and honor due to his Name? His name is above all names, He is above all other gods, and He reign in all the earth. Please join in with me and let us first give honor to our GREAT GOD!!

Let us look at the word honor and see what you and I owe God. According to the American Heritage College dictionary, the word honor means: 1) High respect, as for special merits; esteem. 2) Good name; reputation. 3) A source or cause of credit. 4) Glory or recognition; distinction. 4) To esteem or regard highly.

Given this definition, I know we all would agree that no one else is worthy of the Honor, Glory, and the Praise that is due unto Our Great God.

The word of God has so much to say about giving honor to God. I will give you some of the Scriptures to help you get back into the place of first giving honor to God.

PRACTICAL APPLICATIONS:

1. Because God created the heavens and the earth with His spoken words, honor is truly due unto Him. He also created you and I in his image, for this we should honor Him and give him glory. Sometimes going back to the beginning of something will remind and make us grateful of how, why, and what, we have right now. We must remember what God did in the beginning.

   A. Genesis 1:1-3

   [1]In the beginning God created the heaven and the earth. [2]And the earth was without form, and void; and darkness was upon the face of the deep. And the Spirit of God moved upon the face of the waters. [3]And God said, Let there be light: and there was light.

   B. Genesis 1:26-28

   [26]And God said, Let us make man in our image, after our likeness: and let them have dominion over the fish of the sea, and over the fowl of the air, and over the cattle, and over all the earth, and over every creeping thing that creeps upon the earth. [27]So God created man in his own image, in the image of God created he him; male and female created he them. [28]And God blessed them, and God said unto them, Be fruitful, and

multiply, and replenish the earth, and subdue it: and have dominion over the fish of the sea, and over the fowl of the air, and over every living thing that moves up on the earth.

2. Now we need to be reminded of who this God is? Why must we honor Him? What has God done that should bring Him honor first in my life? There are so many things that can be applied here but I can only address some of them. Let us start with the natural attributes of God, our Supreme Being.

- **God is Unchangeable**

  Numbers 23:19 - [19]God is not a man, that he should lie; Neither the son of man, that he should repent: Hath he said, and shall he do it? Or hath he spoken, and shall he not make it good?

- **God is Incomparable**

  2Samuel 7:22 - [22]Wherefore thou art great, O Lord God: for there is none like thee, neither is there any God besides thee, according to all that we have heard with our ears.

- **God is Invisible**

  John 1:18 - [18]No man hath seen God at any time; the only begotten Son, which is in the bosom of the Father, he hath declared him.

- **Omnipotence (All Powerful)**

  Jeremiah 32:17, 27 - [17]Ah Lord God! behold, thou hast made the heaven and the earth by thy great power and stretched out arm, and there is nothing too hard for thee. [27]Behold, I am the Lord, the God of all flesh: Is there anything too hard for me?

- **Omnipresence (Ever-Present)**

  Psalm 139:7-12 - [7]Whither shall I go from thy spirit? Or whither shall I flee from thy presence? [8]If I ascend up into heaven, thou art there: If I make my bed in hell, behold, thou art there. [9]If I take the wings of the morning, and dwell in the uttermost parts of the sea; [10]Even there shall thy hand lead me, and thy right hand shall hold me. [11]If I say, Surely the darkness shall cover me; Even the night shall be light about me. [12]Yea, the darkness hides not from thee; but the night shines as the day: The darkness and the light are both alike to thee.

- **Omniscience (All Knowing)**

  John 3:20 - [20]For if our heart condemn us, God is greater than our heart, and knows all things.

3. We must give honor to God first because of His moral attributes. God is goodness, holy, impartial, justice, longsuffering, love, mercy, truth, and many other things, but we cannot cover them all. These are the attributes that God bestows upon his people.

- **Goodness**

  Psalm 31:19 - [19]O how great is thy goodness, which thou has laid up for them that fear thee.

- **Holy**

  Revelation 4:8 - [8]And the four beasts had each of them six wings about him; and they were full of eyes within: and they rest not day or night, saying Holy, holy, holy, Lord God Almighty, which was, and is, and is to come.

- **Impartial**

  1Peter 1:17 - [17]And if you call on the Father, who without respect of persons judges according to every man's work, pass the time of your sojourning here in fear.

- **Justice**

  Psalm 89:14 -[14] Justice and judgment are the habitation of thy throne: Mercy and truth shall go before your face.

- **Longsuffering**

  Exodus 34:6-7a - [6]And the Lord passed by before him, and proclaimed, The Lord, The Lord God, merciful and gracious, longsuffering, and abundant in goodness and truth, [7]keeping mercy for thousands, forgiving iniquity and transgression and sin, and that will by no means clear the guilty.

- **Love**

  1John 4:7-8 - [7]Beloved, let us love one another: for love is of God; and everyone the loves is born of God, and knows God. [8]He that loveth not, knows not God; for God is love.

- **Mercy**

  Lamentations 3:22-23 - [22]It is of the Lord's mercies that we are not consumed, because His compassions fail not. [23]They are new every morning: great is thy faithfulness.

- **Truth**

  Psalm 117:1-2 - [1]O praise the Lord, all ye nations: Praise him, all ye people. [2]For His merciful kindness is great toward us: And the truth of the Lord endures forever. Praise ye the Lord.

4. Finally I would like to speak on the ways of God. His ways are not like man's ways. God is Perfect, knowledgeable, righteous, and everlasting.

If for no other reasons you give God honor first, be thankful because of his ways made known to mankind, this should convince you of why we first give honor to our God.

- **God is Perfect**

  Psalm 18:30 - [30]As for God, His way is perfect: The word of the Lord is tried: He is a buckler to all those that trust in him.

- **God is Knowledgeable**

  Psalm 86:11 - [11]Teach me thy way, O Lord; I will walk in thy truth: Unite my heart to fear thy name.

- **God is Righteous**

  Psalm 145:17 - [17]The Lord is righteous in all his ways, and Holy in all his works.

- **God's Ways are made Known to Man**

  Psalm 103:7 - [7]He made known his ways unto Moses, His acts unto the children of Israel.

- **God is Everlasting**

  Habakkuk 3:6 - [6]He stood and measured the earth: He beheld, and drove asunder the nations; And the everlasting mountains were scattered, the perpetual hills did bow: His ways are everlasting.

Now you should always give honor to God first, especially after learning what the Scriptures taught regarding our God! To know that God loves us so much that He forgave us for all of our sinful ways, Lord We will honor You First!!!

Remember: When you admit to yourself that you were an awful sinner and God forgave you of all of your sins, you are now ready to say "First, giving honor to God".

Notes: _____

_____

_____

_____

_____

_____

_____

_____

_____

_____

_____

_____

_____

_____

_____

_____

_____

_____

_____

_____

_____

_____

_____

_____

_____

_____

_____

_____

_____

Week 35

I WILL NOT TAKE GOD'S GLORY

BIBLICAL PRINCIPLES - Revelation 22:8-9 - ⁸And I John saw these things, and heard them. And when I had heard and seen, I fell down to worship before the feet of the angel which showed me these things. ⁹Then said he unto me, See thou do it not: for I am your fellow servant, and of thy brethren the prophets, and of them which keep the sayings of this book: worship God.

In this Scripture the angel had finished showing John (the writer of Revelation), all the things which should come to pass in heaven and upon the earth. Then John fell down to worship the angel, but the angel told him not to do that. The angel wanted John to know that only God is worthy of glory and honor. John was told that he should only worship God. Even the angels in heaven know that nothing and no one is to take God's glory. He made this known to John the apostle of Jesus Christ. The angel had done many great things before John and John felt that he should bow before the angel. But here we see the angel refused to take the glory that is due to God.

This is the same John who was a disciple of Jesus when Jesus lived on earth. He knew the Lord personally and witnessed many of the miracles that were performed during the ministry of Christ. This man stood at the foot of the cross and watched everything that happened to Jesus during the crucifixion and all the days that led up to his ascending up to heaven. Imagine this man being so close to the Son of God, a true friend of Jesus but not expecting to take the glory from the Lord.

John shared many of his memories of the work of Jesus with all of us as the Holy Spirit inspired him to write. But the one thing that stood out to me the most was the fact that John never tried to take any of God's glory. He never made himself as this great person that needed to have some of the glory for himself. This tells me that John understood who Jesus really was. He knew that Jesus was sent to do the will of God and that everything Jesus did brought glory to his Father.

Jesus set the perfect example before his disciples, and his disciples did all they could to bring honor and glory to the name of Jesus Christ. Whatever they went through, endured, suffered, and performed had everything to do with God getting the glory out of their lives. This is a much needed reminder for Christians; we need to understand that our lives should bring honor and glory to the name of Jesus Christ. He alone is worthy of all our glory at all times. Can God depend on you to give him all the glory?

After the angel finished showing John all the things of Revelation, this same John fell on his face to worship the angel and the angel reminded him not to do that. You must always remove yourself from the place call God's throne. It does not matter how great or how worthy you may feel you are, you do not deserve to get God's glory. God's glory is reserved for him and for him alone. You are not deity, you are not the Son of God, and you are not the one to receive the glory.

It is important to know that whatever you do in the ministry or the work you do for God, you are only doing what you were called to do. Many times you feel that people need to honor or praise you for what you do for the Lord, this may not happen but will you continue to give God his glory. God will reward you for your work but you must give God all the glory. Do not take God's glory for yourself.

When you realize that everything you have comes from God and all that you are or ever hope to become is credited to the Almighty God. Paul said in the word of God, "what do you have, that has not been given to you". If God gave you everything you have, why should you take his glory? If God made you who you are, why would you take his glory? If you are nothing without the grace of God, why would you take his glory? If anything, you should give God all of the honor and all of the glory because of who He is and what He has done for you. This is when you shout out "Lord I Will Not Take Your Glory".

The word of God has much to say about giving God the glory due unto Him. We will search the Scriptures to remind us that we must give God all of his glory!

PRACTICAL APPLICATIONS:

1. There are many reasons why you should give God glory. You should give God glory because he is a jealous God and will have no other gods before him. You should give him glory for his work as the author of creation, for him sending His Son to grant us salvation. You should also glorify God because he delivers you from your troubles.

   A. Exodus 20:3-5

      [3]Thou shall have no other gods before me. [4]Thou shall not make unto thee any graven image, or any likeness of anything that

is in heaven above, or that is in the earth beneath, or that is in the water under the earth: ⁵Thou shall not bow down thyself to them, nor serve them: for I the Lord thy God am a jealous God, visiting the iniquity of the fathers upon the children unto the third and fourth generation of them that hate me.

B. Psalm 19:1

¹The heavens declare the glory of God; And the firmament shows his handy work.

C. Hebrews 11:3

³Through faith we understand that the worlds were framed by the word of God, so that things which are seen were not made of things which do appear.

D. Psalm 24:1

¹The earth is the Lord's and the fullness thereof; The world, and they that dwell therein.

E. John 3:16

¹⁶For God so loved the world, that he gave his only begotten Son, that whosoever believeth in him should not perish, but have everlasting life.

F. Psalm 50:15

¹⁵And call upon me in the day of trouble: I will deliver thee, and thou shall glorify me.

2. There are ways that you should and must glorify God. You should give God the glory through your praise and through your service. You must give him glory through your sufferings and through your fruitfulness. God wants you to be fruitful and faithful in your service to Him, this will show by your fruitfulness.

- **Praise**

  Psalm 50:23 - [23]Whoso offers praise glorifies me: and to him that orders his conversation aright will I show the salvation of God.

- **Fruitfulness**

  John 15:8 - [8]Herein is my Father glorified, that you bear much fruit; so shall ye be my disciples.

- **Service**

  1Peter 4:11 - [11]If any man speak, let him speak as the oracles of God; If any man minister, let him do it as of the ability which God gives: that God in all things may be glorified through Jesus Christ, to whom be praise and dominion forever and ever. Amen.

- **Suffering**

  1Peter 4:14-16 - [14]If you be reproached for the name of Christ, happy are you; for the Spirit of glory and of God rests upon you: on their part he is evil spoken of, but on your part he is glorified. [15]But let none of you suffer as a murderer, or as a thief, or as an evildoer, or as a busybody in other men's matters. [16]Yet if any man suffer as a Christian, let him not be ashamed; but let him glorify God on this behalf.

3. You should glorify God in your body and spirit because Jesus paid the price for your eternal life. You must also do good work and let your light shine so others will see your good works and Glorify God and not you.

  A. 1Corinthians 6:20

    [20]For ye are bought with a price; therefore glorify God in your body and in your spirit, which are God's.

A.   Matthew 5:16

[16]Let your light so shine before men, that they may see your good works, and glorify your Father which is ion heaven.

The study and practice of these Scriptures should enable you to become the servant who honors and give God all the glory that is due unto him. Glorify God because of who He is and for all that he has done for you!

Remember: Search the Scriptures daily and see the greatness of God! When you see the magnitude of God's awesomeness and greatness, it should stir in you a level of AWE and RESPECT for God. Only then will you give God the glory due unto Him.

Notes: _____

_____

_____

_____

_____

_____

_____

_____

_____

_____

_____

_____

_____

_____

_____

_____

_____

_____

_____

_____

_____

_____

_____

_____

_____

_____

Week 36

LEARNING HOW TO DENY MYSELF

BIBLICAL PRINCIPLES - Matthew 16:24-26 - [24]Then said Jesus unto his disciples, If any man will come after me, let him deny himself, and take up his cross, and follow me. [25]For whosoever will save his life shall lose it: and whosoever will lose his life for my sake, shall find it. [26]For what is a man profited, if he shall gain the whole world, and lose his own soul? Or what shall a man give in exchange for his soul?

Jesus had just finished teaching his disciples about all the things he was going to suffer for the people of this world to have eternal life. Jesus' ministry had entered into a new phase. Instead of teaching large crowds, he now focuses his attention on his twelve disciples. This he did to prepare them for his denial, sufferings, and death. Jesus wanted them to understand that his time was drawing near and they should know what to expect from the people regarding him and this time in his life. Jesus knew things were going to get really bad before it would get better.

Then Peter, one of Jesus' disciples began to rebuke Jesus telling him, this should not be unto you. But Jesus rebuked Peter and told him he was speaking the things of men and not of God. Peter could not imagine Jesus the Son of God going through anything so awful. Besides this, everyone including the disciples, thought Jesus had come to deliver them from the bondage of the Romans, not to die on a cross for their sins. This was all very new to them, not at all like the ways of men.

Now Jesus looks at his disciples and tells them, if any man will come after me, let him deny himself, take up his cross, and follow me. This is something Jesus truly wanted his followers to understand. He had walked with them for quite some time and they still did not fully understand what Jesus was sent to this world to do. Now it was very important for them to get the full picture of what was about to happen with their Master. After all they would be the men chosen to start the New Testament Church!

Jesus starts this teaching with a direct command that "if any man will come after me, let him deny himself, take up his cross, and follow me". We must take the time to really understand exactly what Jesus meant by this saying.

First, "if any man will come after me, let him deny himself". Jesus is saying, if any man (male or female) will choose to follow him and become his disciple or servant, he must first deny himself. Meaning to, refuse, reject, disavow, to restrain oneself, especially from indulgence in pleasures. Jesus is telling us to forsake all, everyone and everything for him. You must personally count up the cost of discipleship and decide if you are willing to sacrifice all for your relationship with Jesus.

You cannot truly follow Jesus without letting go of everything that will hinder your faithfulness to him. You must be willing to give up all of yourself centered commitments and give yourself to Christ centered commitments. This is a must because God wants all of you!

You are not your own anymore but now you have become the servant of the Almighty, Sovereign God. God has absolute ownership and authority over all of his creation. You are expected to give your life, desires, and will to the desires, work, and will of God, nothing less will do. Jesus gave up his life for you and I, so now you must be willing to give your life for Him. Most of us have a tendency to give up our life for the things we want but now Christ is saying to give up your life for him. This is one of the costs of true discipleship, all or nothing. When we desire something in life we work and give up whatever is necessary to obtain that thing. This is exactly what Jesus is requiring of any man who will come after him.

After deciding to deny yourself, now you are told to take up your cross. The cross was an instrument of death, representing the fact that you are totally surrendered unto God even unto death. When our Lord carried his cross, He took it all the way to death. Jesus gave His life for us and now he is asking us, to give up everything for Him. Is it worth giving up everything for a relationship with Jesus? Our answer should be without hesitation, a loud YES!! Yes Lord, I will give up all for you. Yes Lord, I desire your desires for me in my life. Yes Lord, you are truly worthy of all my love, honor, devotion, time, and everything you desire and want from me. You should cry out, Lord I Surrender All to You!

Now you are ready to follow Jesus. Following Jesus is much more than a profession or confession. It is when your heart belongs totally to Him. It is when you know Jesus is all you want and all you crave deep down in your soul. It is important to deny yourself first so that you will be empty of self and can allow God to fill you up to the brim with his Holy Spirit. In self denial, your focus is not on what God can do for you. Your focus is now, Lord what will you have me to do for you and others.

What a change self denial with bring into your life. You become more interested in what is best for others rather than for yourself. This is one of the lessons Jesus needed so desperately to get his disciples to understand. Just as today he needs to get the body of Christ to understand. We will be able to move many mountains when we become Christ centered rather than self centered.

In following Jesus you become ready and able to do the things of God because you did the first works first. Many will never get to the place of truly following Jesus because they will not deny themselves and take up their cross. Notice, how Jesus place these requirements in a specific order, we must do them in this order to really follow Jesus. One must note that it is hard to pick up your cross if you are still quite concerned about yourself all the time.

After doing all of this, you will not worry so much about saving your life. Now you have received the truth of God's word telling you that your life is hidden in God through Christ Jesus our Lord.

Will you focus this week on denying yourself, taking up your cross, and following Jesus? I will give you some Scriptures that will help you make the transition from self centered to Christ centered.

PRACTICAL APPLICATIONS:

1. You must learn about the cost of discipleship. What does it cost to be a follower of the Lord Jesus Christ? Will you be able to accept

the terms of God to be a true disciple? You can be a disciple but not a true disciple. So let's get ready to count up the cost. Jesus is saying forsake or get rid of everything and follow him. You cannot look or go back into yesterday and your previous life style, or expect God to accept this type of relationship.

A. Luke 14:27-30

[27]And whosoever does not bear his cross, and come after me, cannot be my disciple. [28]For which of you, intending to build a tower, sits not down first, and counts the cost, whether he have sufficient to finish it? [29]Lest haply, after he has laid the foundation, and is not able to finish it, all that behold it begin to mock him, [30]Saying, this man began to build, and was not able to finish.

B. Matthew 19:21

[21]Jesus said unto him, If you will be perfect, go and sell that you have, and give to the poor, and you shall have treasures in heaven: and come and follow me.

C. Luke 9:62

[62]And Jesus said unto him, no man, having put his hand to the plough, and looking back, is fit for the kingdom of God.

D. Luke 18:29-30

[29]And he said unto them, verily I say unto you, there is no man that hath left house, or parents, or brethren, or wife, or children, for the kingdom of God's sake, [30]Who shall not receive manifold more in this present time, and in the world to come life everlasting.

2. A person must give thought to discipleship. You must consider what is most important to you, who is most important to you, and why is it most important to you. You need to have integrity and be honest about giving up your selfish ambitions to follow Jesus. If you are not honest you will began to think that you can bring that same selfish attitude into your relationship with Christ. God will not endorse this type of ambition because pride will bring you to ruins. Humility will bring you into God's desire to exalt you.

A. Proverbs 29:23

   [23]A man's pride shall bring him low: but honor shall uphold the humble in spirit.

B. Proverbs 22:4

   [4]By humility and the fear of the Lord are riches, and honor, and life.

C. James 4:10

   [10]Humble yourselves in the sight of the Lord, and he shall lift you up.

D. Proverbs 11:2

   [2]When pride comes, then comes shame: But with the lowly is wisdom.

E. Proverbs 23:26

   [26]My son, give me your heart, and let your eyes observe my ways.

3. Now it is time for you to change your mind about how you view serving the Lord. You must see God as being worthy of your life and your substance. Because God is the Creator of everything, there is no reason why He should not have first place in your life. You must

consider the true value of all the things you have and decide if it is more important to you than having God in your life. This is called complete self denial. True treasures are treasures that you invest in God and not just earthly gains.

A. Romans 12:1-2

[1]I beseech you therefore, brethren, by the mercies of God, that you present your bodies a living sacrifice, holy, acceptable unto God, which is your reasonable service. [2]And be not conformed to this world: but be ye transformed by the renewing of your mind, that you may prove what is that good, and acceptable, and perfect, will of God.

B. Luke 14:33

[33]So likewise, whosoever he be of you that forsakes not all that he has, he cannot be my disciple.

C. Matthew 6:19-20

[19]Lay not up for yourselves treasures upon earth, where moth and rust doth corrupt, and where thieves break through and steal: [20]But lay up for yourselves treasures in heaven, where neither moth nor rust doth corrupt, and where thieves do not break through nor steal.

4. To take up your cross is when you have decided that you really want God in your life more than anything else. It does not matter how hard the trials, how long the tests, not how many things comes your way, you will not let it separate you from God's love. This is where you make up your mind that you are in this relationship to stay forever. This is true discipleship and true love for your savior.

A. Romans 8:35-39

> [35]Who shall separate us from the love of Christ? Shall tribulation, or distress, or persecution, or famine, or nakedness, or peril, or sword? [36]As it is written, for thy sake we are killed all the daylong; we are accounted as sheep for the slaughter. [37]Nay, in all these things we are more than conquerors through him that loved us. [38]For I am persuaded, that neither death, nor life, nor angels, nor principalities, nor powers, nor things present, nor things to come, [39]nor height, nor depth, not any other creature, shall be able to separate us from the love of God, which is in Christ Jesus our Lord.

B. Romans 6:6

> [6]Knowing this, that our old man is crucified with him, that the body of sin might be destroyed, that henceforth we should not serve sin.

C. Romans 6:13

> [13]Neither yield ye your members as instruments of unrighteousness unto sin: but yield yourselves unto God, as those that are alive from the dead, and your members as instruments of righteousness unto God.

5. You are now ready to follow Jesus. You have become unselfish and your mind is Christ centered. You are no longer seeking self gratification and self ambitions. You are now focused on the things of the eternal God, you want to please Him at all cost. You are not concerned with things going your way anymore because you are sold out to the Lord. You now recognize that this world is not your permanent home and you are preparing for more than what you

see now. You now understand that Jesus is the Best thing that could have ever happened to you.

A. Luke 9:25

25For what is a man advantaged, if he gain the whole world, and lose himself, or be cast away.

B. John 15:16

16Ye have not chosen me, but I have chosen you, and ordained you, that ye should go and bring forth fruit, and that your fruit should remain: that whatsoever ye shall ask of my Father in my name, he may give it you.

C. 1Corinthians 9:27

27But I keep under my body, and bring it unto subjection: lest that by any means, when I have preached to others, I myself should be a castaway.

Now that you see the importance of denying yourself, taking up your cross, and following Jesus, submitting unto His will should be your top priority in life. Take these Scriptures very seriously and practice living them out daily as you go through this life. Keep the will of God first in your life and purpose to please him in everything you do and say.

Remember: Jesus gave his life for you and I, we should be willing to give him our life and service for the rest of our lives. After all, He is the Sovereign God and has total power and authority over us!

Notes: _____

_____

_____

_____

_____

_____

_____

_____

_____

_____

_____

_____

_____

_____

_____

_____

_____

_____

_____

_____

_____

_____

_____

_____

_____

_____

_____

_____

52 weeks of practical application to biblical principles

Week 37

STANDING UP FOR JESUS

BIBLICAL PRINCIPLES - Matthew 10:32-33 - ³²Whosoever therefore shall confess me before men, him will I confess also before my Father which is in heaven. ³³But whosoever shall deny me before men, him will I also deny before my Father which is in heaven.

This Scripture is the type of reminder we all need to stand up and represent our God. Jesus taught that you and I must stand up and confess to others about who He is and what he has done for this whole world. Many times we are afraid or ashamed to speak out about and for Jesus because of what others may think, feel, or say. Notice, Jesus said if you confess him before men, then he would confess you before his heavenly Father. This is so powerful because we all want our heavenly Father to know us personally, so you and I should want others to know this same heavenly Father in a personal way.

We must break away from the feeling of being ashamed to proclaim Jesus to this troubled world. Jesus offers so much to all of mankind, but if no one informs the people of the great gift of God which is eternal life, then how will this world learn of Him? It is the responsibility of Christians to tell the world about Jesus because we have experienced firsthand what the Lord can and will do. Christians know the changes that will happen in a person's life when he/she accept Jesus as his/her personal Savior. This is one of the reasons we must stand up for Jesus.

 Another important reason we must stand up for Jesus is that the love of God constrains us to present God's eternal plan of salvation to everyone. We must care enough for others to the point that we refuse to allow them to enter eternity without Jesus as their Savior. You never would have learned of Jesus if someone did not love you enough to present Jesus to you. Even if it is out of your gratitude to the person who presented Jesus to you, or if it is to Jesus for coming into your life, please stand up for Jesus.

The Lord wants bold soldiers to stand up and proclaim Jesus to this world. Even if you need to pray for some holy boldness to get this done, pray and get busy standing up for Jesus. You may feel that others do not want to hear about your Jesus, tell them anyway. You must remember it is their responsibility to accept or reject Jesus, your responsibility is to tell them. You cannot make anyone receive Jesus as their personal Savior, this is the job of the Holy Spirit. Your only duty is to live the life before them, tell them about Jesus, pray for the people when you witness to them, and leave the rest in God's hand. Jesus never told us that we had to make people accept Him, but he did tell us to Stand up and confess him to this world.

If you and I confess Jesus to this world, He in return, will confess us unto his Father which is in heaven. The more you stand up for Jesus the more he will stand up for you. Stand firm, bold and faithfully confess your Savior. Jesus deserves this and much more from us especially after all he suffered for you and me.

I remember in the book of Jeremiah, God spoke to Jeremiah and told him not to be afraid of the people faces and this same word applies to us. We need not be afraid or ashamed to speak out boldly about the God who is supreme ruler over this entire universe. God is due my confessing and my standing up for Him.

So now you should show your God that you will stand up for Him at all times. You will let Him know that he can depend on you to deliver this Gospel to the people whenever given the chance. Make the stand for the Savior who hung, bled, died, and rose for you, and has given you eternal life.

Here are some Scripture to encourage you to stand up boldly for Jesus. Study and live them in your everyday life, show Jesus how much you really love Him.

PRACTICAL APPLICATIONS:

1. Never, ever, should you feel ashamed to stand up and confess Jesus to other people. People are humans just as you are, so do not let them intimidate you about your relationship and standing up for your Savior.

    A. Mark 8:38

    [38]Whosoever therefore shall be ashamed of me and of my words in this adulterous and sinful generation; of him also shall the Son of man be ashamed, when he comes in the glory of his Father with the holy angels.

    B. Luke 9:26

    [26]For whosoever shall be ashamed of me and of my words, of him shall the Son of man be ashamed, when he come in his own glory, and in his Father's, and of the holy angels.

C. Acts 4:29-30

> [29]And now, Lord, behold their threatening: and grant unto thy servants, that with all boldness they may speak your word. [30]By stretching forth your hand to heal; and that signs and wonders may be done by the name of thy holy child Jesus.

2. You do not have to fear what others may try to do unto you because you confess or stand up for Jesus. God does not want you to be afraid of their faces as to how they look at you nor the things they may say unto you. You must always remember they are only humans just as yourself and that your God will take care of you.

A. Matthew 10:28

> [28]And fear not them which kill the body, but are not able to kill the soul: but rather fear him which is able to destroy both soul and body in hell.

B. Luke 12:4-5

> [4]And I say unto you my friends, be not afraid of them that kill the body, and after that have no more that they can do. [5]But I will forewarn you whom you shall fear: Fear him, after which he hath killed hath power to cast into hell; yea, I say unto you, fear him.

C. Jeremiah 1:8

> [8]Be not afraid of their faces: for I am with thee to deliver thee, says the Lord.

3. We all have been commissioned by Jesus to go into the entire world to preach and teach the Gospel to every living creature. We are to give them the chance to know of Jesus for themselves. This is the

one decision every individual must make for him/her selves. You can witness, teach, and pray for them, but your greatest witness will be the way you walked before them and the way you loved them.

A. Mark 16:15

[15]And he (Jesus) said unto them, Go ye into all the world. And preach the gospel to every creature.

B. Matthew 28:19-20

[19]Go ye therefore, and teach all nations, baptizing them in the name of the Father, and of the Son, and of the Holy Ghost: [20]Teaching them to observe all things whatsoever I have commanded you: and lo, I am with you always, even unto the end of the world. Amen.

C. Matthew 10:33

[33]But whosoever shall deny me before men, him will I also deny before my Father which is in heaven.

Let us avoid disappointing our God by not standing up for Him before this world. We have been sent out to stand boldly and present Jesus as the only begotten Son of God who gave his life as the perfect payment and sacrifice for every man's sin. Now we must stand up for this same Jesus!

Remember: Life is full of twists and turns, successes and failures, and many other things, but imagine you being able to do something for the God of Creation that will make the difference in someone else's life. Yes, you can STAND UP and NOT BE AFRAID to tell this world about JESUS!!

Notes: _____

_____

_____

_____

_____

_____

_____

_____

_____

_____

_____

_____

_____

_____

_____

_____

_____

_____

_____

_____

_____

_____

_____

_____

_____

_____

_____

Week 38

THE POWER AND AUTHORITY OF GOD'S WORD

BIBLICAL PRINCIPLES - Psalm 119:9-12 - ⁹Wherewithal shall a young man cleanse his way? By taking heed thereto according to thy word. ¹⁰With my whole heart have I sought thee: O let me not wander from thy commandments. ¹¹Thy word have I hid in mine heart, that I might not sin against thee. ¹²Blessed art thou, O Lord: Teach me thy statutes.

In this particular psalm, the author was giving instructions on godly living. How a young man would be able to cleanse his way from all types of immoral living. He knew something about the power and the authority that exist in the word of God. In fact the writer tell us that by taking heed (pay attention to; listen to and consider; close attention) to God's word, a man's way would be cleansed.

The word of God also teaches that a man must seek God with his whole heart, not part but all of his heart. To be able to keep or heed the word of God, your entire heart must be involved as the highest role in your relationship with God. You must understand that God is not like man, looking at or on the outward appearance of what you present. Your God is so all knowing, that he knows and sees exactly what is going on in your heart. Therefore God arrives to his decision by your true motives and your true heeding to his word. The true results of whether or not you are heeding the word of God will play out in how you walk in his will.

When you began to seek God with your whole heart as the word of God requires, your whole person will produces the changes which are spoken of in His word. This is the power and authority of the word of God. In your life, the fruit of the Spirit, the mind of Christ, walking circumspectly, obeying the will of God, and honoring God as your Savior will become so active and real, that others will notice the changes also. If your whole heart is involved, you will not wander away from God's commandments and his will.

Once you hide the word of God in your heart, it will prevent you from actively sinning against God. This same word will help you desire to learn of God's will and desires for your life. Only the power and authority of the word of God is able to produce such transformation in the life of any human.

It is a very serious matter to try the power and authority of God's word in your life. When God spoke his written word, he meant everything he said in it, with no exceptions. Therefore you and I must by faith, receive, believe, and walk according to all that is written. We must recognize that the whole heart is to be involved in the production of the results that we receive. If you do not apply your whole heart in your walk through the word of God, as you study, read, and practice living, you will not experience the complete activation of the power and authority that is meant to be received through the Word.

Get busy activating the power and authority that has been given to you in God's word by hiding the word in your heart.

I will give you some Scriptures that will help you in your study of God's word. These Scriptures should also help you in transforming your walk and your mind in Christ Jesus.

PRACTICAL APPLICATIONS:

1. The first reason for applying the word of God in and to your life is for you to understand what the word has the power and authority to do in your life. The reason for this is to desire something that is good and profitable for you. There are many things you can and will do in this life that will not be to your best interest, but applying God's word to your life is one of the best things you will ever do. The word will order your steps and become a light and lamp to your feet, helping you to take the correct paths in life.

   A. Psalm 119:105

   [105]Thy word is a lamp unto my feet, and a light unto my path.

   B. Psalm 119:133

   [133]Order my steps in thy word: and let not iniquity have dominion over me.

2. The word of God will make you more productive in the work God has called you to do. It will also produce in you the fruit of the Spirit, transforming your character, attitude, your mind, and the way you walk before God. The word is so powerful that it will clean you up and present you righteous before our Holy God.

A. Galatians 5:22-23

²²But the fruit of the Spirit is love, joy, peace, longsuffering, gentleness, goodness, faith, ²³Meekness, temperance: against such there is no law.

B. Philippians 2:5

⁵Let this mind be in you, which was also in Christ Jesus.

C. Ephesians 5:15-19

¹⁵See then that you walk circumspectly, not as fools, but as wise, ¹⁶Redeeming the time, because the days are evil. ¹⁷Wherefore be not unwise, but understanding what the will of the Lord is. ¹⁸And be not drunk with wine, wherein is excess; but be filled with the Spirit; ¹⁹Speaking to yourselves in psalms and hymns, and spiritual songs, singing and making melody in your heart to the Lord.

D. John 15:3

³Now you are clean through the word which I have spoken unto you.

3. The word of God has the power and the authority to cut things that are offensive to God, off and out of your body, soul, and spirit. This is so powerful to know and understand because many things you have suffered through in this life, can be removed through proper applications of God's word. You can try and depend on the Word of God because it is settled in Heaven, meaning God's word will not change. The word of God will accomplish all that it has been sent out to perform.

A. Hebrews 4:12

¹²For the word of God is quick, and powerful, and sharper than any two edged sword, piercing even to the dividing asunder of

soul and spirit, and of the joints and marrow, and is a discerner of the thoughts and intents of the heart.

B. 1Peter 1:25

   [25]But the word of the Lord endures forever. And this is the word which by the Gospel is preached unto you.

C. Psalm 119:89-90

   [89]Forever, O Lord, Thy word is settled in heaven. [90]Thy faithfulness is unto all generations: Thou has established the earth, and it abides.

D. Isaiah 55:11

   [11]So shall my word be that goes forth out of my mouth: It shall not return unto me void, but it shall accomplish that which I please, and it shall prosper in the thing whereto I sent it.

4. For you to experience all the benefits of God's powerful and authoritative word, you must receive it with gladness, obey it, do it, and respect it. It is a good thing to stand in AWE of GOD"S WORD because the word of God is God!!

A. Acts 2:41

   [41]Then they that gladly received his word were baptized: and the same day there were added unto them about three thousand souls.

B. Psalm 119:161-162

   [161]Princes have persecuted me without a cause, but my heart stands in awe of thy word. [162]I rejoice at thy word, as one that finds great spoil.

C. James 1:22-25

> ²²But be a doer of the word, and not hearers only, deceiving your own selves. ²³For if any be a hearer of the word, and not a doer, he is like unto a man beholding his natural face in a glass: ²⁴For he, beholds himself, and goes his way, and straightway forgets what manner of man he was. ²⁵But whoso looks into the perfect law of liberty, and continues therein, he being not a forgetful hearer, but a doer of the work, this man shall be blessed in his deed.

Now that you understand the power and authority that is in the word of God, you should be able to liv1`e a more perfect life in God through Jesus Christ our Lord. You should begin to walk a more committed, powerful, and holy life in God.

Remember: God is not looking for excuses but he is looking for more obedient and productivity from his Christians. Will you be one of the ones who will fall into this category?

Notes: _____

_____

_____

_____

_____

_____

_____

_____

_____

_____

_____

_____

_____

_____

_____

_____

_____

_____

_____

_____

_____

_____

_____

_____

_____

_____

_____

Week 39

YES, GOD LOVES ME

BIBLICAL PRINCIPLES -John 3:16 - [16]For God so loved the world, that he gave his only begotten Son, that whosoever believeth in him should not perish, but have everlasting life.

This Scripture paints such a perfect picture of how much God the Father and God the Son loves us all. This entire world was operating under the curse of sin, not one human, but all of us. God loves this world so much that he gave his only begotten Son to die a brutal and cruel death for all of us, to satisfy the penalty of sin. God knew that mankind would never be righteous enough in his sight to pay this debt. The debt needed to be paid by someone perfect, righteous, and holy, Jesus is the only one who qualified to meet the need. So God sent His Son to provide the perfect sacrifice that would appease our debt for sin. For this I say thank you Lord!

Jesus loves us so much that he came to this earth and did just as his Father commanded him to do. Jesus, the perfect Son of God agreed to die for the sins of the world. He could have chosen another path but he became obedient to the will of his Father and fulfilled God's eternal plan of salvation for all mankind. This alone proves to you and I, that yes, God loves us.

So many times in life you feel as if no one cares or thinks about you. But here is such great information you need to know, that even if you do not receive the love you expect from others, your heavenly Father is always giving you all the love you need. The problem with us is that we are so busy trying to get others to love us for who we are, until we constantly ignore the love God is standing by to give us daily. God has no problems with loving us as we are because he created us and knows all there is to ever know about the real individual.

In saying this, we should be very excited to get to know this wonderful God who is ready, willing, and able to love us so unconditionally. Also, he has proven this love through the sacrifice of his only Begotten Son on the cross to die just for you and me. Now this is truly what love is all about.

Sometimes we expect others to love us in ways that they are not capable of doing. When people have not experienced the love of God in their life, they cannot give you what they do not have. To be honest with you, some of us have difficulty loving ourselves. So if you find it hard to love yourself, others will have the same problem. Now the question is, how much do you love the person God has made you to become? As a Christian, do you have problems accepting who God has called you to be? Are you trying to please everyone else instead of following the path God has established for you? Receive the love of God deep within your heart and let the will of God rule your entire life, this can really happen because the word of God says so.

Start falling in love with the individual you are, accept the fact that you are not someone else. Stop trying to be who you are not, because you are unique and there is no one else on this earth like you. Enjoy the skin that God has placed you in and stop trying to fit the mandates of someone else's skin. Realize the fact that if God meant for you to be like someone else, he would have placed you inside of their skin and not the skin you are in!! Be thankful that you are who you are, find acceptance in you being you, and walk in the newness of your God given life, full of love, grace, and mercy!

When you are able to get alone with you, then you will be able to start getting alone with others also. This will solve many of the problems you are facing. Many of your problems are not found so much in the things you need to do. But it is the fact that you sometimes worry, or you are concerned about the way others will react and what they will say regarding God's will in your life.

Live in the love of God, grow in the love of God, and reap the benefits of the perfect love of God. This is what God desires for your life. Experience the freedom of the love of God and live the life you were meant to live.

Yes, God really does love me and this will never change. I may choose to walk away from his love but God will always love me.

We will take a look at the Scriptures to find out how much God really loves you.

PRACTICAL APPLICATIONS:

1. Many times it is hard for people to accept the fact that God loves them. They will sometimes ask, "how can God love someone like me?" The truth of the matter is: how can he not love someone like

you, being that he made you? God is love, so love is what He does. This is a part of God's character and he is true to his word.

A. Ephesians 2:4-7

> [4]But God, who is rich in mercy, for his great love wherewith he loved us, [5]even when we were dead in sins, hath quickened us together with Christ (by grace ye are saved); [6]And hath raised us up together, and made us sit together in heavenly places in Christ Jesus: [7]That in the ages to come he might show the exceeding riches of his grace in his kindness towards us through Christ Jesus.

B. 1John 4:9-10

> [9]In this was manifested the love of God towards us, because that God sent his only begotten Son into the world, that we might live through him. [10]Herein is love, not that we loved God, but that he loved us, and sent his Son to be the propitiation (appeasing or conciliation) for our sins.

2. It is important that you understand how much God loves you because this is what will motivate you to love others. Since God loves you so much, it is only proper that you love others also and tell them of the great love God has towards them.

A. 1John 4:7-8

> [7]Beloved, let us love one another: for love is of God; and everyone that loves is born of God, and knows God. [8]He that loves not, knows not God; for God is love.

B. 1John 3:18

> [18]My little children, let us not love in word, neither in tongue; but in deed and in truth.

C. 1John 3:1

   ¹Behold, what manner of love the Father hath bestowed upon us, that we should be called the sons of God: Therefore the world knows us not, because they knew him not.

D. 1John 4:19

   ¹⁹We love him, because he first loved us.

3. It is one thing to say you love God, but it is proven by how you walk and obey Him. This is also true pertaining to how you know that God loves you. God loves you so much that he gave his Son to die for you and now you should show your love to him by obeying this same God and loving others.

   A. 1John 5:2-3

      ²By this we know that we love the children of God, when we love God, and keep his commandments. ³For this is the love of God, that we keep his commandments: and his commandments are no grievous.

   B. 1John 4:11-12

      ¹¹Beloved, if God so loved us, we ought also to love one another. ¹²No man hath seen God at any time. If we love one another, God dwells in us, and his love is perfected (mature) in us.

Jesus took the time to come and redeem us back to his Father because of his great love for us. Let us never forget the depth and the price that was paid for this great love that has been given unto us. We must always embrace it with all respect, humility, and reverence, and give honor to our Awesome God for loving us so completely!!

Remember: Everything God did for us was not done because he had to do it, but because he loved us all so much. Now this is what you call LOVE unconditionally!!

Notes: _____

_____

_____

_____

_____

_____

_____

_____

_____

_____

_____

_____

_____

_____

_____

_____

_____

_____

_____

_____

_____

_____

_____

_____

_____

_____

Week 40

GOD IS YOUR PROTECTION IN THE STORMS

BIBLICAL PRINCIPLES - Psalm 91:1-6 - ¹He that dwells in the secret place of the most High, Shall abide under the shadow of the Almighty. ²I will say of the Lord, He is my refuge and my fortress: My God; in him will I trust. ³Surely he shall deliver thee from the snare of the fowler, and from the noisome pestilence. ⁴He shall cover thee with his feathers, and under his wings shall thou trust: His truth shall be thy shield and buckler. ⁵Thou shall not be afraid for the terror by night; Nor for the arrow that flies by day; ⁶Nor for the pestilence that walks in darkness; Nor for the destruction that wastes at noonday.

These Scriptures teaches about the protection plan of the Most High God. Many of us are not aware of the protection that God gives us all the time. You have a personal protection plan in God that covers you through any and all types of storms. There is a secret place where you can go and hide, but it is found only in God. Christians have a place called the shadow of the Almighty where they can go for protection, and it does not matter what type of storm you are facing.

We Christians can say that God is our refuge (a shelter against harm) and our fortress (a fortified place), where we can trust that He will take great care of us. Not only this, but God is our deliverer from all types of traps, dangers seen and unseen, even for all manners of diseases and sicknesses.

You can rest assured that God will cover you with his wings of protections and you can trust God in all things. Because God is truth, his truth shall be your Shield (a protective armor) and buckler (a round shield worn on the arm). You need not be afraid or worried about anything at night nor do you need to be concerned or have anxiety during the day of God not protecting you. God has your situations under control, let him handle it.

This Scripture is saying, that you can put all of your trust in the Almighty God because he cares for you and will take great care of you at all times. This is the promise of God and God cannot lie. If God said he will protect you, sit back and watch God move, He does not need your help to fix it.

So many times you find yourself worrying about things you have no control over, only to find out that God took care of it anyway. This should give you the confidence you need to put all your trust in the one and only God who can keep his promises. You are limited in what you can do but God is not limited to time, space, or anything, so He can do all things.

Let us talk about storms. What exactly are storms? Storms are: A violent disturbance or upheaval; To assault, capture, or captivate by storm; To move or rush tumultuously. In relation to life, storms happen when life takes some difficult turns and you do not know what to do. Sometimes there is nothing you can do except trust that God will work it all out for your good. Storms can hit at any time in your life and can last for quite some time. This is why you must trust God to fix them.

We have all types of insurance policies to cover many things, but you will never find a policy so complete that covers every area of your life, like the protection plan of God! When it comes to storms, there are many kinds, and to purchase an insurance policy for total coverage, you will probably end up paying a large premium. But when you accept Jesus as your personal Savior, your premiums will never increase. In fact you get more coverage as time go on, and the value of your policy increases without any chance of you being turned down for coverage.

In the natural, there are policies that cover floods, rain, wind damages and many other things, but most of the time you must elect to purchase these coverage for extra premiums. With God, every type of storm that can happen to an individual during this lifetime, is totally covered and there is not waiting period. Once you become a member of the family of God, your coverage starts right then. You now have full coverage and you do not have to worry any more about the things that have kept you awake at night before. Your benefits in Jesus are a lifetime policy and can only be cancelled by you. Go to sleep, rest well, and know that God have you covered!!

Storms will happen but, you do not have to allow your storms to define who you are. When storms arise in your life, hide under the shadow of the Almighty God and let Him take care of you and your storms.

The Scriptures will give you the confidence you need to trust God in your storms. Here are a few to show you that God wants to take of you.

PRACTICAL APPLICATIONS:

1. It is so typical of us to think that we are the only ones going through a storm. Many times when you are riding out a storm, someone else is riding out something much worse than your storm. Jesus' disciples weathered storms also but, they knew to call on the Jesus for the help they so desperately needed. You will gain confident in the power and authority Jesus has over everything as you read about Jesus calming their storm. Please know, if Jesus can calm the wind and the sea, surely he can calm all of your storms!

    A. Mark 4:35-41

> [35]And the same day, when the evening was come, he (Jesus) said unto them, Let us pass over unto the other side. [36]And when they had sent away the multitude, they took him even as he was in the ship. And there was also with him other little ships. [37]And there arose a great storm of wind, and the waves beat into the ship, so that it was now full. [38]And he was in the hinder part of the ship, asleep on a pillow: and they awake him, and say unto him, Master, cares thou not that we perish? [39]And He arose, and rebuked the wind, and said unto the sea, Peace be still. And the wind ceased, and there was a great calm. [40]And he said unto them, Why are ye so fearful? How is it that you have no faith? [41]And they feared exceedingly, and said one to another, what manner of man is this, that even the wind and the sea obey him?

2. When you confess that you trust the Lord to take care of you, there should come a time in your relationship with Jesus that you stop laying awake all night crying and wondering what to do. Trusting God means you will cast all your cares upon him because He cares for you. At some point you must come to realize that if there is

nothing you can do about the situation, this is one for the Lord to fix! Turn it all over to him and watch God move.

A. Proverbs 3:24-26

[24]When thou lie down, thou shall not be afraid: yea, thou shall lie down, and thou sleep shall be sweet. [25]Be not afraid of sudden fear, neither of the desolation of the wicked, when it comes. [26]For the Lord shall be your confidence, and shall keep thy foot from being taken.

B. Psalm 121:7-8

[7]The Lord shall preserve thee from all evil: He shall preserve thy soul. [8]The Lord shall preserve thy going out and thy coming in from this time forth, and even for evermore.

C. Psalm 4:8

[8]I will both lay me down in peace, and sleep: For thou Lord makes me dwell in safety.

D. 1Peter 5:7

[7]Casting all your cares upon him; for he cares for you.

3. When you make the Lord your Savior and Master, he will not allow the evil to overtake you. God will show Himself strong in your situations. It is God's good pleasure to show Himself great and strong for his servants.

A. Psalm 91:9-10

[9]Because thou has made the Lord, which is my refuge, even the most High, thou habitation; [10]There shall no evil befall thee, neither shall any plague come nigh thy swellings.

A. 2Chronicles 16:9a

> [9a]For the eyes of the Lord run to and fro throughout the whole earth, to show Himself strong in behalf of them whose heart is perfect towards Him.

Now you see that God is your protection in the storms. All you must do is choose to walk upright before Him and trust that he will take care of you.

Remember: Storms will come, life will happen, but they that put their trust in the Lord will always have full coverage protection.

Notes: _____

_____

_____

_____

_____

_____

_____

_____

_____

_____

_____

_____

_____

_____

_____

_____

_____

_____

_____

_____

_____

_____

_____

_____

_____

_____

_____

_____

_____

_____

Week 41

KEEPING MY MIND ON JESUS

BIBLICAL PRINCIPLES - Romans 8:6-8 - [6]For to be carnally minded is death; but to be spiritually minded is life and peace. [7]Because the carnal mind is enmity against God: for it is not subject to the law of God, neither indeed can be. [8]So then they that are in the flesh cannot please God.

In this particular passage of Scripture, Paul the Apostle is writing to the Christians in the Romans Church regarding their mindset, and how it does affect their walk and relationship with God. He began by informing them that to be carnally minded (mind of the flesh) is death. Paul is saying, when you choose to follow the desires and cravings of what you want to do, you have chosen the path of death in the end. The Scripture is so clear on the fact that to be fleshly minded, will make life hard and eventually destroy you.

As you read the word of God you will notice that the human mind has always been against the will of God. Since then, nothing has changed regarding our human mindset. Many activities takes place in the mind, this is why it is so important to keep your mind on Jesus. When you keep your mind on Jesus you will avoid many dangerous situations that can cause you much grief. As you see in Scripture, the earthly mind is always concerned with self but the spiritual mind is concerned with the things of God. So in all reality, if you follow the mind of your flesh, you cannot please God because he is a Spirit, and they that worship Him must do it in Spirit and in truth.

Christians are always to be concerned about pleasing God and this should be on a daily basis. This is what living for Christ is all about. With the mind of Christ, you will be able to live this way. It becomes hard to keep your mind on Christ when you are always trying to do whatsoever you please. I know you do not want to spend your entire life on being selfish and doing only the things that makes you happy.

Start living to please God and see how different and wonderful you will feel when you are caring for others. We were not created to be concerned only for self, but to be of value to others. When you keep your mind on Jesus, you began to develop the mind and character of Christ and the rest will fall in place. You will find yourself wanting to be used by God and feeling good about the person you are.

Many times you hear people saying it is so hard to live this life, but this is only because you must change and adjust your mind to the things of Christ. When you think spiritually, you walk and live spiritually. But when you think fleshly, you walk and live fleshly. Yes, it truly is that simple, the way you think will determine how you live and walk. So, if you keep your mind on Jesus, you will walk like Jesus, if you keep your mind on you, you will walk like you!

If you are tired of walking without the approval of or pleasing Christ, you can do something about it. Allow Jesus to fill your mind daily and you will start seeing the difference this will make in your life. You will find yourself making better choices and doing things that will cost you less problems. You will even see that getting along with others is not as difficult as it seemed. Give it a chance, start keeping your mind on Jesus, and watch yourself grow in the grace of God.

I will give you some Scriptures to help you make the transformation of your mind from carnal (flesh) to Spiritual (godly).

PRACTICAL APPLICATIONS:

1. One of the things you must consider is transforming your mind to the mind of Christ. You are responsible for this; no one else can do this for you. In fact the bible says be ye transformed by the renewing of your mind, you must change the way you think, feel, see, and do things. The old ways must cease to be, it was the wrong way and now you must live by the new ways of God. This is the beginning of your new mindset.

    A. Romans 12:2

        ²And be not conformed to this world: but be ye transformed by the renewing of your mind, that you may prove what is that good, and acceptable, and perfect will of God.

    B. 1Corinthians 2:16

        ¹⁶For who has known the mind of the Lord, that he may instruct him? But we have the mind of Christ.

2. When you keep your mind on Jesus, you will find complete joy, peace, and your love for God will increase. This is one way that growth takes place in a Christian's life. If you start walking in the ways of Christ you will began to live in the ways of Christ. However a man thinks; is how a man lives.

A. Philippians 4:7

7And the peace of God, which passes all understanding, shall keep your hearts and minds through Christ Jesus.

B. Proverbs 23:7a

7aFor as he thinks in his heart, so is he.

C. Philippians 2:1-2

1If there be therefore any consolation in Christ, if any comfort of love, if any fellowship of the Spirit, If any bowels and mercies (intense care and deep sympathy), 2Fulfill you my joy, that you be like minded, having the same love, being of one accord, of one mind.

3. When you have the mind of Christ, you are sure to do the things of Christ. Many desire to do the things of Christ but are unable due to the state of their minds. You must purpose to have the mind of Christ and work towards this goal. Having the mind of Christ will help you in every area of your Christian walk and you will not have to be condemned, because your mind is now controlled by the Spirit of Christ. The mind of Christ prevents you from being double minded, never knowing exactly what you want.

A. Philippians 2:5

5Let this mind be in you, which was also in Christ Jesus.

A. Ephesians 4:21-23

21If so be that you have heard him, and have been taught by him, as the truth is in Jesus: 22That you put off concerning the former conversation (your old lifestyle) the old man, which is corrupt according to the deceitful lusts; [23]And be renewed in the spirit of your mind.

A. Colossians 3:1-2

[1]If ye then be risen with Christ, seek those things which are above, where Christ sits on the right hand of God. [2]Set your affections on things above, not on things on the earth.

B. James 1:8

[8]A double minded man is unstable in all his ways.

4. Pure love for the Lord will always push you towards keeping your mind on Jesus. When you love someone it is hard to keep your mind off of that individual, this is how it should be with your love for God. Loving Jesus is what you were meant to do, and keeping your mind on him will happen because you love him.

A. Luke 10:27

[27]And he answering said, Thou shall love the Lord thy God with all thy heart, and with all thy soul, and with all thy strength, and with all thy mind; and thy neighbor as thyself.

B. Deuteronomy 6:5-6

[5]And thou shall love the Lord thy God with all your heart, and with all thy soul, and with all thy might. [6]And these words, which I command thee this day, shall be in your heart.

I do hope you understand the importance of keeping your mind on Jesus. Your mind is your reasoning faculty and is responsible for your perception, intent, remembrance, reasoning, feelings, desires, and purpose. Keeping your mind on Jesus will assure you of the proper applications of all these faculties.

Remember: Your mind is a terrible thing to waste, so keep it on Jesus and you will get proper usage out of it.

Notes: _____

_____

_____

_____

_____

_____

_____

_____

_____

_____

_____

_____

_____

_____

_____

_____

_____

_____

_____

_____

_____

_____

_____

_____

_____

_____

_____

_____

Week 42

I WILL HUMBLE MYSELF BEFORE YOU LORD

BIBLICAL PRINCIPLES - 1Peter 5:5b-6 5bFor God resists the proud, and gives grace to the humble. 6Humble yourselves therefore under the mighty hand of God, that he may exalt you in due time.

Learning how to be humble before God is something that can never be expressed or stressed enough. Scripture teaches us to humble ourselves under the mighty hand of God that he may exalt us in due time. It is a requirement of the Lord that his disciples will humble themselves to the authority of God. There are reasons why God instructs the Christians to humble themselves under his full authority. To walk in a mature relationship with the Lord, you must walk humbly before God not in proud and arrogance. When you began to walk in arrogance, you cannot obey or please God because everything becomes all about you, and nothing about God.

God resists (stands against) the proud (the defiant and haughty), meaning, God stands against the selfish, defiant, and haughty Christians. To be proud is to think of oneself as being better than others and feeling a sense of superiority above them. This is one of the behaviors that is spoken against so often in Scriptures. Pride will put you in a place where God will have to abase or bring you down. It is also spoken of as one of the six things that the Lord hates in Proverbs 6:16-17. What you must know and understand is that, before an individual becomes proud, it must happen in the heart first, then it will display itself outward. By the time you see the pride display of an individual, it has been going on inside of the heart for a while.

God gives grace or unmerited favor to the humble. If you want to walk constantly in the favor and anointing of the Most High God, please start humbling yourself under the mighty hand or authority of God. God gives you favor that you will not deserve or that you cannot earn, simply because you humbled yourself to God and the things of God. Stop resisting the will of God and began to obey the word of God by submitting yourself to what God requires of you. It does not matter who you think you are, but everything is riding on who God knows you are. You cannot impress God walking in pride, but humility will grant you God's authority in your life. Humility will bring you before great men and will allow you to walk in places with God that you never would have thought possible. God is always standing by to exalt you when you have learned how to humble yourself before Him.

Walking in pride will bring you to ruins and cause you to fall from where you have exalted yourself. Many people may brag and pat you on your back, but if you do not have the approval of the Almighty God because of your selfish pride, you really have not accomplished much. Yes, it may seem as if you are at the top of your game, but if pride becomes your daily garment, you have really lost it all. Why would you work so hard to attain so many things and allow pride to cause you to lose it all? This is something you really need to think about before pride becomes your end.

So go forth in this life seeking to please the Almighty God by adorning yourself in the garment of humility and watch God move in your life. Do not allow pride to remove you from the favor of God, but do walk in the spirit of humility and see how different and content you will become in every area of your life.

I would like to leave you with Scriptures to read and study regarding the subject of humility, on how and why you need to walk humbly before God.

PRACTICAL APPLICATIONS:

1. Many times in life you will find yourself being tested in areas of pride versus humility. If you are not careful, you will choose to walk in pride and not humility. When you are challenged, you may have the option to take the quiet way out or to walk away from a situation. But the pride inside of you will push you to speak out or stay and try to defend yourself. It is okay to walk away or keep silent to humble yourself and not develop a fighting attitude. You know whether you are right or wrong, you do not have to prove that to anyone else. Hold your peace and let the Lord fight your battles.

   A. Proverbs 29:22-23

   [22]An angry man stirs up strife, and a furious man abounds in transgression, [23]A man's pride shall bring him low: but honor shall uphold the humble in spirit.

B. Proverbs 16:19-20

> [19]Better is it to be of an humble spirit with the lowly, than to divide the spoil with the proud. [20]He that handles a matter wisely shall find good: and whosoever trusts in the Lord, happy is he.

2. Pride is a deceiver, it will make you think you are so very important when in fact; you are really setting yourself up for a great fall. The Scriptures teaches you that before destruction happens, pride comes first. Christians must always keep pride and arrogance far from their hearts, if they want to walk in God's favor. This too, is a choice that you must make if you are genuinely interested in a mature, Spirit-led relationship with the Lord.

A. Proverbs 16:18

> [18]Pride goes before destruction, and a haughty spirit before a fall.

B. Matthew 18:4

> [4]Whosoever therefore shall humble himself as this little child, the same is greatest in the kingdom of heaven.

C. Matthew 23:12

> [12]And whosoever shall exalt himself shall be abased; and he that shall humble himself shall be exalted.

D. Proverbs 18:12

> [12]Before destruction the heart of man is haughty, and before honor is humility.

3. Christians must know the benefits of walking daily in humility. Once you have chosen to walk in humility, the favor of God

becomes present in your life. The spiritual and natural exaltations begin to also happen in your life, and no one can prohibit God from moving. Humility will also bring you before great men and take you places you never thought possible. This alone should prompt you to continue on in this walk of humility and watch the Lord continue moving in your life.

A. Proverbs 22:4

[4]By humility and the fear of the Lord are riches, and honor, and life.

B. Proverbs 15:33

[33]The fear of the Lord is the instruction of wisdom; and before honor is humility.

C. James 4:5-6

[5]Do you think that the Scriptures says in vain, the spirit that dwells in us lusts to envy? [6]But he gives more grace. Wherefore he says, God resists the proud, but gives grace unto the humble.

D. James 4:10

[10]Humble yourselves in the sight of the Lord, and he shall lift you up.

Please read and study these Scriptures with a purpose of not falling into the spirit of pride. Also read Proverbs 6:16-17:

[16]*These six things does the Lord hate: yes, seven are an abomination unto him: [17]A proud look, a lying tongue, and hands that shed innocent blood.*

Notice that a proud look is at the top of the list, and this is just the look of pride. Now that you know how much God hates pride, keep it out of your heart.

Remember: If you do not want to fall, put a guard or spiritual fence around your heart with a sign stating "KEEP OUT, YOU ARE NOT WANTED HERE".

Notes: _____

_____

_____

_____

_____

_____

_____

_____

_____

_____

_____

_____

_____

_____

_____

_____

_____

_____

_____

_____

_____

_____

_____

_____

_____

_____

_____

_____

_____

_____

_____

_____

Week 43

I CAN SEE GOD WORKING ON MY INSIDE

BIBLICAL PRINCIPLES - 2Corinthians 5:17-18 -
**¹⁷Therefore if any man be in Christ, he is a new creature: old
things are passed away; behold, all things are become new.
¹⁸And all things that are of God, who has reconciled us to
himself by Jesus Christ, and has given to us the ministry of
reconciliation.**

After you have become a child of God, there should be some great
changes in your life. All of these changes must first happen in
the inside of your heart, then radiate to the outside in your walk as this
new creature. Others will be able to see your good works and glorify
your Father who is in heaven.

This Scripture confirms that you are not the same person you once
were. There is a new Spirit living inside of you, He is known as the
Holy Spirit of Jesus Christ. It is important that you recognize this is
the Spirit of power, authority, deliverance, and truth. Therefore, He

demands great respect, honor, and obedience because He is sent to instruct you on the will of God. He will not speak of his own but of the Will of God.

Now, you are a new individual and as Scripture teaches, old things are passed away, meaning the old spirit who once lived inside of you has been evicted, gone, and crucified forever. Not only is he gone, but the power and authority he once held over your life is also gone! You are no longer held captive to do the things that you could not stop doing before this new birth. You have been reconciled (no longer God's enemy) and God's Spirit and peace is now present inside of you.

You have no reason why you cannot live the life of power and authority in Christ Jesus. Excuses have been removed, power has been given, and a fresh new start is living inside of you. You are the first person who should be able to see and recognize that you are a new creature. Your conversations, way of living, the way you treat yourself and others, and the way you see God, should all be different now. You are not a slave to sin any longer, you are God's free servant! God took the initiative to call you into a new walk and lifestyle because of his great love for you.

What a wonderful display of the love of God toward his children. Now it is your chance to show your gratitude for all that God has done for you. Your life and love for God should move you into the direction God has chosen for you. When God is working on the inside of you, life takes on a whole new meaning. You are no longer obligated to your flesh and the things of your flesh. God working on the inside of you, jump starts the process of liberating you from your old ways. Now you must continue to live this process out by the way you submit to the leading of the Holy Spirit.

God is not looking for or listening to excuses as to why you cannot do righteous living. The reason being, you have been given everything you need to accomplish this in your life. When you start making and accepting your excuses, you are saying that the Spirit of the Most High God does not have the power and authority to continue to change you. As you embrace the truth of God's Word, you will find that the word is more than able to keep you from falling and present you faultless before this very same God.

So, can you see God working on the inside of you daily? Can you agree with the facts of Scripture that God's Holy Spirit is able to keep you until the day of Jesus Christ's return? Why would God pass old things away that were already in your life, and give you all things new, if you would not be able to live this new life? Take the time out to reflect back on all the positive changes that you see in your new life and remind yourself, that if God did it then, he surely can do it now. Is there anything too hard for God?

Changes are happening everyday inside of you, even if you don't see them. Because God is abiding in you, he will continue to do all the necessary changes, adjustments, and deleting if needed, to bring you to his expected end for you. You must do your part in this relationship. There is the reading, studying, eating (ingestion), and digestion (absorption or processing) of God's word. Do not just read but do all the steps needed to walk out the word.

Also, when the Holy Spirit reveal things to you that need to be removed, do not ignore Him and continue to do those things. But start praying, submitting, and allowing Him the authority to do whatever he needs to do, so you will get the deliverance you may need. To walk free in the power and authority of your new life, you must obey and submit to the entire will of God as you see him working inside of you. Be that

Christian who will make God so proud to call you his own. Have a desire to be the best child of God you can possibly be. Let your life strongly display the power and authority of the great God of creation. Let the world see how **GREAT** your God really is.

We will go into God's word for more Scriptures and strengthening as you understand how to allow God to work on the inside of you.

PRACTICAL APPLICATIONS:

1. To see God working on the inside of you, there must be a commitment and dedication to living by the Word of God. Your sins have been cast away from you and God does not remember them anymore, you are free to live a pure and holy life for Him. If it took the word to save you, it will also take this same word to keep you from stumbling. All Christians should have a desire to really please God.

    A. Isaiah 38:17

    [17]Behold, for peace I had great bitterness: But thou has in love to my soul delivered it from the pit of corruption: For thou has cast all my sins behind thy back.

    B. Micah 7:19

    [19]He will turn again, he will have compassion upon us; He will subdue our iniquities; and thou will cast all their sins into the depths of the sea.

    C. Jeremiah 31:34

    [34]And they shall teach no more every man his neighbor, and every man his brother, saying, know the Lord: For they shall all know me, from the least to them unto the greatest of

them, says the Lord: For I will forgive their iniquity, and I will remember their sin no more.

2. Now that you no longer have to worry about your old sins, because they are removed and forgiven, you have the rest of your life with a new spirit inside of you. Your new Spirit is now renewed with the knowledge of the image of your God. For this you say thank you Lord!!! Only God could do such a wonderful thing for his people. This is your chance to show God how great you know he is, and how much you want to serve him for the rest of your life. Your old man has been pulled off, you do not have to put him back on anymore.

   A. Ephesians 4:21-25

> [21]If so be that you have heard him, and have been taught by him, as the truth is in Jesus: [22]That you put off concerning the former conversation the old man, which is corrupt according to the deceitful lusts; [23]And be renewed in the spirit of your mind; [24]And that you put on the new man, which after God is created in righteousness and true holiness. [25]Wherefore putting away lying, speak every man truth with his neighbor: for we are members one of another.

   B. Colossians 3:7-10

> [7]In the which you also walked sometime, when you lived in them. [8]But now you also put off all these: anger, wrath, malice, blasphemy, filthy communication out of your mouth. [9]Lie not one to another, seeing that you have put off the old man with his deeds; [10]And have put on the new man, which is renewed in knowledge after the image of him who created him.

C. Romans 6:4

> ⁴Therefore we are buried with him by baptism into death: That like as Christ was raided up from the dead by the glory of the Father, even so we also should walk in newness of life.

3. You have been given a new heart! The old heart you once had is gone, now you have been given a new heart that can be groomed in the will of God. All of your old evil ways are removed but it is now up to you to keep them away from you. You have been given the power and authority to fill your new heart with nothing but the things of God. The choice is up to you to place the will of God in your heart. No one else can do this for you, they can pray for you, teach the word of God to you, and desire the things of God for your life, but only you can make it happen.

A. Ezekiel 11:19-20

> ¹⁹And I will give them one heart, and I will put a new spirit within you: And I will take the stony heart out of their flesh, and will give them a heart of flesh: ²⁰That they may walk in my statues, and keep mine ordinances, and do them: and they shall be my people, and I will be their God.

B. Ezekiel 36:26-27

> ²⁶A new heart also will I give you, and a new spirit will I put within you: and I will take away the stony heart out of your flesh, and I will give you a heart of flesh. ²⁷And I will put my Spirit within you, and cause you to walk in my statues, and you shall keep my judgments, and do them.

C. John 4:23-24

> [23]But the hour will come, and now is, when the worshippers shall worship tie Father in spirit and in truth: for the Father seeks such to worship him. [24]God is a Spirit: and they that worship him must worship him in spirit and in truth.

Since you are now seeing God working in the inside, you should be able to show others how it is done. Also do as Psalm 33:3a says "Sing Unto God a New Song", for he alone is worthy.

Remember: All of your sins are forgiven, you have a new heart, and the Holy Spirit now resides within you! Live the powerful and authoritative life that you have been given, with God working on the inside of you.

Notes: _____

_____

_____

_____

_____

_____

_____

_____

_____

_____

_____

_____

_____

_____

_____

_____

_____

_____

_____

_____

_____

_____

_____

_____

_____

_____

_____

_____

Week 44

MY BODY BELONGS
TO YOU LORD

BIBLICAL PRINCIPLES - 1Corinthians 6:19-20 - [19]What? Know ye not that your body is the temple of the Holy Ghost which is in you, which ye have of God, and you are not your own? [20]For ye are bought with a price: therefore glorify God in your body, and in your spirit, which are God's.

This passage of Scripture teaches you that your body belongs to the Almighty God. You do not own the rights to your body. In fact, as a Christian, you are bought with a price; the blood of Jesus Christ. When Jesus went to the cross he paid the entire cost of your redemption, now instead of you obeying the works of your flesh, you now owe your obedience to God. Once you have accepted Jesus as your personal Savior, you are now filled with His Holy Spirit, which make your body the temple of God.

Since your body is now housing the Holy Spirit, you are responsible for keeping your vessel pure before God. This is the reason why you should read, live, listen and obey God's word. The more Scriptures you feed the Holy Spirit, the more obedient you become to His leading and guiding you. The Holy Spirit is sent to dwell inside of you from the Almighty God, therefore you are not your own. You are to yield your body to the glorifying of God and not for your very own pleasures.

Once you can accept and program this vital piece of information in your mind, heart, and spirit, you will become a very powerful servant of God. God is requiring and expecting you to glorify Him in your body and your spirit. Why? Because the entire you belongs to God, and only God.

This is when you must make the decision that your body belongs to God, and you are going to honor, obey, live, and give God all the glory that belongs to him, in your body. You must value your body, and understand that you are responsible for housing the Spirit of God inside of you. Do you not know and understand what an awesome honor and privilege it is to have God's Holy Spirit living and abiding inside of your natural body, right here on earth? You must see the honor in this great provision God has done for all mankind. This could not have been done without the Hand of God making it possible.

 You are to make and keep your body as a sacred place where the power and Spirit of God now resides. Yes, it is possible for you to live a holy and sacred life, honoring God everyday in your body. You can live like this because the same Spirit that is inside of you, will not only live in you, but will also assist you in making this lifestyle possible. You are not able to fulfill this tall order on your own. The Holy Spirit must be given the authority from you to do the work that needs to be done, to make your body a sacred dwelling place for Him.

You are not to let sin rule in your body, and you are not to fulfill the lusts that comes with sin. Your mind must be transformed to do what is right, and you must train your body to live this holy way. This is what I call spiritual body and mind conditioning. Just as athletes must train and condition their bodies for the sports they desire to compete in, you and I must do the same with our mind and body.

God does not approve of you yielding to your fleshly cravings, and it does not matter how often you say God understands and he knows you. You cannot keep on committing sinful acts in and with your body, without insulting and grieving the Holy Spirit who abides in you.

Purpose to live the way God delights to see you live and make the Holy Spirit feel very welcomed in His bodily temple, your body. Imagine living in a house that made you feel nasty and unwelcomed, would you desire to remain in that house?

Walk with me in the word of God to see how to preserve your body as the living house or temple of the Holy Spirit.

PRACTICAL APPLICATIONS:

1. As a Christian, you are not to continue in the sinful lifestyle you once lived. It is taught in Scripture that once you have died spiritually to sin, meaning, you have accepted Jesus as your personal Savior, you cannot live any longer therein. You must leave that old lifestyle and condition yourself to live the new life that you have been given, starting fresh.

   A. Romans 6:1-4

      ¹What shall we say then? Shall we continue in sin, that grace may abound? ²God forbid. How shall we, that are dead to sin,

live any longer therein? [3]Know ye not, that so many of us as were baptized into Jesus Christ were baptized into his death? [4]Therefore we are buried with him by baptism into death: that like as Christ was raised up from the dead by the glory of the Father, even so we also should walk in newness of life.

A. Romans 6:11-13

[11]Likewise reckon ye also yourselves to be dead indeed unto sin, but alive unto God through Jesus Christ our Lord. [12]Let not sin reign (rule) in your mortal (human) body, that you should obey it in the lusts thereof. [13]Neither yield ye your members (body) as instruments of unrighteousness unto sin: but yield yourselves unto God, as those who are alive from the dead, and your members as instruments of righteousness unto God.

2. You must start working on transforming your mind to reject the things of the flesh, and receive the things of the Spirit. For years, your mind has been used for evil thoughts and entertaining evil things. Now you must start replacing and exchanging the evil thoughts with holy thinking and holy entertainment. The way to get this done is to fill your mind with holy spiritual things. Confessing your sins are not enough for you to start walking in the Spirit, you must become a yielded body for God's service. This includes your body and your mind daily.

A. Romans 12:1-2

[1]I beseech (call) you therefore, brethren, by the mercies of God, that ye present your bodies a living sacrifice, holy, acceptable unto God, which is your reasonable service. [2]And be not conformed to this world: but be ye transformed by the

renewing of your mind, that ye may prove what is that good, and acceptable, and perfect, will of God.

B. Ephesians 5:15-19

[15]See then that ye walk circumspectly, not as fools, but as wise, [16]Redeeming the time, because the days are evil. [17]Wherefore be ye not unwise, but understanding what the will of the Lord is. [18]And be not drunk with wine, wherein is excess; but be filled with the Spirit; [19]Speaking to yourselves in psalms and hymns and spiritual songs, singing and making melody in your heart to the Lord.

C. 1 Thessalonians 4:7-8

[7]For God has not called us unto uncleanness, but unto holiness. [8]He therefore that despises, despises not man, but God, who has also given us His Holy Spirit.

3. There are the works of the flesh, which you are to avoid always. Then there are the fruit of the Spirit, which you are to embrace always. The Holy Spirit desires the fruit of the Spirit and the word of God to be active in your life. There is nothing in the works of the flesh that will prosper the Holy Spirit. So stay away from the things of your flesh and run wholeheartedly towards the things of the Spirit.

A. Galatians 5:18-21

[18]But if you are led by the Spirit, you are not under the law. [19]Now the works of the flesh are manifest, which are these; Adultery, fornication, uncleanness, lasciviousness, [20]Idolatry, hatred, variance, emulations, wrath, strife, seditions, heresies, [21]Envyings, murders, drunkenness, revellings, and such like:

of the which I tell you before, as I have also told you in time past, that they which do such things shall not inherit the kingdom of God (these are a list of the sins of the flesh which are forbidden by God for Christians to commit).

See week #14 for the definitions of the works of the flesh

B. Galatians 5:22-25

[22]But the fruit of the Spirit is love, joy, peace, longsuffering, gentleness, goodness, faith, [23]Meekness, temperance: against such there is no law. [24]And they that are Christ's have crucified the flesh with the affections and lusts. [25]If we live in the Spirit, let us also walk in the Spirit.

Your body belongs to God and you should do everything possible to make God glorified of the way you maintain your temple of the Holy Spirit!

Remember: God did an honorable thing when he gave you his Holy Spirit. Now, you do an honorable thing by making a sacred and holy place for his Spirit to dwell.

Notes: _____

---

52 weeks of practical application to biblical principles

Week 45

SPENDING VALUABLE TIME WITH GOD

BIBLICAL PRINCIPLES - Jeremiah 29:12-14a - ¹²Then shall ye call upon me, and ye shall go and pray unto me, and I will hearken unto you. ¹³And ye shall seek me, and find me, when ye shall search for me with all your heart. ^{14a}And I will be found of you, says the Lord.

There will come a day in every Christian's life when they will need to spend some very valuable time with the Lord. Life has a way of bringing you to a place where only the presence and the word of God will do. Sometimes hard circumstances, difficult decision making, and just trying to walk with the Lord, will require some unrushed time with the Master. There are really no particular time frames when this may occur in your life or relationship with the Lord, but you will recognize the need when it is presented.

As you began to mature in your Christian walk, you will come to realize that you desire more from God than what you have been getting. You began to experience a yearning for more of God's touch, wisdom, knowledge, understanding, and his anointing. It does not matter what you do, or how long you do it, you still feel that your soul is craving for something that money, shopping, gadgets, or anything else will satisfy. This is when you desperately need to spend some quality time with God.

You are now in a place where all you want is God and more of him. You want his conversations, his presence, being under the shadow of his power, and his Abba Father tender care. You know there is more to your relationship with God than what you have been experiencing, you just want and need more of the Almighty!

God is saying to you at that time that he needs you to call upon Him and pray unto Him, and He will hearken unto you. The word hearken means that God will listen to you attentively and give heed to your call. God is saying: "I want you to disconnect yourself from all of the things that you feel are so important to you and connect yourself to the call for a deeper experience with Me". You need to focus your attention to the things that God is calling for NOW, and focus less on the things you have completed in the past.

You must also realize that life in Christ is a life of progress for every Christian. God does not want you to become complacent, and feel like you don't need to do anything else. This is why periodically, you will feel this great urge to draw closer to God, and spending more time with him will bring you to that place. You are to bear fruit and your fruit should remain, but when you start getting into a rut, sometimes your productivity slows down or may even cease. You need a powerful reconnect with your power source, Jesus the Christ!

In the fruit stage, you have no fruit, fruit, more fruit, and much fruit. Only God knows the stage of fruit bearing you are in and at what stage you should be producing. This is why you must with all your heart, take the time to call upon him, go and pray unto him, seek him, and find him in his word. There is the promise made unto you that the Lord will be found of you. God is always waiting for you to come to Him, He will make Himself available to you if you search for Him with your whole heart. God deserves you undivided attention with only Him on your mind and heart.

Turn off everything, remove every distraction, fall down on your knees and give yourself totally unto the Lord. I know this may sound like a onetime encounter, but the truth is, this should be happening in your Christian relationship all the time. There should always be a strong desire inside of you to call on and be in a place where God's rule is first in your life. Every day you should spend special time with God and keep this a priority in your life. The more time you spend with God the more Godly you will become. You will become more powerful, more knowledgeable, and more informed of God's will for your life.

Do not wait to go into the Church to have an encounter with God, do this in your home, in your automobile, or anytime of your day. Because the Holy Spirit lives in you, you are responsible for feeding him the Word of God on a daily basis. You must give him everything he desires from you so that He can produce in you the perfect will of God for your life.

Scripture teaches us that there were times when Jesus would get to himself and talk with his Father in heaven to get whatever it was he needed at the proper time. He would actually leave the crowds and his disciples, sending them away because He knew the importance of spending valuable time with God the Father. Now you and I must also recognize the importance of spending this same valuable time with God!! When you say you want to be more like the Lord, this is how it happens.

The more time you spend with someone, gives you the opportunity to learn more about them and their ways. It will also help in your decision as to whether you want this person in your life or at what level will they be placed in your life. This is true with God! Do you really want him in your life and if so at what level will you place him? Will He be first, second, or where will he be placed? Will he get the time that is left over out of your busy day, or will he get the time from the first of your day? These are questions every Christian needs to personally ask so they can commit to spending more valuable time with God. It is to your advantage if you choose to give God more of your time, rather than give less time.

Since the Word of God is your authoritative voice in all you do, let us search the Scriptures regarding this matter.

PRACTICAL APPLICATIONS:

1. Jesus is our perfect example regarding all matters in life. Let us see how he handles the matter of spending time with his Father. He knew His life was not His own because He was sent by His Father to redeem mankind back to the Father, so He constantly separated himself to talk with and give God glory. After ministering to many people Jesus knew the value of praying alone to his Father.

   A. Matthew 14:22-23

   [22]And straightway Jesus constrained his disciples to get into a ship, and to go before him unto the other side, while he sent the multitudes away. [23]And when he had sent the multitudes

away, he went up into a mountain apart to pray: and when the evening was come, he was there alone.

B. John 6:15

[15]When Jesus therefore perceived that they would come and take him by force, to make him a king, he departed again into a mountain himself alone.

C. Luke 6:12-13

[12]And it came to pass in those days, that he went out into a mountain to pray, and continued all night in prayer to God. [13]And when it was day, he called him his disciples: and of them he chose twelve, whom also he named apostles.

D. Mark 6:45-46

[45]And Straightway he constrained his disciples to get into the ship, and go to the other side before unto Bethsaida, while he sent away the people. [46]And when he had sent them away, he departed into a mountain to pray.

2. Spending valuable time with God is required for study of the word of God. It is imperative that as a servant of God, you study to show yourself approved unto God. You are responsible for telling and teaching others about the things of God, so you must first be proficient to make others the same.

A. 2Timothy 2:14-15

[14]Of these things put them in remembrance, charging them before the Lord that they strive not about words to no profit, but to the subverting of the hearers. [15]Study to show thyself

approved unto God, a workman that need not to be ashamed, rightly dividing the word of truth.

B. Psalm 119:11

[11]Thy word have I hid in my heart, that I might not sin against thee.

C. Psalm 119:33

[33]Teach me, O Lord, the way of thy statues; and I shall keep it unto the end.

3. There is the matter of fruit productions in the Christians' life. To be productive in your work for the Lord, sometimes you must meditate on the Word of God. You must understand that you are connected to Jesus and he is connected to his Father. Your nutrients for growth, production of fruit, and cleansing is by the word and therefore you must abide in the word and the word will abide in you. This calls for spending valuable time with the Lord.

A. John15:1-4

[1]I am the true vine, and my Father is the husbandman. [2]Every branch in me that bears not fruit he takes away: and every branch that bears fruit, he purges it, that it may bring forth more fruit. [3]Now you are cleansed through the word which I have spoken unto you. [4]Abide in me, and I in you. As the branch cannot bear fruit of itself, except it abide in the vine; no more can you, except you abide in me.

B. Psalm 19:14

[14]Let the words of my mouth, and the meditation of my heart, be acceptable in thy sight. O Lord, my strength, and my redeemer.

4. During times of testing and pruning, it is good to still away to Jesus! Get into the habit of talking less, praying more, and obeying the call to spend time with God. Spending valuable time with God will teach you how to wait on God, how to trust in his will for you, and seek to be closer to him in this time of testing. Many times during testing and pruning, the desire to draw back from God presents itself. But the attention you give to God and his word will determine whether you draw back or grow closer to him. Do not give in to complaining and grumbling, but give thanks unto the Lord for he is GOOD!

A. 2Chronicles 15:2b

[2b]The Lord is with you, while you be with him; and if you seek him, he will be found of you; but if you forsake him, he will forsake you.

B. Lamentations 3:21-26

[21]This I recall to my mind, therefore have I hope. [22]It is of the Lord's mercies that we are not consumed, but because his compassions fail not. [23]They are new every morning: great is thy faithfulness. [24]The Lord is my portion, says my soul; therefore will I hope in him. [25]The Lord is good unto them that wait for him, to the soul that seeks him, [26]It is good that a man should both hope and quietly wait for the salvation of the Lord.

C. Deuteronomy 4:29

[29]But if from thence thou shall seek the Lord thy God, thou shall find him, if thou seek him with all thy heart and with all thy soul.

D. Psalm 107:1

[1]O give thanks unto the Lord, for he is good: For his mercy endures forever.

This week, begin setting aside special time to spend with God. It does not matter if all is well with you or if you are in a time of testing, make time for God. You will prosper from the time spent in his presence.

Remember: God is always waiting to spend time with you, are you desiring to spend time with him? Give yourself totally to knowing your Great Creator!!!

Notes: _____

_____

_____

_____

_____

_____

_____

_____

_____

_____

_____

_____

_____

_____

_____

_____

_____

_____

_____

_____

_____

_____

_____

_____

_____

_____

_____

_____

_____

_____

Week 46

BEING A DOER OF THE WORD

BIBLICAL PRINCIPLES - James 1:21-24 -²¹Wherefore lay apart all filthiness and superfluity (overflow) of naughtiness, and receive with meekness the engrafted (implanted) word, which is able to save your soul. ²²But be ye doers of the word, and not hearers only, deceiving your own selves. ²³For if any be a hearer of the word, and not a doer, he is like unto a man beholding his natural face in a glass: ²⁴For he beholds himself, and goes his way, and straightway forgets what manner of man he was.

Being a doer of the word (Bible) of God is one of the most important things you will ever do in this life. It is not enough to know the word, tell the word, and memorize the word, especially if you cannot do what the word says. Being a doer of the word means you are obeying what God is saying to you. If you ever want to deceive yourself, learn the word of God and do nothing with it.

This Scripture text is instructing us to lay aside all unrighteousness and overflow of wickedness, and receive the engrafted (implanted) word of God. The reason the word is spoken of as the implanted word, is because you are to allow the word of God to take root in your heart, and show it outwardly in the way you live. People often quote Scriptures and find joy in doing so, but very few enjoy living what they have learned and now know. It is wonderful to know the written word, but it is more profitable to be doers of the word.

These Scriptures are teaching on conduct of true religion and what it really means to have it. The word is saying, both the receiving of and doing the word will produce the promises of what is written in the word. The promises made in the word only apply to those who perform what is instructed. You cannot make charges to God regarding his word if you are not doing what the word says. The word of God has the power to show the real you while reading or studying it. But if you fail to produce the necessary changes that are required and written in the word, you are not an active doer. Now you have become as a man who looked in the mirror, then went on his way and forgot what he looked like while in the mirror.

This is when you began to deceive your own self. No one else is fooled by you, because they know what they see, it is you who forgot what was seen in the mirror. Many things are covered when you speak of being a doer of the word. When people are doers of God's word, there will be restraints in the areas where needed, the guiding of the Holy Spirit will be noticeable in their life, they will have joy unconditionally, and the standard of conduct will be different from that of the world. You will also see a source of new life, and they will desire the word as their spiritual food.

You cannot call yourself a pear tree when you are producing peaches. Doers of the word will produce the fruit of the Spirit which is, love, joy, peace, longsuffering, gentleness, goodness, faith, meekness, and temperance. If the fruit of the Spirit is not present, you are not looking at a doer of the word.

So now that you understand why it is so important to be a doer of the word and not a hearer only, we will take the word and enforce what has been taught.

PRACTICAL APPLICATIONS:

1. In the Christian's life we must do more than say Lord I believe, we must do whatever the word of God instructs or command us to do. Being a doer of the word means displaying in your life whatever is taught in Scripture.

    A. Matthew 7:21

        [21]Not everyone that says unto me, Lord, Lord, shall enter into the kingdom of heaven; but he that does the will of my Father which is in heaven.

    B. Luke 6:47-49

        [47]Whosoever comes to me, and hear my sayings, and do them, I will show you to whom he is like: [48]He is like a man which built a house, and dug deep, and laid the foundation on a rock: and when the flood arose, the stream beat vehemently upon that house, and could not shake it: for it was founded upon a rock. [49]But he that hears, and does not, is like a man that without a foundation built a house upon the earth; against which the stream did beat vehemently, and immediately it fell; and the ruin of that house was great.

    C. Romans 2:13

        [13]For not the hearers of the law are just before God, but the doers of the law shall be justified.

D. 1John 3:7

> [7]Little children, let no man deceive you: he that does righteousness is righteous, even as he is righteous.

2. The love of God is made manifest by the love you show towards God and others. You cannot say from your heart that you truly love God if you do not keep his sayings. Doing the word of God teaches you how to love. In fact the word will teach you restraints in all areas of your life. It will set a standard of conduct in side of you that will cause others to desire a closer walk with the Lord.

A. John 14:23

> [23]Jesus answered and said unto them, if a man love me, he will keep my words: and my Father will love him, and we will come unto him, and make our abode with him (live in him).

B. Psalm 119:9,11

> [9]Wherewithal shall a young man cleanse his way? By taking heed thereto according to thy word. [11]Thy word have I hid in my heart, that I might not sin against thee.

C. Deuteronomy 29:9

> [9]Keep therefore the words of this covenant, and do them, that ye may prosper in all that ye do.

D. John 13:17

> [17]If ye know these things, happy are ye if you do them.

E. Philippians 4:9

> [9]Those things, which ye have both learned, and received, and heard, and seen in me, do: and the God of peace shall be with you.

3. God declares blessings to the doers of God's word. So be a doer and not a hearer only.

   A. Revelations 1:3

   ³Blessed is he that reads, and they that hear the words of this prophecy, and keep those things which are written therein: for the time is at hand.

   B. Acts 20:32

   ³²And now, brethren, I commend you to God, and to the word of his grace, which is able to build you up, and to give you an inheritance among all them which are sanctified.

Always practice being a doer of the word of God, saying less and doing more. It is not how many words you know and speak, but how many deeds you perform from what you know.

Remember: God is always aware of the way you do and obey his word. You will never convince God that you were a doer, if all you did was hear. You will be rewarded for everything you do in your body, whether good or bad.

Notes: _____

_____

_____

_____

_____

_____

_____

_____

_____

_____

_____

_____

_____

_____

_____

_____

_____

_____

_____

_____

_____

_____

_____

_____

_____

_____

_____

_____

Week 47

SHARING GOD'S WORD WITH OTHERS

BIBLICAL PRINCIPLES - Matthew 28:18-20 - [18]And Jesus came and spoke unto them, saying, All power is given unto me in heaven and in earth. [19]Go ye therefore, and teach all nations, baptizing them in the name of the Father, and of the Son, and of the Holy Ghost: [20]Teaching them to observe all things whatsoever I have commanded you: and lo, I am with you always, even unto the end of the world. Amen.

After the resurrection of Jesus, he showed himself alive to his disciples and many others on several different occasions. This gave the disciples and other followers the confidence, knowledge, and desire to go out and spread what they had learned and experienced with Jesus. Now the disciples were being prepared by Jesus, the resurrected Savior, for their responsibilities toward their fellow man and the rest of the world. They were getting ready to lay the foundation and start the New Testament Church. Jesus was informing them that He would always be there with them, and that all power in heaven and earth was now given into His hands.

Jesus' disciples had no reason to fear anything or anyone because he loved them so much and would be there for them always even unto the end of the world. The instructions were very clear, precise, and to the point. They did not have to guess about anything that Jesus was saying, only do what was instructed. The same is true for you; there is no reason to fear anyone when you feel the need to introduce them to Jesus. Just remember, Jesus is still saying "Lo, I am with you always", this means forever.

In the Bible, this passage of Scripture is known as the Great Commission, and it is also given to all Christians as a direct command from Jesus. These are some very important commands, and you must receive them as such. You were commanded to go into the entire world and teach this Gospel to all nations. You were not given the options to pick or choose who you would teach, but to go into all nations. You are given the charge to share God's word with others. You may think going is only for the leaders, but according to this particular Scripture, all Christians are instructed to go. Will you or will you not GO?

As a Christian, there should be such enthusiasm and excitement inside of you regarding all that Jesus did for your eternal salvation, so you will began to spread the good news to everyone. Jesus took the time to let you know that all power has been given unto him in both heaven and earth. Now he has the divine power and authority to command you to spread this Gospel to every living creature.

You have been instructed to teach and baptize them in the name of the Father, the Son, and the Holy Ghost. Also to observe all things whatsoever Jesus has commanded you. There is so much work to be done in the earth regarding teaching people about God's eternal plan of salvation. The Church has a very large order to fill, and must know the importance of fulfilling this order. Sometimes you may think your leader is the one trying to get you to go out witnessing, but the truth is they are only enforcing what Jesus has already commanded. You must accept this charge for what it really is, a command from the Almighty God.

We need to remember all that Jesus did for us, when he came to the earth to die for all of mankind on Calvary. He knew there was no other way to complete the plans of God regarding our sin infested future. Jesus also knew that nothing or no one was holy or perfect enough to pay our debt except the only begotten Son of God. After completing the charge to die for man's sin and pay the penalty for sin, Jesus is now sitting on the right hand of his Father making intercession constantly for you and me.

This is the great news that we have been charged by Jesus, to share with the entire world. Some of us may be sent overseas for mission work, while others may be called to share in your home area. It really does not matter where you have been call to serve, just get busy and serve. Because someone thought enough of you to tell you about Jesus and all he did, you should feel responsible enough, to share this Jesus with someone else so that they will have the option to accept Jesus as their personal Savior, or reject him for whatever reason they may have. At least give them the option, and the knowledge they need to make a right decision.

We have not been charged or sent to make people choose Jesus, but to give them the choice to fall in love with Jesus or to run away from him. Jesus knew we would not be able to make people accept Him as their Savior, but what he did know was that we would come into contact with people and have the chance to share the Gospel with them.

Get busy, show Jesus how much you love Him by informing or witnessing to others about their eternal salvation, so that they do not lose their soul. Ask yourself, where would you be if someone did not take the time to share this Gospel with you? What condition would you be in at this present moment, and what would your life look like without Jesus Christ as your personal Savior?

The best instructor you will ever have on sharing God's word with others, would be the Word of God himself. We will now go into the Word to see what is written on this matter.

PRACTICAL APPLICATIONS:

1. Can you remember when you first heard about Jesus and how you felt after accepting Him as your personal Savior? Remember the joy and excitement that flooded your entire soul. On that day, you were so happy that Jesus gave you a whole new life and wiped all of your sins away. With this in mind, when was the last time you took the opportunity to go and tell someone about Jesus? Were you happy or delighted to share your God with someone else, and tell them about how great Jesus is?

   A. Mark 16:15-16

   [15]And he said unto them, Go ye into all the world, and preach the Gospel to every creature. [16]He that believes and is baptized shall be saved; but he that believes not shall be damned.

   B. John 3:3-7

   [3]Jesus answered and said unto him, verily, verily, I say unto thee, Except a man be born again, he cannot see the kingdom of God. [4]Nicodemus said unto him, how can a man be born when he is old? Can he enter the second time into his mother's

womb, and be born? [5]Jesus answered, verily, verily, I say unto thee, Except a man be born of water and of the Spirit, he cannot enter into the kingdom of God. [6]That which is born of the flesh is flesh; and that which is born of the Spirit is spirit. [7]Marvel not that I said unto thee, Ye must be born again.

A. Acts 1:8

[8]But ye shall receive power, after that the Holy Ghost is come upon you: and ye shall be witnesses unto me both in Jerusalem, and in all Judea, and in Samaria, and unto the uttermost part of the earth.

2. It is important to know what you are to tell others about Jesus. You must tell them that Jesus loves them very much. And, that the wages of sin is death, but Jesus came to give them eternal life. You must also tell them that they must repent of all their sins and accept Jesus as their personal Savior.

A. John 3:16-17

[16]For God so loved the world, that he gave his only begotten Son, that whosoever believeth in him should not perish, but have everlasting life. [17]For God sent not his Son into the world to condemn the world; but that the world through him might be saved.

B. Romans 6:22-23

[22]But now being made free form sin, and become servants to God, ye have your fruit unto holiness, and the end everlasting

life. ²³For the wages of sin is death; but the gift of God is eternal life through Jesus Christ our Lord.

C. Acts 2:37-39

³⁷Now when they heard this, they were pricked in their heart, and said unto Peter and to the rest of the apostles, men and brethren, what shall we do? ³⁸Then Peter said unto them, Repent, and be baptized everyone of you in the name of Jesus Christ for the remission of sins, and ye shall receive the gift of the Holy Ghost. ³⁹For the promise is unto you, and to your children, and to all that are afar off, even as many as the Lord our God shall call.

3. The love of God in your heart will make you concerned about others in ways you never thought possible. You will have a desire and a burden in your heart for the lost. This is the true connection of a Christian to God, because if you do not love others you cannot love God. In fact, the Scriptures teach "How can you say you love God and not love your brothers", the love of God is not in you. Your love should compel you to draw others unto your God.

A. Romans 9:1-3

¹I say the truth in Christ, I lie not, my conscience also bearing witness in the Holy Ghost, ²That I have great heaviness and continual sorrow in my heart. ³For I could wish that myself were accursed from Christ for my brethren, my kinsmen according to the flesh.

B. 1John 5:10-12

¹⁰He that believeth on the Son of God has the witness in himself: he that believeth not God has made him a liar;

because he believeth not the record that God gave of his Son. [11]And this is the record, that God has given to us eternal life, and this life is in his Son. [12]He that has the Son has life; and he that has not the Son of God has not life.

C. 1John 4:19-21

[19]We love him, because he first loved us. [20]If a man say, I love God, and hates his brother, he is a liar: for he that loves not his brother whom he has seen, how can he love God whom he has not seen? [21]And this commandment have we from Him, that he who loves God love his brother also.

D. 1John 4:13-16

[13]Hereby know we that we dwell in him, and he in us, because he has given us of his Spirit. [14]And we have seen and do testify that the Father sent the Son to be the Savior of the world. [15]Whosoever shall confess that Jesus is the Son of God, God dwells in him, and he in God. [16]And we have known and believed the love that God hath to us. God is love; and he that dwells in love dwells in God, and God in him.

Because you love God so much, and are so grateful to Jesus for laying down his life for you, the command to go into the entire world and teach this Gospel is the least you can do for Him. You will never be able to repay the debt for the price Jesus paid for you, but you can go and tell others all about His eternal plan of SALVATION!!

Remember: Do not be a selfish Christian, go out and tell someone about Jesus and all that he has to given to this world. Let them know that "The wages of sin is death but the Gift of God is eternal life, through Jesus Christ our Lord".

Notes: _____

_____

_____

_____

_____

_____

_____

_____

_____

_____

_____

_____

_____

_____

_____

_____

_____

_____

_____

_____

_____

_____

_____

_____

_____

_____

_____

_____

_____

_____

Week 48

LEARNING TO PUT OTHERS FIRST

BIBLICAL PRINCIPLES - Philippians 2:3-4 - ³Let nothing be done through strife or vainglory: but in lowliness of mind let each esteem other better than themselves. ⁴Look not every man on his own things, but every man on the things of others.

In these days and time we find so many selfish people, always concerned about themselves. Never really noticing the conditions of others or what they may need. In this passage of Scripture, we are instructed to esteem others (to regard with respect) better than yourself. We are to do nothing through strife or vainglory, meaning we are not to do anything through selfish motives or conceit. This is very powerful for day to day living. If we all could do what this Scripture instructs, imagine the changes we all will see and experience in this world.

One of the main enemies in the Church and the world is selfish motives. We find that unity is broken because of this type of behavior, also disagreements and many disputes are due to selfish and conceited behavior. If we as a people could understand that the world is not all about me, and that there are many other people in the world besides myself, we could advance in life, a long distance.

Because the Lord gave the Church these types of instructions, there had to be this type of behavior present in the body of Christ. We are to do things with the proper attitude and recognize others more than self. This will keep down a lot of confusion and problems. Each one of us is to esteem others better than ourselves in lowliness of mind. This does not mean that everyone else is more talented or more superior than you are, but it places all of us with the same self worth.

Many problems occur because of selfish people looking down on or treating others with less respect than what they desire for themselves. One of the things Jesus taught in Scripture was to do unto others as you would have them do unto you and love your neighbors as yourself. Keeping this in mind, would you like for others to treat you with less respect or look down on you as though you were nobody? The answer would be no to this question, so why would you do this to someone else?

Stop comparing people to others, this only causes more problems in the individual's life. Everybody is unique and have their very own personality, so allow them the respect they deserve for being themselves. This is how you learn to put others first and respect people as they are. When you put others first you start to grow because you began to learn that your way is not always the best way to get things done. Selfishness will make you think you are the smartest tool on the shed, but lowliness of mind will remind you that others got to where they are because they knew something too. Recognize that there is always someone who just might know a little more than you do.

Stop pumping yourself up so high and allow someone else to brag on you. Your bragging is partial because it is coming from you, but when someone else speaks highly of you, they speak from what they see in you. This is how unity begins to grow and grow, because people begin to see the good in you and you will see the good in them. Relationship will form and blossom when we stop putting self up so high and allow God to promote us. Promotions comes from God, so it does not matter how high you exalt yourself, only what God approves will last.

You must also remember that everyone is not meant to have the same things in life, so accept where you are and embrace others where they are. Learn how to lift others up because you never know what they may be going through at the time you make them feel little. Stop looking at what you have. Instead, look on the things of others and give God the glory. What is it that you have, that was not given to you by the Almighty God? You are who you are because of God and others are who they are because of God.

Try to think with the mind of Christ, because if it had not been for the Lord on your side where would you be, what would you be doing, and how would others be treating you? I call this great food for thought, so think about it and treat others better or shall I say treat them right. It does not cost you anything to be humble, kind, and loving to others, because in return you will get it back.

Teaching about learning to put others first, reminds me of small children before they learn how to share their toys. You will constantly hear them say that's mine, give it to me. But as they grow older and have been taught to share their toys, you will hear them say, you want to play with this, you can hold this. Since we are to come unto Christ as little children, let us stop saying, that's mine and give it to me. Instead, let us say you can have it, it is your turn, not mine. Never feel like your things are better than others, this is selfishness and very rude behavior.

Will you take the time to start putting others first? Give others the chance to feel special too and not you all the time. Let us all purpose to esteem others higher than ourselves. We will search the Scriptures to see what Jesus has to say about these things.

PRACTICAL APPLICATIONS:

1. Jesus had a special way of teaching things to the crowds. He taught in one setting about taking the best seat when you are invited to a gathering. Just because you felt that you were a special guest, someone else may show up who may be a little more special than you. Always wait to be exalted so that you will not have to face embarrassment and given a lower seat.

   A. Luke 14:8-11

   [8]When you are bidden of any man to a wedding, sit not down in the highest room; lest a more honorable man than you be bidden of him; [9]And he that bade you and him come and say to you, Give this man place; and you begin with shame to take the lowest room. [10]But when you are bidden, go and sit down in the lowest room; that when he that bade you comes, he may say unto you, friend, go up higher: then shall you have worship in the presence of them that sit at meat with you. [11]For whosoever exalts himself shall be abased: and he that humbles himself shall be exalted.

2. Jesus always put us first in whatever he did for his Father. Every decision He made was in our best interest, and he never neglected to get it done. He came for one purpose to die for our sins to redeem us back to his Father. Since Jesus has this much unconditional love and concern for us, we should have love and concern for others unconditionally. Because of the Holy Spirit inside of us, we can do it.

A. Matthew 1:21

21And she shall bring forth a son, and thou shall call his name JESUS: for he shall save his people from their sins.

B. Ephesians 1:7

7In whom we have redemption through his blood, the forgiveness of sins, according to the riches of his grace.

C. Romans 3:24-25

24Being justified freely by his grace through the redemption that is in Christ Jesus: 25Whom God has set forth to be a propitiation (conciliation) through faith in his blood, to declare his righteousness for the remission of sins that are past, through the forbearance of God.

D. 1John 3:16-17

16Hereby perceive we the love of God, because he laid down his life for us: and we ought to lay down our lives for the brethren. 17But whoso has this world's good, and sees his brother has need, and shuts up his bowels of compassion from him, how dwells the love of God in him?

3. Putting others first should be a mark for all Christians, because we have been instructed to deny ourselves. This was so important to

Jesus that he taught this at several gatherings. He realized that we cannot be faithful disciples until we learn to deny self and that it is not all about us. To see the will of God, we must see pass ourselves first.

A. Matthew 16:24

   24Then said Jesus to his disciples, If any man will come after me, let him deny himself, and take up his cross, and follow me.

B. Mark 8:34

   34And when he had called the people unto him with his disciples also, he said unto them, Whosoever will come after me, let him deny himself, and take up his cross, and follow me.

C. Luke 9:23

   23And he said unto them all, If any man will come after me, let him deny himself, and take up his cross daily, and follow me.

D. Matthew 10:38

   38And he that takes not his cross, and follows me, is not worthy of me.

4. Pride is something that all Christians must deal with on a daily basis. Pride will have you thinking you really are better than others. Not only will you think this but you will start acting this way. You will feel like certain things are below you and people you think you are better than, should be the ones to do the below you jobs. This type of pride happens to you inside and outside of the Church. Be on the lookout for this deceitful enemy, he will destroy you fast.

A. Proverbs 21:4

   ⁴A high look, and a proud heart, and a plowing of the wicked is sin.

B. Proverbs 11:2

   ²When pride comes, then comes shame: But with the lowly is wisdom.

C. Proverbs 16:18

   ¹⁸Pride goes before destruction, and a haughty spirit before a fall.

D. Proverbs 29:23

   ²³A man's pride shall bring him low: but honor shall uphold the humble in spirit.

E. 1John 2:16

   ¹⁶For all that is in the world, the lust of the flesh, and the lust of the eyes, and the pride of life, is not of the Father, but is of the world.

The world will know if you put others first, by the way you deny yourself. When people see that you are not the center of your own conversation, they will know what you have learned from the Scriptures. Learning something is not just reciting it, to learn something is to put it into action! Do not allow pride to bring you low.

Remember: Just because you learned something one way, does not mean you cannot change your mind, and learn it the right way. Kill your pride, humble yourself, and let the Holy Spirit set you on the right course.

Notes: _____

_____

_____

_____

_____

_____

_____

_____

_____

_____

_____

_____

_____

_____

_____

_____

_____

_____

_____

_____

_____

_____

_____

_____

_____

_____

_____

Week 49

HAVING A THANKFUL ATTITUDE

BIBLICAL PRINCIPLES - Ephesians 5:20 - ²⁰Giving thanks always for all things unto God and the Father in the name of our Lord Jesus Christ.

This week I would like to remind you of the importance of having a thankful attitude. Since attitude plays an important role in your walk with God, you must commit to being thankful. Not having an attitude of complaining, being mad about life, and murmuring for whatever reasons. Learning to be thankful regardless of whatever is going on in your life is a must because believe it or not, there is always someone in a much worse situation than you.

In this Scripture, we are instructed to give thanks to God always and for all things, in the name of Jesus Christ our Lord. This may seem impossible when life gets hard, but it can be done. Many times when your way seems dark, the first thing you must do is tell the Lord thank you. This is a very positive step you should not skip because, it will help you focus on the things that are good in your life. You are responsible for not allowing negative thoughts to enter into your mind. Remember you have the mind of Christ, and he was always thankful to his Father in every situation, even unto death on the cross.

To be unthankful for whatever God has done and is doing for you is very disrespectful to Him. You must always know that life will happen and so will problems, but God is able to take care of you. He did not bring you this far to leave you all alone. God is always aware of every situation you will ever encounter, and he has the power and resources to deliver you at the right time. You must trust him with your whole heart, and remember his history of faithfulness to his people down through every generation. He never failed them and he will never fail you.

When you are thankful to God, it shows that you are submitting unto his authority. It also make known unto God and others that you trust God to do whatever he knows is best for you. Sometimes you may forget that God is not governed by time, space, or things, and that He is always at work in your life, for the good. Because you do not see things happening, does not mean God is not working in your favor. This alone should point you into the direction of giving thanks unto the Lord, for He is good.

There are times when Christians may feel they are not supposed to weather any storms, or suffer through discouraging situations. This is not what the word of God teaches us in the James 1:2-3. In fact this Scripture tells you to count it all joy when you fall into divers temptations; knowing this that the trying of your faith works patience. So everything you go through is not always a bad thing, God is teaching you patience or maybe the fruit of the Spirit, since you must have the fruit of the Spirit maturing in your life. To become a mature Christian you must have a thankful attitude and give thanks to God in all things because he commands you do this.

A thankful attitude is also developed when you have to trust God in areas you thought were already perfected. Make it a priority to tell God thank you upon waking up in the morning, all through the day, when you think of something he did for you, at night, and at all times. There is no such thing as saying thank you too much to the Almighty God. You will never be able to thank him enough for all of his goodness, mercies, love, and grace he has showered down on you. The more you thank God, the more you realize you need to thank him, because he is always doing something for you.

I would like to give some Scriptures that will help you to develop a thankful attitude. Also these Scriptures will show you how much you have been complaining when you should have been giving thanks unto the Lord!

PRACTICAL APPLICATIONS:

1. You need to understand that giving thanks unto the Lord is something you must do at all times and in all circumstances because it is the will of God. Never under estimate the power of giving thanks to the Lord. Giving thanks to God, in the name of Jesus Christ will bring you peace through troubled times, and keep your mind on him. Avoid complaining and murmuring, keep a praise of thanksgiving in your mouth at all times and bless the Lord. You must be aware of the blessings of God in your life and thanksgiving will come from deep feelings and convictions.

    A. 1 Thessalonians 5:18

    [18]In everything give thanks: for this is the will of God in Christ Jesus concerning you.

B. Psalm 107:1

> ¹O give thanks unto the Lord, for he is good: For his mercy endures forever.

A. Colossians 3:15

> ¹⁵And let the peace of God rule in your hearts, to the which also you are called in one body; and be ye thankful.

B. Psalm 103:1-3

> ¹Bless the Lord, O my soul: And all that is within me, bless his holy name. ²Bless the Lord, O my soul, and forget not all his benefits: ³Who forgives all your iniquities: and heals all thy diseases.

C. Philippians 2:14

> ¹⁴Do all things without murmurings and disputing.

2. It is not the will of the Lord for you to be anxious about anything. God is so concerned about you and your affairs personally, he will not let you down. You may ask God to do things for you that are against his will, but God cannot go against his word. Therefore you will think that God has let you down or failed you, but the truth is he knows what is best for you, and he worked it all out for your good, in his time.

A. Philippians 4:6-7

> ⁶Be careful for nothing; but in everything by prayer and supplication with thanksgiving let your requests be made known unto God. ⁷And the peace of God, which passes all understanding, shall keep your hearts and minds through Christ Jesus.

B. Psalm 105:1

> [1]O give thanks unto the Lord; call upon his name: Make known his deeds among the people.

C. Psalm 119:89

> [89]Forever, O Lord, Thy word is settled in heaven.

3. Give thanks unto God for his steadfast love, for his mercy endures forever, and because he is God. Be thankful to him for his presence and his awesome powers in all the earth. Also give thanks unto the Lord for he is good. When you go into his house, enter with thanksgiving and praise.

A. Psalm 106:1

> [1]Praise ye the Lord. O give thanks unto the Lord; for he is good: For his mercy endures forever.

B. Psalm 116:17

> [17]I will offer to thee the sacrifice of thanksgiving, and will call upon the name of the Lord.

C. Psalm 93:1-5

> [1]The Lord reigns, he is clothed with majesty; The Lord is clothed with strength, wherewith he girded himself: The world also is established, that it cannot be moved. [2]Thy throne is established of old: thou art from everlasting. [3]The floods have lifted up, O Lord, the flood have lifted up their voice; the flood lifted up their waves. [4]The Lord on high is mightier than the noise of many waters, Yes, than the mighty waves of the sea. [5]Thy testimonies are very sure: Holiness becomes your house, O Lord, forever.

D. Psalm 100:3-5

> [3]Know ye that the Lord he is God: it is he that hath made us, and not we ourselves; we are his people, and the sheep of his pasture. [4]Enter into his gates with thanksgiving, and into his courts with praise: Be thankful unto him, and bless his name. [5]For the Lord is good; his mercy is everlasting; and his truth endures to all generations.

This is one area that all Christians need to give special attention and care. With all the stressors and problem we all face from time to time, do not get caught up in what things looks like, but in what the word of God promises to all of his children. Life is going to happen for all of us, but if we keep a thankful attitude towards God, the challenges will not take you out, only make you stronger.

Now I challenge you to start giving thanks and more thanks unto the Lord, then watch your attitude shift to being thankful.

Remember: Only you know all the things God has done for you, and why you should give thanks unto the Lord. Be active in giving thanks and praise to your God, thinking about it will not be enough, you must do it daily!!!

Notes: _____

_____

_____

_____

_____

_____

_____

_____

_____

_____

_____

_____

_____

_____

_____

_____

_____

_____

_____

_____

_____

_____

_____

_____

_____

_____

_____

_____

_____

_____

Week 50

I WILL BLESS THE LORD AT ALL TIMES

BIBLICAL PRINCIPLES - Psalm 34:1-3 - ¹I will bless the Lord at all times: His praise shall continually be in my mouth. ²My soul shall make her boast in the Lord: The humble shall hear thereof, and be glad. ³O magnify the Lord with me, and let us exalt his name together.

This is a psalm of David when he had been driven away from his home, into a foreign land because of hate from King Saul. David prayed and cried out unto the Lord, and God heard him and answered his prayer. David made a vow to bless (to bestow blessings upon) the Lord at all times, meaning for the rest of his life. He also vowed to continually keep praise in his mouth. He knew within his heart, if it had not been for the Lord on his side, the enemy would have swallowed him up quickly. God's grace, love, and mercy delivered David from the hands of his enemies, now all he wanted to do was bless the name of the Lord forever.

What does it mean to bless the Lord? How do you bless the Lord? Can you give God something that he already possesses? What can you offer unto God that will bless him at all times? These are questions that need to be answered so that you can actually bless the Lord at all times and keep praise in your mouth.

Blessing God means to, speak well of Him, to praise and to celebrate him for what is addressed to God (everything). It also means to acknowledge his goodness, with desire for his glory. You can bless God by consecrating (dedicating) yourself unto him, by setting yourself apart to be used only by him, and by walking humbly and obedient to his will. Even though God owns you, proper reverence, obedience, and acknowledgement of who God really is and what he has done, will bless him at all times. God wants all of you with your whole heart involved in the process.

You must understand that God is not like man, he does not require earthly materials to be happy or fulfilled. He owns this entire universe so everything you have or so called owns, belongs to God. You cannot give God what He already owns, therefore, you must give him something from the depth of your heart, soul, mind, and strength. Whatever you choose to give to God, will not be accepted if your entire heart is not involved in blessing Him.

Because God looks at the heart of a man, and knows the motive behind whatever is done for him, God is the only one to accept or reject your blessings. Whatever you do for the Lord, let it be real and full of honesty. Blessing God will be one of the greatest acts of worship you will ever accomplish. You are giving God something for himself, instead of asking God for things to advance you and you agendas. This is where you remove your wants and desires from this act and time, then allow God be the center of this special offering you are dedicating to Him. You are dedicating all of you unto the Lord God Almighty, for Him to be honored, adored, magnified, worshipped, and glorified. All of this must come directly from a surrendered and faithful heart, nothing else will do.

You are giving God blessings of thanksgiving for his goodness toward you. Adoration is given to him for being the one and only great God Almighty. Worship is now done in reverence and respect for being God, commitment to be his child for the rest of your life, with holding nothing from him. You are giving him all that you are, all that you would ever hope to be, and everything that will ever come of you. You are saying with your heart, Lord I surrender all unto you!

David also said, his soul shall make her boast in the Lord. David knew he had nothing to boast about within himself. Considering his encounters with the enemies, all his boastings belonged only to God! He would take great pleasure in boasting before others about what God had done for him. His testimonies would also humble others and make them glad to have the Lord as their God. Now David invites the people to magnify the Lord with him and exalt the name of the Lord together.

Stir up the desire within you to bless the Lord at all times. Do not with hold your act of blessing from God. Please do not take upon yourself to trade blessings with God, thinking when you bless Him, surely he will bless you back. Bless God with a selfless, humbled, unconditional heart, not looking or expecting something in return.

The word of God is a true guide to help and instruct you on the things of God. Always refer to the Bible for all of your needs, and find out what God is saying in His Word. As a Christian, you should always seek out ways and times in your live to bless the Lord. Also prepare your heart and mind to continually keep a praise in your mouth, this will honor God greatly.

PRACTICAL APPLICATIONS:

1. Knowing who God is and what he has done in your life, should give you the reason to bless the Lord at all times. Prepare your heart to surrender totally to the will of God and start blessing the Lord right now. Imagine the God of creation allowing you to come humbly into his presence, to bless him!

   A. Micah 6:8

   [8]He hath shown thee, O man, what is good; And what does the Lord require of thee, but to do justly, and to love mercy, and to walk humbly with thy God.

   B. Psalm 16:7-9

   [7]I will bless the Lord, who hath given me counsel: My reins (mind) also instruct me in the night seasons. [8]I have set the Lord always before me: because he is at my right hand. I shall not be moved. [9]Therefore my heart is glad, and my glory rejoices.

   C. Psalm 63:1-4

   [1]O God, thou art my God; early will I seek thee: My soul thirsts for thee, My flesh longs for thee, in a dry and thirsty land, where no water is; [2]To see thy power and thy glory, so as I have seen thee in the Sanctuary. [3]Because thy loving kindness is better than life, my lips shall praise thee. [4]Thus will I bless thee while I live: I will lift up my hands in your name.

2. God has forgiven all of your sins and iniquities, never to remember them again. He has given you a new life, new beginning, and a fresh new praise for life. You now have so many benefits, healing from diseases, love, grace, mercy, and all that comes with the name of Jesus. God is so great and clothed in honor and majesty.

   A. Psalm 103:1-5

> [1]Bless the Lord, O my soul: And all that is within me, bless his holy name. [2]Bless the Lord O my soul, and forget not all his benefits: [3]Who forgives all your iniquities; who heals all your diseases; [4]Who redeems thy life from destruction; who crowns you with loving kindness and tender mercies; [5]Who satisfies your mouth with good things; so that your youth is renewed like the eagle's.

   B. Psalm 104:1-2

> [1]Bless the Lord, O my soul. O Lord my God, thou art very great; Thou art clothed with honor and majesty. [2]Who covers thyself with light as with a garment: who stretches out the heavens like a curtain.

   C. Psalm 145:1-6

> [1]I will extol (exalt, praise highly) thee, my God, O king; And I will bless thy name forever and ever. [2]Everyday will I bless thee; And I will praise thy name forever and ever. [3]Great is the Lord, and greatly to be praised; And his greatness is unsearchable. [4]One generation shall praise thy works to another, and shall declare thy mighty acts. [5]I will speak of the glorious honor of thy majesty, and of thy wondrous works. [6]And men shall speak of the might of thy terrible acts: And I will declare thy greatness.

3. There are so many things regarding your salvation, why God should be blessed. He has blessed you with spiritual blessings in heavenly places. He has chosen you to be his servant. God has justified you through the blood of his son, Jesus Christ. He has given you everlasting life and his Holy Spirit. God also gives you physical and material things, he supplies all your needs.

A. Ephesians 1:3-4

[3]Blessed be the God and Father of our Lord Jesus Christ, who hath blessed us with all spiritual blessings in heavenly places in Christ: [4]According as he hath chosen us in him before the foundation of the world, that we should be holy and without blame before him in love.

B. Romans 4:7-8

[7]Saying, blessed are they whose iniquities are forgiven, and whose sins are covered. [8]Blessed is the man to whom the Lord will not impute (charge) sin.

C. John 3:16

[16]For God so loved the world, that he gave his only begotten Son, that whosoever believeth in him should not perish, but have everlasting life.

D. Acts 1:8a

[8a]But ye shall receive power, after that the Holy Ghost is come upon you these things. [33]But seek ye first the kingdom of God, and his righteousness; and all these things shall be added unto you.

As you complete this week of applications, get into the habit of blessing the Lord without looking or expecting God to send down a blessing for you. God is worthy of all the blessing you will ever be able to give him.

Remember: It is a great honor and privilege for you and me, to be able to bless the great God of creation, and for him to accept our blessings. "O Lord my God, you are so wonderful and great is your name above the earth."

Notes: _____

_____

_____

_____

_____

_____

_____

_____

_____

_____

_____

_____

_____

_____

_____

_____

_____

_____

_____

_____

_____

_____

_____

_____

_____

_____

_____

_____

_____

_____

Week 51

I HAVE HOPE IN CHRIST JESUS

BIBLICAL PRINCIPLES: Hebrews 6:18-19 - [18]That by two immutable (unchangeable) things, in which it was impossible for God to lie, we might have a strong consolation (comfort fortified with encouragement), who have fled for refuge to lay hold upon the hope set before us: [19]Which hope we have as an anchor of the soul, both sure and steadfast, and which enters into that within the vail.

Never, ever lose your hope! Always know that your hope is in Jesus Christ, the Son of the living God! It does not matter how good or how bad your life may be or seem, always know that God cares for you, and in him there is always hope.

When you look at the word hope, you must understand that it means the expectation of future good. It is so important that you always have expectations of good things happening to and for you, even into your future. It may not be happening right now, but have expectations for your future. In life, you cannot only receive bad things all the time, especially if your hope is in Christ Jesus. Yes, you will experience highs and lows in this life, things will sometimes go wrong, some friends will disappoint you, and some may even walk away, but you can still have hope for a better day in Jesus Christ. He also said, "I came that you might have life and have it more abundantly."

Scripture instructs you to have a sure and steadfast hope in God. When you fled or walked away from the sins of this world, you found refuge (a shelter against harm) in Jesus as your personal Savior, to lay hold on a future hope that is set before you. Your hope should be as sure and steadfast as an anchor that is let down into the deep waters to keep the ship from moving. Your hope rests firmly with assurance in your Great God and your Savior Jesus Christ. You do not have to be moved because things are not going your way. Be steadfast and unmovable, standing directly on the word and promises of Jesus Christ our Lord.

Keep high expectations because your God cannot lie, if he spoke a word, it is sure to happen. The power of God's word assures you of the fact that God will do just what he said he would do. You must have faith, patience, and hope in every word that is written in the Scriptures. Your confidence is placed in the God of impossibilities, who can do anything but fail. God will never lose control of anything, even your future outcomes. He already knows what your future holds.

Faith in God is needed to enable you to look pass what you think you see or know, and trust God for future deliverance. Faith will remind you that you can only see but so much, whereas God sees everything. He already knows when your day will come. Search Scriptures on faith and see the reputation of God, how he has never failed! You serve the eternal God who knows everything and has all power in his hands! Lose your anxieties and rest your hope in this powerful eternal God!

Patience is a much needed virtue to have, especially, when you think all hope is gone, or when you just cannot see your way. It takes patience to wait on God, you cannot rush him, nor can you demand him to move when you think he should move. You must trust that he knows the correct time to move in your favor. Do not lose hope; learn how to wait on the Lord. While you are waiting, keep on praising, worshipping, and thanking God for your break through. Do not give in to worrying and wavering about what God is able to do. Stand firm on what is written in Scripture and know that God is God!

Now your hope is needed, with great expectations for God to move. Hold on to your expectations, never let go or allow someone to tell you that God will not do what he said he would do. Search the Scriptures to see if your desires are within the boundaries of God's will and promises. Sometime you may desire things that are against the will of God and Scriptures, or things that will cause you harm, do not expect the Lord to go against his word. This is the time for you to adjust your will and desires to the will of God.

Surround yourself with positive hopeful people who have also experienced dark times, but waited patiently on the Lord, and saw God move in their lives. This will help you gain more trust in God's faithfulness and his abilities to come through for you.

You have so much hope in Christ Jesus but you must be convinced that God is who he said he is and will do exactly what he promised he would do.

We will explore the word of God and find supporting Scriptures about you having hope in Christ Jesus our Lord!

PRACTICAL APPLICATIONS:

1. You are now a Child of God and do not have to walk around with your head hung down as if you have no hope. Your hope is in Christ Jesus and he has the power and the authority to speak to your situations and changes must occur. When you pray for the Lord to move in your life, do not make the typical mistake of expecting God to move by your plans. Allow God to be creative and in control of how he desires to move. God is the only one who knows the plans he has designed for your expected end.

    A. Jeremiah 29:11-12

    [11]For I know the thoughts that I think towards you, says the Lord, thoughts of peace, and not of evil, to give you an expected end. [12]Then shall you call upon me, and ye shall go and pray unto me, and I will hearken unto you.

    B. Psalm 42:11

    [11]Why art thou cast down, O my soul? and why art thou disquieted within me? Hope thou in God: for I shall yet praise him, who is the health of my countenance, and my God.

    C. Psalm 31:24

    [24]Be of good courage, and he shall strengthen your heart, all ye that hope in the Lord.

    D. 1Peter 1:3

    [3]Blessed be the God and Father of our Lord Jesus Christ, which according to his abundant mercy hath begotten us again unto a lively hope by the resurrection of Jesus Christ from the dead.

2. You may feel like your hope is in vain because you do not see any results. Do not waver in your faith in the Lord, because faith is needed at this time to produce the substance you are expecting. If you began to waver back and forth, God cannot do anything for you, because you are not sure of what you want done.

   A. James 1:6-8

> 6But let him ask in faith, nothing wavering: for he that wavers is like a wave of the sea driven with the wind and tossed. 7For let not that man think that he shall receive anything of the Lord. 8A double minded man is unstable in all his ways.

   B. Psalm 16:9

> 9Therefore my heart is glad, and my glory rejoices: my flesh also shall rest in hope.

   C. Psalm 39:7

> 7And now, Lord, what wait I for? My hope is in thee.

3. There are times when you will need to learn how to wait on the Lord. Developing patience is one way this will happen. You cannot control the time or the way God is going to move in your life, but what you can do is learn to wait until God decides to move. Your expectation for a better day is in Jesus, so you must wait for his move, because his time is always the perfect time.

   A. Romans 5:1-5

> 1Therefore being justified by faith, we have peace with God through our Lord Jesus Christ: 2By whom also we have access by faith into this grace wherein we stand, and rejoice in hope of the glory of God. 3And not only so, but we glory

in tribulations also: knowing that tribulation works patience; [4]and patience, experience; and experience, hope: [5]And hope makes not ashamed; because the love of God is shed abroad in our hearts by the Holy Ghost which is given unto us.

B. Galatians 6:9

[9]And let us not be weary in well doing: for in due season we shall reap, if we faint not.

C. Hebrew 10:36

[36]For ye have need of patience, that after ye have done the will of God, ye might receive the promise.

D. Romans 8:25

[25]But if we hope for that we see not, then do we with patience wait for it?

4. When you are sure of your hope in Christ Jesus, you will stand against all the odds, knowing how faithful and trustworthy your God really is. Stand firm, be unmovable, and allow yourself to see God move in your favor. Your hope is built on nothing less than the faithfulness of Jesus Christ.

A. 1Corinthians 15:58

[58]Therefore, my beloved brethren, be ye steadfast, unmovable, always abounding in the work of the Lord, for as much as you know that your labor is not in vain in the Lord.

B. Colossians 1:23a

[23a]If ye continue in the faith grounded and settled, and be not moved away from the hope of the Gospel, which ye have

heard, and which was preached to every creature which is under heaven.

C. Titus 1:2

²In hope of eternal life, which God, that cannot lie, promised before the world began.

I encourage you to hold on to your hope, even when you cannot see anything happening. Just know that God is always at work in your life, bringing you to an expected end that he has planned just for you. Have faith in him and trust every word that God said he would do. Never lose your expectations in your Great God, He will come through for you.

Remember: Hope that can be seen is not hope at all. You cannot trust God if all you believe is what you see. Trust beyond what you see and believe in the God you trust! Never lose your hope in Christ Jesus!!!

Notes: _____

_____

_____

_____

_____

_____

_____

_____

_____

_____

_____

_____

_____

_____

_____

_____

_____

_____

_____

_____

_____

_____

_____

_____

_____

_____

_____

_____

_____

Week 52

LIVING IN THE KINGDOM OF GOD RIGHT NOW

BIBLICAL PRINCIPLES: Colossians 1:13-14 - ¹³Who hath delivered us from the power of darkness, and hath translated (transferred) us into the kingdom of his dear Son: ¹⁴In whom we have redemption through his blood, even the forgiveness of sins.

This is one of my favorite Scriptures in the Bible. It reminds me of the fact that through the bloodshed of Jesus Christ, I am truly delivered from the bondage of sin and the negative affects it had in my life. I am no longer in bondage, praise the Lord I am free!

God, has delivered us from the power of darkness, and has translated (transferred) us into the kingdom of his dear Son, Jesus Christ. You may wonder how this could have happened. All of this took place on the cross at Calvary, when Jesus gave his life for you and I. Jesus had to present himself as the perfect sacrifice without sin, to pay the high price for the penalty of our sins. God knew we would never be able to redeem ourselves, no matter how hard we tried, we could not eliminate our sin problems. So through his love for us, Jesus came and gave what we could not give, which was his Life, for the forgiveness of sin. Right now, this day, we are the righteousness of God through his Son Jesus Christ, if we accept his sacrifice for the remission if sin.

We are transferred into the kingdom of Jesus Christ right now. This is a completed action and is now made available to anyone who will accept it. You do not have to be enslaved to the works and demands of Satan anymore. You have a new master, a new owner, and a new place of residence. You now belong to Jesus, the one who paid your debt for sin, and removed you for the kingdom of darkness, and transferred you into His private kingdom. In the kingdom of God, Satan has no authority over anything, not even you.

The problem with all of this is, now you must transform your mind from the rule and kingdom of Satan, which is darkness. Be transformed to your new Lord and Master, in the kingdom if Jesus the Christ. The old rule book you once lived by in darkness is of no value to you now. You cannot use any of it in your new life and kingdom. Remember Jesus said, old things are passed away and behold all things are become new. Now you are living by the rules and laws of God's kingdom. This may take some getting used to because you have been in bondage for so long. Living as you please, saying whatever you thought you should say, and being rebellious to any kind of authority is no longer allowed in your new place of residence.

You once lived by the laws of the flesh, obeying the lust thereof, and every command given to you by Satan. Now you must live by the fruit of the Spirit, walking not after the flesh but after the recommendation of the Spirit. These are changes you must learn to abide by in the kingdom of God. You must now present your body a living sacrifice, holy and acceptable, which is your reasonable service unto God. There cannot be joint loyalty to the old master and your new master. You must decide to commit yourself to one Lord, one faith, and one baptism, you cannot serve two masters.

The new life you have chosen now is so much easier than your old life, if you learn all the laws to the kingdom. You have the laws of love, faith, grace and mercy, spiritual adoption, forgiveness, humility, justification, redemption, and so many others that will profit you in your new life. You must take the time to read the word of God to understand what is required of you regarding your attitude, actions, your service, and your relationship with your new King, in his kingdom.

In the world you have constitutions, declarations, and other principles that are set in place to keep equality, stability, unity, and balance in the Country. Believe it or not, you have this in the kingdom of God also. Just as any citizen in a country must abide by the constitution to remain a citizen, so must the citizens of the kingdom of God abide by God's constitution. It is very simple, you must obey what God has ordained as his standards for his people in the kingdom. You cannot come into God's kingdom trying to take over, do what you want to do, and try to change what God has established as his kingdom rules.

In every kingdom, there is only "One King", you may have many subjects working under the king, but you only have one king. In God's kingdom, there is only one King, and he is the governing authority. You must submit to that authority at all times to be called a child of his kingdom.

Knowing now that you are an active citizen of the kingdom of God, it is important that you govern yourself to your new position. You do not have to fear what Satan is doing anymore, because Jesus has disarmed him of his powers over you, once you accepted Him as your personal Savior. Now all you have to do is accept what the Lord requires and rest in peace in your new kingdom.

There are many things I will share with you from the word of God regarding Living in the kingdom of God right now.

PRACTICAL APPLICATIONS:

1. All Kingdom Citizens must be born again, must repent of our rebellion against God, must turn back to God and accept Him as our personal Savior, and must acknowledge that He is Lord, Savior, and Owner of our lives.

   A. John 3:3

   > ³Jesus answered and said unto him, verily, verily, I say unto thee, Except a man be born again, he cannot see the kingdom of God.

   B. John 3:5-7

   > ⁵Jesus answered, verily, verily, I say unto thee, except a man be born of water and of the Spirit, he cannot enter into the kingdom of God. ⁶That which is born of flesh is flesh; and that which is born of the Spirit is spirit. ⁷Marvel not that I said unto thee, Ye must be born again.

2. Now we are naturalized citizens of the kingdom of God, we are now returned to our original natural status before the fall of Adam. We are no longer strangers or enemies of God, but are fellow citizens with the members of the household of God. God is our King, the King of the Kingdom, and we are his citizens.

A. Ephesians 2:19

> [19]Now therefore ye are no more strangers and foreigners, but fellow citizens with the saints, and of the household of God.

B. Philippians 3:20

> [20]For our conversation (citizenship) is in heaven; from whence also we look for the Savior, the Lord Jesus Christ.

3. We are no longer citizens of this world, our citizenship is now in Heaven, and as citizens of Heaven we are govern by new laws.

- **The law of love**

  John 15:17 - [17]These things I command you, that ye love one another.

- **The law of Faith**

  Hebrews 11:6 - [6]But without faith it is impossible to please him: for he that cometh to God must believe that he is, and that he is a rewarder of them that diligently seek him.

- **The law of Grace**

  Romans 6:15 - [15]What then? Shall we sin, because we are not under the law, but under grace? God forbid.

- **The law of Mercy**

  Matthew 5:7 - [7]Blessed are the merciful: for they shall obtain mercy.

- **The law of Spiritual Adoption**

  Romans 8:15 - [15]For ye have not received the spirit of bondage again to fear; but ye have received the Spirit of adoption, whereby we cry Abba (expressive of an especially close relationship to God), Father.

- **The law of Forgiveness**

   <u>Matthew 6:14-15</u> - [14]For if ye forgive men their trespasses, your heavenly Father will also forgive you: [15]But if ye forgive not men their trespasses, neither will your Father forgive your trespasses.

4. Your citizenship in heaven is ACTIVE NOW while you are on earth. At the time of the new birth your kingdom citizenship is activated, you are a child of God now, God has brought you into the Kingdom of His Son now. God is active in the earth NOW and so is your citizenship. Kingdom citizenship is never postponed, it starts immediately.

   A. Colossians 1:12-13

   [12]Giving thanks unto the Father, which hath made us meet to be partakers of the inheritance of the saints in light: [13]Who hath delivered us from the power of darkness, and hath translated us into the kingdom of his dear Son.

   B. Colossians 1:21-23a

   [21]And you, that were sometimes alienated and enemies in your mind by wicked works, yet now hath he reconciled [22]In the body of his flesh through death, to present you holy and blameless and irreproachable in his sight: [23a]If ye continue in the faith grounded and settled, and be not moved away from the hope of the Gospel, which ye have heard, and which was preached to every creature which is under heaven.

5. As kingdom citizens we join the royal family heritage and inheritance, we are now sons of God positionally. The Word of God is our heritage, pure Bible doctrine produces the mind of Christ because it is our constitution for the kingdom of God. We are now in the family of God.

A. Ephesians 2:13-16, 19

[13]But now in Christ Jesus ye who sometimes were far off are made nigh by the blood of Christ. [14]For he is our peace, who hath made both one, and hath broken down the middle wall of partition between us; [15]Having abolished in his flesh the enmity, even the law of commandments contained in ordinances; for to make in himself of twain one new man, so making peace; [16]And that he might reconcile both unto God in one body by the cross, having slain the enmity thereby. [19]Now therefore ye are no more strangers and foreigners, but fellow citizens with the saints, and of the household of God.

B. Romans 8:14-17

[14]For as many as are led by the Spirit of God, they are the sons of God. [15]For ye have not received the spirit of bondage again to fear; but ye have received the Spirit of adoption, whereby we cry Abba, Father. [16]The Spirit itself bears witness with our spirit, that we are the children of God: [17]And if children, then heirs of God, and joint heirs with Christ; if so be that we suffer with him, that we may be also glorified together.

6. Spiritual Blessings are included in our citizenship, and there are 7 categories of spiritual blessings: 1) Being in God's eternal, historical, and daily plans; 2) A solution to the sin problem; 3) A new home and citizenship; 4)A new relationship; 5) A new status; 6) Provision

for living the Christian way of life (God's daily plan); 7) A future, a new home and grace support for proper relationships with God and one another. The main supports on the human level are humility toward self and love toward others.

A.   Romans 8:28

[28]And we know that all things work together for good to them that love God,   to them who are called according to his purpose.

B.   Ephesians 1:7

[7]In whom we have redemption through his blood, the forgiveness of sins, according to the riches of his grace.

C.   Colossians 1:13

[13]Who hath delivered us from the power of darkness, and hath translated us into the kingdom of his dear Son.

D.   1John 3:1-2

[1]Behold, what manner of love the Father hath bestowed upon us, that we should be called the sons of God: Therefore the world knows us not, because it knew him not. [2]Beloved, now we are the sons of God, and it does not yet appear what we shall be: But we know that, when he shall appear, we shall be like him; for we shall see him as he is.

E.   2 Corinthians 5:17

[17]Therefore if any man be in Christ, he is a new creature: old things are passed away, behold, all things are become new.

F.   Ephesians 1:3

³Blessed be the God and Father of our Lord Jesus Christ, who hath blessed us with all spiritual blessings in heavenly places in Christ.

G. Romans 13:8

⁸Owe no man anything, but to love one another: For he that loves another hath fulfilled the law.

7. Your inheritance also includes physical blessings. These are the grace blessings from God for life in physical bodies on earth.

A. Matthew 6:31-32

³¹Therefore take no thought, saying, What shall we eat? or, What shall we drink? or, Wherewithal shall we be clothed? ³²(For after all these things the gentiles seek): for your heavenly Father knows that ye have need of all these things.

B. Philippians 4:19

¹⁹But my God shall supply all your need according to his riches in glory by Christ Jesus.

8. God commands kingdom citizens to reflect Him and be loyal to Him, we must:

- **Seek His kingdom first**

  Matthew 6:33 - ³³But seek ye first the kingdom of God, and his righteousness; and all these things shall be added unto you.

- **Live like heavenly citizens**

  Philippians 1:27 - ²⁷Only let your conversation (conduct) be as it becomes the Gospel of Christ: that whether I come and see you, or else be absent, I may hear of your affairs, that ye stand fast in one spirit, with one mind striving together for the faith of the Gospel.

- **Walk worthy of God**

  1 Thessalonians 2:12 - [12]That ye would walk worthy of God, who hath called you unto his kingdom and glory.

- **Walk worthy of calling**

  Ephesians 4:1 - [1]I therefore, the prisoner of the Lord, beseech you that ye walk worthy of the vocation wherewith ye are called.

- **Do everything in the name of the Lord Jesus**

  Colossians 3:17 - [17]And whatsoever ye do in word or deed, do all in the name of the Lord Jesus, giving thanks to God and the Father by him.

- **Do everything for the Lord**

  Colossians 3:23-24 - [23]And whatsoever ye do, do it heartily, as to the Lord, and not unto men; [24]Knowing that of the Lord, ye shall receive the reward of the inheritance: for ye serve the Lord Christ.

9. The kingdom citizen has certain responsibilities:

   A. To God: we must Learn from, obey, love, and represent him at all time.

   1. Deuteronomy 6:5

      [5]And thou shall love the Lord thy God with all your heart, and with all thy soul, and with all thy might.

2. Ephesians 5:1-2

   [1]Be ye therefore followers of God as dear children; [2]And walk in love, as Christ also hath loved us, and hath given himself for us an offering and a sacrifice to God for a sweet smelling savor.

A. To the Bible: Learn and apply the word to your life daily.

3. Psalms 119:9-11

   [9]Wherewithal shall a young man cleanse his way? By taking heed thereto according to thy word. [10]With my whole heart have I sought thee: O let me not wander from thy commandments. [11]Thy word have I hid in my heart, That I might not sin against thee.

4. James 1:21-24

   [21]Wherefore lay apart all filthiness and superfluity (overflow) of naughtiness, and receive with meekness the engrafted (implanted) word, which is able to save your soul. [22]But be ye doers of the word, and not hearers only, deceiving your own selves. [23]For if any be a hearer of the word, and not a doer, [24]he is like unto a man beholding his natural face in a glass: For he beholds himself, and goes his way, and straightway forgets what manner of man he was.

5. 2Peter 3:18

   [18]But grow in grace, and in the knowledge of our Lord and Savior Jesus Christ. To him be glory both now and forever. Amen.

B. To God's Plan: You must follow all of it.

1. Ephesians 2:10

    [10]For we are his workmanship, created in Christ Jesus unto good works, which God hath before ordained that we should walk in them.

2. Philippians 2:12-13

    [12]Wherefore, my beloved, as ye have always obeyed, not as in my presence only, but now much more in my absence, work out your own salvation with fear and trembling. [13]For it is God which works in you both to will and to do his good pleasure.

3. Colossians 3:9-10

    [9]Lie not one to another, seeing that ye have put off the old man with his deeds; [10]and have put on the new man, which is renewed in knowledge after the image of him that created him.

C. To authority: As kingdom citizens you are to obey authority.

1. Hebrews 13:17

    [17]Obey them that have the rule over you, and submit yourselves: for they watch for your souls, as they must give account, that they may do it with joy, and not with grief: for that is unprofitable for you.

2. 1 Thessalonians 5:12-13

    [12]And we beseech you, brethren, to know them which labor among you, and are over you in the Lord, and admonish you;

^{13}And to esteem them very highly in love for their work's sake. And be at peace among yourselves.

3. 1 Peter 2:18

^{18}Servants be subject to your masters with all fear; not only to the good and gentle, but also to the forward.

D. To our Nation: Live under the laws of divine establishment and have respect.

1. Romans 13:1-3

^{1}Let every soul be subject unto the higher powers. For there is no power but of God: the powers that be are ordained of God. ^{2}Whosoever therefore resists the power, resists the ordinance of God: and they that resist shall receive to themselves damnation. ^{3}For rulers are not a terror to good works, but to the evil. Will thou then not be afraid of the power? Do that which is good, and thou shall have praise of the same.

2. 1 Peter 2:13-16

^{13}Submit yourselves to every ordinance of man for the Lord's sake: Whether it be to the king as supreme; ^{14}Or unto governors, as unto them that are sent by him for the punishment of evildoers, and for the praise of them that do well. ^{15}For so is the will of God, that with well doing ye may put to silence the ignorance of foolish men: ^{16}As free, and not using your liberty for a cloak of maliciousness, but as the servant of God .

E. To creation: Rule it, bring it under God's control and care.

1. **Genesis 1:27-28**

^{27}So God created man in his own image, in the image of God created he him; male and female created he them. ^{28}And

God blessed them, and God said unto them, Be fruitful, and multiply, and replenish the earth, and subdue it: and have dominion over the fish of the sea, and over the fowl of the air, and over every living thing that moves upon the earth.

2. Psalms 8:3-6

[3]When I consider thy heavens, the work of thy fingers, the moon and the stars, which thou hast ordained; [4]What is man that thou art mindful of him? And the son of man, that thou visits him? [5]For thou hast made him a little lower than the angels and hast crowned him with glory and honor. [6]Thou made him to have dominion over the works of thy hands; thou hast put all things under his feet.

F. To people: Witness as God's representative motivated by your love for God and love to people.

1. Matthew 28:19-20

[19]Go ye therefore, and teach all nations, baptizing them in the name of the Father, and of the Son, and of the Holy Ghost: [20]Teaching them to observe all things whatsoever I have commanded you: and lo, I am with you always, even unto the end of the world. Amen.

2. Acts 1:8

[8]But ye shall receive power, after that the Holy Ghost is come upon you: and ye shall be witnesses unto me both in Jerusalem, and in all Judea, and in Samaria, and unto the uttermost part of the earth.

3. 1 Corinthians 13:4-7

[4]Charity (love) suffers long, and is kind: charity does not envy; charity does not parade itself, is not arrogant. [5]Does not behave

itself unseemly, seeks not her own, is not easily provoked, thinks no evil; ⁶Rejoice not in iniquity, but rejoices in the truth. ⁷Bears all things, believes all things, hopes all things, endures all things.

G. To the local church: Most consistently under the authority of the pastor/teacher to be equipped.

4. Ephesians 4:12-13

   ¹²For the perfecting of the saints for the work of the ministry, for the edifying of the body of Christ: ¹³Till we all come in the unity of the faith, and of the knowledge of the Son of God, unto a perfect man, unto the measure of the stature of the fullness of Christ.

5. Hebrews 10:25

   ²⁵Not forsaking the assembling of ourselves together, as the manner of some is; but exhorting one another: and so much the more, as ye see the day approaching.

After you have learned how to access your royal rights as a citizen of God's Kingdom; you have labored as an ambassador of Christ in your life; and you have understood your responsibility as a representative of Heaven; you are now ready to experience life on a new supernatural level! You are a citizen of an Unshakeable Kingdom, The Kingdom of God! So access your Kingdom inheritance today and fulfill your divine destiny on Earth!!!

Remember: You are living in the kingdom of God right now! Walk in it with all the authority given unto you by your Lord and Savior Jesus Christ!!!

Notes: _____

_____

_____

_____

_____

_____

_____

_____

_____

_____

_____

_____

_____

_____

_____

_____

_____

_____

_____

_____

_____

_____

_____

_____

_____

_____